John Calvin's
Sermons
on the
Ten Commandments

Edited and Translated by
Benjamin W. Farley

Foreword by
Ford Lewis Battles

6749 Remington Cir
Pelham AL 35124

Solid Ground Christian Books
6749 Remington Circle
Pelham, AL 35124
205-443-0311
mike.sgcb@gmail.com
www.solid-ground-books.com

SERMONS ON THE TEN COMMANDMENTS

John Calvin (1509-1564)

Translated by Benjamin W. Farley in 1980

First Solid Ground edition is September 2011

Copyright © 1980 by Baker Book House
Originally published in English under the title
   John Calvin's Sermons on the Ten Commandments
   By Baker Books, a division of Baker Book House
   Company, Grand Rapids, MI 49516, USA.
All rights reserved.

Cover design by Borgo Design
Contact them at borgogirl@bellsouth.net

ISBN- 978-159925-261-2

to
my Mother and Father

and to
Margaret, John, and Bryan

In memory of Ford Lewis Battles

Acknowledgments

I should like to express gratitude to Dr. John Haddon Leith for the inspiration, supervision, helpful criticism, and encouragement he provided throughout the work on this volume. Also, I wish to thank Dr. Ford Lewis Battles for his invaluable criticism and advice, as well as his warm encouragement. Especially do I thank Mrs. B. D. Aycock, Reference Librarian, Union Theological Seminary, Richmond, Virginia, for locating and acquiring critical information and key resources; Mrs. Gordon B. English for typing the final draft and assisting with manuscript corrections; Mrs. Carolyn Henderson for typing the bibliography; and the Reverends Messrs. Palmer M. Patterson and James W. White, Jr. for assisting with the indexes.

Above all, I am indebted to my wife, Margaret, who shared the entire project with me and patiently typed and retyped the many drafts of this manuscript.

Foreword

This work represents, in terms of the history of preaching, a chastening of the often diffuse and long-winded homilies containing continuous exegesis of a particular book or portion of Scripture, a method first developed by Origen of Alexandria. Out of all the available models, it was perhaps the New Testament exegeses of John Chrysostom of Antioch and Constantinople that most appealed to Calvin. But it was neither the allegorical method (whether in the lush style of an Origen or the more tempered manner of Augustine) nor the more responsible historical-grammatical method of Antioch that Calvin used as a model; always keeping in sight his twin principles of *perspicuitas* and *brevitas*, Calvin made use of the whole exegetical tradition—Jewish as well as Christian—down to his day. Yet in the end, Calvin remained his own man concerning Scripture.

Calvin usually preached in Geneva every other week, twice on Sunday (New Testament and Psalms) and daily during the week. It was at these weekday services that series such as those on Deuteronomy were preached, chapter by chapter, as each book of the Bible was exegeted. There is a sense in which such preaching could be viewed as actual commentary, commentaries as impressive in their own way as Calvin's Latin commentaries were.

This prompts a few words about the unity of Calvin's labors, both in the field of action—whether in the pulpit or in municipal affairs—and in that of writing. It is usually this latter image of

7

Calvin as theological scholar and writer that most readily comes to mind. Upon a closer examination, however, one will find this image to be only one part of his accomplishments. The scope of Calvin's labors embodies a deep unity. This unity, asserted by Calvin in regard to his *Institutes* and *Commentaries,* can be applied as well to his sermons, whereby the teachings of his writings are elaborated in answer to the spiritual needs of the people. In a sense, these sermons represent a living bridge between the scholarly exegete and the Christian man of action.

The critical introduction to this book amply demonstrates this relationship by a careful if brief comparative study of the *Institutes,* the *Commentary on the Last Four Books of Moses* (arranged as a harmony), and the sixteen sermons featured in this work. Herein lies one very important feature of Dr. Farley's study: it restores to modern students of Calvin that long-lost sense of unity in Calvin's devoted service to God. Even those students who have concentrated their studies on a narrow consideration of Calvin's theology can no longer neglect the study of the sermons in favor of the *Institutes* and the *Commentaries.* Farley's study points the way to a fuller and more unified understanding of Calvin's works.

This work would not be as helpful as it is, however, without the aid of other Calvin scholars, both past and present. One good example is the *Supplementa Calviniana,* which shows the careful editing of Calvin's text; it is an inspiration to modern researchers. Would that all the sermons printed in *Opera Calvini* had had the same care! (Of course, this does not in any way detract from our lasting appreciation for what the Strasbourg editors did to draw Calvin's corpus together.) Although Farley's critical labors do not rest on a text edited to demanding modern standards, his utilization of the printed text is careful, discriminating, and sufficient for his purpose. His introduction will show how modern scholarship has aided him in this.

Another strong point of this book is its effort to place the sermons in the context of historical Geneva. This is an important feature for the newcomer to Calvin the preacher; in presenting the sermons as they were preached from the pulpit to the people of Calvin's Geneva they are given flesh and blood. After all, sermons are written for preaching to people, a situation in this case long since lost in the womb of history; thus printed transcriptions or translations by themselves lack this element of human context. As a result of this, Dr. Farley, dissatisfied with what he considered the woodenness of his first efforts of translation, appealed to me for help. In reply, I asked my former student, Dr. François Gérard of Toronto, to tape one of the sermons in its original language. Perhaps some of the flowing quality of Dr. Farley's final translation came from an ear attuned to the sound of the French as spoken, not read from the printed page. Let all translators heed this lesson!

The series of 200 sermons on Deuteronomy, of which the sixteen concerning the Decalogue here presented constitute the heart and core, is a veritable treasure-trove in that it contains Calvin's critical study of the economic and social aspects of ancient Israel. Could one expect any less from someone taught by the great Guillaume Budé, author of *De Asse*, a pioneer work of the Renaissance on the economic and social history of the ancient classical world? This fact has been recognized by the noted Genevan scholar André Biéler, whose great work, *La pensée économique et sociale de Jean Calvin*, is still lamentably locked up in its original language. Biéler studied the whole corpus of Calvin's writings in preparing his magistral study, but found no source of greater importance than the *Sermons on Deuteronomy*. Out of such evidence Biéler has, in another work, *Calvin: prophète de l'ère industrielle*, more succinctly expounded Calvin's exegetical method and extrapolated its use into our own time. It is to be hoped that this recently translated book will be published soon. Dr. Farley is sensitive to this aspect of the Deuteronomy sermons, although of course this does not represent his chief concern. To him, this painstaking study of ancient Israel and its life and institutions is used by Calvin to adumbrate the message of salvation which he emphasized to his hearers.

This foreword must close with a personal note. The genesis of this study, in a sense, was in a conversation with Benjamin Farley in the summer of 1973, while I was lecturing in the Union Theological Seminary Pastor's School. I commended to him the Decalogue sermons as his field of research. His study has indeed exceeded my expectations expressed in our first meeting.

This book is a venture of faith, not only for its author, but also for its publisher, Baker Book House, whose willingness to undertake its publication in these stringent and uncertain times will, I hope, be honored by a wide and enthusiastic response.

Grand Rapids   FORD LEWIS BATTLES
16 October 1979

Contents

12

Introduction

General

Calvin began his series of sermons on the Ten Commandments on Friday, June 7, 1555.[1] They belong to a larger corpus of sermons on Deuteronomy, which Calvin had initiated on March 20 earlier that year[2] and which he would not conclude until the following summer in July, 1556. The series on the Decalogue, however, dates only from June 7 to July 19, 1555.[3]

Historically, 1555 was a momentous year for both Calvin and the Genevan Republic. It saw the collapse of Calvin's opponents, the ratification of the Consistory's right to ban delinquent members from the Lord's Supper, and the renewal of political-theological disputes between Bern and Geneva. All of these developments either preceded Calvin's sermons on the Decalogue or occurred on the very eve of the series. The reformer's correspondence amply testifies how extensively these matters weighed on his mind throughout the period.

[1]See John Calvin, *Ioannis Calvini Opera quae supersunt omnia*, vols. 1–59, ed. Guilielmus Baum, Eduardus Cunitz, Eduardus Reuss, Corpus Reformatorum, vols. 29–87 (Brunsvigae: C. A. Schwetschkte et filium, 1863–1900), vol. 26, col. 235. (Hereafter cited as *CO* vol. and col.)

[2]See Nicholas Colladon, *Vie de Calvin, CO* 21, col. 79. (Hereafter cited as Colladon, *Vie, CO* 21, col.)

[3]See *CO* 26.236 n. 432. Specifically, the Decalogue series comprises Calvin's sermons on Deuteronomy 4:44–6:4.

Theologically, Calvin's interest in the Commandments was nothing new. Calvin had discussed the Ten Commandments as early as his first edition of the *Institutes* and in each successive edition thereafter.[4] Thus the sermons were based on a theological context as well as an historical one.

In general, one can say that the sermons popularized material that is more clearly and succinctly stated in the *Institutes*. The sermons are not inferior to the *Institutes*, however, for they do an excellent job of applying Calvin's theological acumen to the issues of his times. As a result, the sermons enhance the *Institutes* in a rewarding fashion, while at the same time displaying the reformer's socioeconomic thought.

Historical Background and Sociopolitical Repercussions

In the early months of 1555, three developments took place which were integral to Calvin's Decalogue sermons. The first and perhaps the most important was the collapse of the so-called "Libertine" party, a political faction which had opposed Calvin and the unfolding reformation of the Genevan Republic. This dual note is sounded insofar as "Libertine" opposition was directed against the transformation of Geneva as much as it was against Calvin himself.[5] The "Libertines" simply wanted to see Geneva march to the beat of a different drum.

According to Theodore Beza, the central leader of these antagonists was the syndic Ami Perrin.[6] Beginning in the March of

---

[4]See n. 43 below.

[5]See P. E. Hughes' general reminder to this effect in the *Register of the Company of Pastors of Geneva in the Time of Calvin*, ed. and trans. Philip Edgcumbe Hughes (Grand Rapids: Eerdmans, 1966), pp. 3–13. (Hereafter cited as *Register of the Company* vol. and p.) For the original French and Latin volumes of this work, see *Registres de la Compagnie des Pasteurs de Genève au Temps de Calvin*, publies sous la direction des Archives d'Etat de Genève, vol. 1, 1546–1553 ed. Jean-Francois Bergier; vol. 2, 1553–1564 ed. Robert Kingdom, avec la collaboration de Jean-Francois Bergier et Alan Dufour (Genève: Librairie E. Droz, 1962 and 1964). (Hereafter cited as *Registres de la Compagnie* vol. and p.) Also see Emile Doumergue, *Jean Calvin, Les Hommes et les Choses de Son Temps* (7 vols., vols. 1–5: Lausanne: Georges Bridel & Cie., 1899–1917; vols. 6–7: Neuilly-sur-Seine: Editions de "La Cause," 1926–1927), vol. 6, pp. 91–119. (Hereafter cited as Doumergue vol. and p.)

[6]Theodore Beza, *Ioannis Calvini Vita, CO* 21, col. 150. (Hereafter cited as Beza, *Vita, CO* 21, col.) The English translation is from *The Life of John Calvin*, trans.

1546, a series of "indignities" began to occur between Calvin and Perrin's family, which resulted in a long decade of conflict. A brief history of this conflict is important, as allusions to the struggle frequently appear in the sermons.

The chain of events began on March 21, 1546, when Perrin and his wife, the daughter of Francois Favre, a Genevan man of wealth, attended a betrothal at which there was dancing. Since dancing was prohibited in Geneva, the offending parties were arrested by the Little Council and made to appear before the Consistory. Echoes of this incident appear in "The Ninth Sermon."

In early 1547, another incident occurred, in which Favre was charged with violating the seventh commandment.[7] A loud echo of this resounds in "The Ninth Sermon," which has to do with the prohibition against adultery and fornication.

In 1546, Perrin was elected to the office of captain-general.[8] From this position he championed the popular target-festival of the Arquebusiers, requesting on May 9, 1547, that the Little Council permit the Society to celebrate its ancient festival. The Council approved but reminded participants of the city's injunction against the wearing of indecent hose, the traditional garb of the festivals. The issue soon required a meeting of the Council of Two Hundred which, convening on May 25, ultimately accepted Calvin's argument that to yield to the Society's request would only result in abuses that would later prove difficult to curb.[9] An allusion to this matter also appears in "The Ninth Sermon."

By 1548, Perrin's influence was having a detrimental effect on Calvin's ministry. Beza reports that some Genevans openly flaunted their disrespect of the reformer by calling their dogs "Calvin"; others shortened his name to Cain; many stopped taking the Lord's Supper, citing their "hatred of Calvin" as justification.[10]

With the election of February, 1549, Ami Perrin rose to first syndic. As the leader of the opposition party, he became more and

Francis Sibson, with copious notes by an American editor (Philadelphia: J. Whetham, 1836), p. 63. (Hereafter cited as Beza, *Life*, p. Unless otherwise noted, all English quotations from the *Life* are from the Sibson translation.)

[7]See the *Annales*, *CO* 12.395–96. See Doumergue 6.91–95. See also Williston Walker, *John Calvin: The Organiser of Reformed Protestantism 1509–1564* (New York: Schocken Books, 1969), pp. 303–4.

[8]Beza, *Vita*, *CO* 21.138.

[9]See Calvin's argument as reported in the *Annales*, *CO* 21.405–6. Cf. Calvin's letter to Viret, May 28, 1547, *CO* 13.531. Noted by Doumergue 6.101, n. 5. See Walker's summary in Walker, *John Calvin*, pp. 304–5.

[10]Beza, *Life*, p. 44.

more able to challenge Calvin's aims. Chief among his supporters were Pierre Vandel, Philibert Berthelier, and his younger brother, Francois Daniel. All were sons of an older political *esprit d'independence* and were defiant of Calvin's spiritual reformation.[11] Their efforts did much to shape the politics of conflict that constantly put Calvin's theology and courage to the test and added to his personal burdens.

In the following years up to 1555, the Perrinists fought to keep the swelling refugee population unarmed and disenfranchised (as this group favored Calvin),[12] acted as Michael Servetus's defense attorney,[13] sought repeatedly to extinguish the Consistory's power,[14] and openly insulted Calvin as occasion permitted.[15]

By 1555 the Perrinists were synonymous with all that seemed "seditious," at least in the eyes of Calvin's proponents.[16] Therefore, when in February of 1555 the Little Council's newly elected syndics were predominantly Calvinists[17] and the balance of power favored the reformer's cause, the "riot" that occurred on the evening of May 16 (involving Perrin and some of his followers) understandably precipitated the "Libertines' " fall.

This "riot" occurred roughly three weeks prior to Calvin's sermons on the Ten Commandments, but its intensity was such that it haunted Calvin throughout his series. His letters to Farel and Bullinger, dated June 5 through July 24[18] (which fall upon the eve and within the range of the sermons), confirm his preoccupation with the disturbance and provide nuances that surface in the sermons.

Specifically, the May 16[19] tumult was the result of several

[11]See the interesting reports of March 8 and 22, 1554, in the *Registres de la Compagnie* 2.54. Also see Walker, *John Calvin*, p. 311.

[12]Beza, *Vita, CO* 21.143, 145, 146; *Life*, pp. 51, 54, 55.

[13]Walker, *John Calvin*, p. 333.

[14]More shall be said of this in the subsequent section.

[15]Beza, *Vita, CO* 21.143; *Life*, p. 51.

[16]Ibid., col. 145; ibid., p. 54.

[17]Walker, *John Calvin*, p. 344.

[18]Calvin to Farel, July 16 and 24, 1555; *CO* 15.686, 693–94. Calvin to Bullinger, June 5 and 15, 1555; *CO* 15.640–43, 676–85. The English translation of these letters may be found in Jules Bonnet, ed., *Letters of John Calvin*, trans. Marcus Robert Gilchrist (Philadelphia: Presbyterian Board of Publication, 1858), vol. 3, pp. 204–5, 205–6, 185–87, 192–202 respectively. Vols. 1–2 of this collection were translated by David Constable. (Unless otherwise noted, all English quotations from Calvin's letter are from this collection.)

[19]The major sources for this drama are Calvin's letters cited in n. 18 above; Colladon, *Vie, CO* 21.79; Beza, *Vita, CO* 21.150; the *Annales, CO* 21.604–5; *Registres de la Compagnie* 2.63. Modern discussions abound. See Doumergue 7.26–66;

months of increasing disenchantment on the part of Perrin and his followers. Calvin saw this drift in his own assessment which he shared with Bullinger at the latter's request.[20] As Calvin explains, Perrin and Vandel were the principal agitators. Having controlled Genevan politics until the recent election in February of that year, the two were no longer in positions of influence. Adding to their sense of powerlessness, the Little Council, under the impetus of fresh leadership,[21] had begun granting citizenship to well-known French refugees who had long resided in the city.[22] The Perrinists reacted by assembling a mob. They persuaded the prefect of the city to protest this new course before the Little Council (May 13 and 14)[23] and to demand a hearing before the Two Hundred. The Little Council stood its ground.

It was in the despondency of these setbacks that, on Thursday evening, May 16, after two earlier dinner parties sponsored by Vandel and Perrin, guests began wandering through the streets in a raucous manner. In the darkness, Calvin explains, a stone was hurled and a man's cry rang out. The night sentries rushed to the quarter behind the market place where the call for help had originated. Here they were immediately assailed by two brothers, the Comparets, and a host of others.[24] Aroused by the scuffle, the syndic Henry Aulbert[25] made his way to the scene and raised his syndical mace to restore order. The crowd ignored his authority, and one of the Comparets threatened him with a sword. Perrin then appeared and attempted to seize Aulbert's mace on the pretext of pacifying the mob. Aulbert resisted. Cries were then raised that the French refugees had taken up arms. When a second syndic appeared, Perrin seized his baton, but the man set up such a

Walker, *John Calvin*, pp. 350 ff.; E. William Monter, *Calvin's Geneva*, New Dimensions in History, Historical Cities (New York: John Wiley & Sons, Inc., 1967), pp. 86–88.

[20]Calvin to Bullinger, June 15, 1555; *CO* 15.676–85; Bonnet, *Letters*, vol. 3, pp. 192–202.

[21]See Monter, *Calvin's Geneva*, p. 86.

[22]See Walker, *John Calvin*, p. 349. Monter presents evidence that indicates that some of these newly-enfranchised refugees had not been in Geneva as long as Calvin's letter suggests. See Monter, *Calvin's Geneva*, p. 87, n. 40.

[23]Calvin does not provide dates. See the *Annales*, *CO* 21.604–5. The *Registres du Conseil* (cited by the *Annales*) identifies Hudroit du Moclard as the prefect. The dates given are May 13 and 14.

[24]Calvin does not identify the brothers in his letter. Their identity is reported in the *Annales*, *CO* 21.605.

[25]Ibid.

howl that Perrin had to return it. The Comparet brothers were finally arrested and the crowd dispersed. But the damage had been done. The Little Council wasted no time and called a night meeting.

Calvin explains that the Council ordered an inquiry; after allowing for a sufficient time in which witnesses were summoned, the Two Hundred met. Perrin and Vandel actually attended the earlier sessions but fled once they realized the mounting danger to themselves.[26] The Two Hundred supported the Little Council, which decreed the arrests of Perrin and four of his close associates. The fugitives were given fifteen days in which to appear. The accused wrote letters refusing to return unless provided assurance of safe passage. This being denied, on June 3 (only four days before Calvin's first sermon in the Decalogue series) they were sentenced to be beheaded. The grisly verdict may still be read in the *Register of the Company*.[27]

Far more could be said of the defeat of the "Libertine" party, or of the Perrinists, or of the "conspiracy" of May 16. But the collapse of Calvin's opponents is emphasized here, as the tumultuous events that belong to that decade of conflict can be sensed in almost every passage of the Decalogue sermons. Throughout the series Calvin never tired of stressing the importance of a God-fearing and well-ordered state, supported by a responsible and decent citizenry, led by a pious and accountable magistracy.

The defeat of Calvin's opponents represents but one cord in that tight web of historical context which underlies the sermons on the Ten Commandments. There are two other developments that took place in 1555 which also deserve mention: the ratification of the Consistory's right to excommunicate and Bern's renewal of political-theological differences between herself and Geneva. Both developments preceded Calvin's sermons and received attention in his correspondence during the series.

The Consistory's struggle with the Little Council over the right to ban unrepentant communicants from the Lord's Table belongs to a long chapter in the history of the separation of church-state powers in Geneva. Although the struggle was in part aggravated by "Libertine" assaults, the problem was principally one of the proper delineation between church and state functions at a time

---

[26]See Monter's analysis in Monter, *Calvin's Geneva*, p. 87.
[27]*Registres de la Compagnie* 2.63; *Register of the Company*, p. 309.

when the Genevan Republic was anxious to control so powerful a force as religious faith.

Readers should recall that Geneva was already committed to the Reformation before Calvin journeyed there in 1536. Her civil authorities had participated in the ouster of papal rule and had prohibited the celebration of the mass. In fact, nothing was exempt from their purview.[28]

Although Calvin did not want the Little Council to interfere in ecclesiastical policy, the *Ecclesiastical Ordinances* adopted in 1541 required the Consistory to report obstinate cases of discipline to the Little Council.[29] This meant that the final power to ban delinquent members from the Lord's Table belonged to the Little Council. The provisions of the *Ordinances,* however, were equivocal, and the Consistory resented so blatant a concession of power. As a result, bitter disputes usually erupted whenever the Consistory referred controversial cases to the Little Council.

The most celebrated case involved the "Libertine" Philibert Berthelier, the brother of Francois Berthelier, the man who threw the stone in the May 16 disturbance. The Little Council sought to have him reinstated, but during the hearings his conduct was so belligerent they affirmed the Consistory's decision.[30]

Other incidents also issued in disputes between the two groups, concerning whose prerogative it was to ban persons from the Lord's Table. The matter, however, was not finally resolved until January 24, 1555.[31] At that time, the Little Council and the Council of Two Hundred settled it in favor of the Consistory. This decision signaled the victory of the Church's right to discipline its own members and to wield the spiritual sword in its own domain.

Thus the state's ratification of the Consistory's work as a whole vitally underscores Calvin's appeals throughout the series for Genevans to acknowledge their need of discipline and to submit to the "yoke" of God. The very opening sentence of the first sermon sounds this appeal with unequivocal power.

---

[28]See *Register of the Company,* pp. 3–13; Monter, *Calvin's Geneva,* pp. 49–58. For Calvin's own development of church-state relationships, see his *Institutes of the Christian Religion,* ed. John T. McNeill and trans. Ford Lewis Battles, The Library of Christian Classics, vols. 20–21 (Philadelphia: The Westminster Press, 1960), vol. 21, pp. 1485–1521. (Hereafter cited as *LCC* vol. and p. Future references to the *Institutes* will also include bk., ch. and sec.)

[29]See *Registres de la Compagnie,* 1.6, 11–13; *Register of the Company,* pp. 41, 47–49.

[30]See *Register of the Company,* pp. 11–12.

[31]See Beza, *Vita, CO* 21.150–51; *Life,* pp. 63–64. Cf. *Registres de la Compagnie* 2.59.

> Recognizing how difficult it is for the world to be retained under his sub-
> jection, God chose a people and willed to govern them not simply for a lim-
> ited period, but continuously that they might become sufficiently accustomed
> to his yoke—which is how he daily makes use of the same in his Church.

From this perspective, then, the triumph of the Consistory's right to function as a responsible and independent ecclesiastical board supplied inestimable psychological force to Calvin's series. Certainly the congregation that heard these sermons would not have failed to sense the justice and relevance of Calvin's message as opposed to the maelstrom through which they had all passed.

In connection with the above development is the significance of the role that the Consistory played in Geneva's social and political life. According to the *Ordinances,* the Consistory was composed of twelve elders and the ministers of Geneva. The group met every Thursday under the chairmanship of a syndic, and its disciplinary powers were both of a spiritual and political nature. One historian has boldly suggested that the Consistory ultimately enforced the law that Calvin's theology inspired.[32] That would mean that the social theology exhibited in the Decalogue sermons provides, in part, a clue as to what the Consistory sanctioned as acceptable social behavior. If so, the converse of this might also be true: that what the Consistory deemed as socially acceptable behavior influenced Calvin's social and economic views as expressed in the Decalogue sermons.

More moderate in his appraisal is the view of Daniel Buscarlet. In his book, *Genève Citadelle de la Réforme,* Buscarlet maintains that the rigor and austerity which we associate with Geneva was not peculiar to that republic alone. What was distinctly Genevan was "a discipline at the interior of the Church," viz., the Consistory with its insistence on the power to excommunicate.[33] Buscarlet explains:

> Excommunication—the privation of the Lord's Supper—is not a punish-
> ment like others, imprisonment or the pillory. It represents a pedagogical
> measure, a sanction for a limited time, which makes men take seriously the
> Christian faith, leads them to seek instruction concerning truths they poorly
> grasp, and forces them to mend their lives when they swerve from the law of
> God.[34]

---

[32]Eugène Choisy, *La Théocratie à Genève au temps de Calvin* (Genève: Imprimerie J. G. Fick, 1897), p. 187.

[33]Daniel Buscarlet, *Genève Citadelle de la Réforme* (Genève: Comité du Jubilé Calvinien, 1959), p. 50.

This is suggestive, for it reinforces the possibility that the Decalogue sermons reflect the social philosophy that the Consistory labored to instill in Genevan hearts and minds. The Consistory may not have created that theology, but it certainly championed it and sought to enforce it.

Buscarlet interprets the Consistory's work as a form of "Christian socialism."[35] He sees it as an agent actively engaged in maintaining the social orders that underlie the whole Second Table of the Law. If this seems repressive, Buscarlet observes, we must remember that it was the sixteenth century and not the twentieth; it was an epoch when individual liberty meant less than it does today and when a city was an indivisible community. Was it good to live in Geneva? he asks. Yes, if you loved the Bible, wanted to battle for Christ's stead, and considered your first occupation "the honor of God."[36] It is not too far afield to state that this is ultimately what the Decalogue sermons are about.

Finally, Buscarlet stresses that Geneva served as a citadel for the entire French Reformation. As a citadel it both protected and equipped those who fled there for sanctuary. Beginning with the repressive measures of Francis I in 1535 and continuing through Calvin's life, 5,000 refugees found safety and hope in that fortress.

Although Buscarlet does not develop it, this "chateau-fort" character of the city intensified its destiny as a republic in which Calvin's "right rule for living" became a hallmark. Consequently, it is something of a mystery that Calvin's sermons on the Ten Commandments appeared as late as they did. Yet their appearance at the very time that the Consistory's right to ban was ratified, the Perrinists had been defeated, and the refugees were being enfranchised in increasing numbers signaled the end of an old era and the commencement of a new, pledged to the will and honor of God as revealed in the Decalogue.

A third issue that erupted in 1555 involved religious disputes of a controversial nature which contained embarrassing political ramifications for Calvin and Geneva. These disputes were instigated by certain Swiss pastors whose parishes were under Bernese jurisdiction. The issue was aggravated by the fact that Bern and Geneva had long been antagonists over basic ecclesiastical practices

[34]Ibid., pp. 50–51.
[35]Ibid., p. 52.
[36]Ibid., p. 53.

and by the fact that the political alliance between the two repub-
lics, dating back to August 7, 1536, was due to expire in March
1556. A significant number of Calvin's letters between February
and July 1555 directly address these disputes, reflecting the extent
to which Calvin's thoughts and energies were engaged by this
issue.[37]

Beza's summary of the affair provides a brief introduction and
calls attention to its fundamental aspects:

> Another circumstance prevented Calvin from experiencing uninterrupted
> joy this year. A faction arose of a few neighboring ministers, who were of
> their own accord opposed to Calvin, and under the influence of Bolsec.
> These persons, though of infamous characters, thinking to acquire reputa-
> tion by attacking so illustrious an adversary, accused him, in scurrilous lan-
> guage, of making God the author of sin, because he taught that nothing is
> excepted from the eternal providence and appointment of God. Calvin de-
> spised at first these calumnies . . . but compelled at last by their railings, solic-
> ited permission to repair to Berne, accompanied by envoys from the republic
> to maintain the cause of truth before the inhabitants of that city. After ad-
> vocating his cause, Castellio was banished with infamy from the territory of
> Berne, and Bolsec was also ordered to depart; . . .[38]

Briefly, then, the issue involved attacks against Calvin's doctrine
of providence and predestination, prompted by Jerome Bolsec
and reinforced by Sebastian Castellio's position on toleration,
through the agency of certain Swiss clergymen, notably, André
Zebédée and Jean Lange.[39] The matter resulted in Calvin having
to risk his personal prestige by twice journeying to Bern to redress
the situation (March 6 and 29). As late as June 6 (the eve of Calvin's sermons on the Ten Commandments), the issue had still not
been resolved, and Pastor Macar, one of Geneva's delegates, had
just returned to report that hostilities between the two parties had
only increased.[40]

Many points were in dispute, but the heart of the matter was
the Bernese attitude that Calvin's doctrine of predestination was

[37]See Calvin's letters, *CO* 15.430–41, 449–50, 537–42, 572–73, 599–604, 605–8;
Bonnet, *Letters*, vol. 3, pp. 136–37, 151–52, 160–69, 169–71, 171–76, 176–81 respectively. For a general sketch of these disputes and their background, see
Monter, *Calvin's Geneva*, pp. 2–70, 81–82, 87–89, 97; Walker, *John Calvin*, pp.
165–215.

[38]Beza, *Vita, CO* 21.151–52; *Life*, p. 65.

[39]All four of these names appear in letters sent to the Bern magistrates on
behalf of Calvin by the Company of Pastors of Geneva, Oct. 4, 1555. See *Register of
the Company*, pp. 298–304.

[40]*Registres de la Compagnie* 2.63–64; *Register of the Company*, pp. 309–10.

too radical. It showed "too much curiosity" and wanted "to enter too deeply into the secrets of God."[41]

These controversies directly spill over into the sermons. The impact of this struggle is especially visible in those passages where Calvin affirms the doctrine of predestination, for affirm it he does. Certainly it would be unfounded to conclude that he voiced his affirmations in response to his Bernese critics, but their assaults must surely have been uppermost in his thoughts.

There are at least four sections in the sermons where this controversy is mirrored. The Second, Third, Sixth, and Fifteenth Sermons, dated June 12, 17, 21, and July 18, all reflect Calvin's unhappiness over this issue. The following quotation best exhibits his frame of mind and running argument with his Bernese detractors.

> Seeing then that God can utterly ruin and destroy us, if it pleases him to use his goodness and clemency toward anyone and call them to himself and rescue them from their abyss, what fault can anyone find with that? Why reproach him for that? Why should we raise our eyebrows if he has pity on his creatures? And although he does not use an equal standard toward all, nevertheless it is necessary to keep our mouth closed. Indeed, it is even necessary for us to open it to confess that what he does is within reason and equitable, even though it might transcend our grasp. For we do not always understand why in fact God decrees what he does for men. But it is proper for our *(curiosité)* to be abated and for us to learn to worship God in his judgments when they are too lofty and secret for us.[42]

Theological Considerations

The sermons on the Ten Commandments are first and foremost an exposition of the moral law. As such they were delivered against the background of no less than nineteen years of persistent reflection. Coming as they do in 1555, one cannot read them critically without weighing them against the content of Calvin's *Institutes,* for the latter serve as their theological foundation.

The *Institutes* passed through five major editions: 1536, 1539, 1543, 1550, and 1559.[43] Obviously, four of these precede the

---

[41] Ibid., 62; ibid., p. 308. Italics for emphasis.

[42] See "The Third Sermon," n. 46.

[43] For an excellent brief sketch of this history, see Francois Wendel, *Calvin: The Origins and Development of His Religious Thought,* trans. Philip Mairet (New York: Harper & Row, 1950), pp. 112–22. Cf. Doumergue 4.1–11.

Decalogue sermons. In fact, the major outline of Calvin's thought on the Decalogue had already received expression prior to the sermons. For example, the opening chapter of the 1536 edition was entitled "On the law"[44] and dealt specifically with the Ten Commandments. Moreover, the preponderance that would both survive and substantially constitute the definitive edition of 1559 had clearly appeared by 1539.[45] The final edition would add four new sections and reorganize the material, but on the whole, Calvin's thought on the Law was not that radically affected.

With regard to the sermons, one can say that they develop in a popular and engaging manner what the *Institutes* define with clarity and brevity. This in no way denigrates them or suggests that they have nothing to contribute of their own. On the contrary, they reveal a vivacity and application that make them significant in their own right. But the theological content of the sermons had been established by Calvin before 1555. What the sermons exhibit is the compelling manner in which Calvin sought to apply what his *Institutes* more systematically discuss.

In the *Institutes,* Calvin designated the moral law as the crucial locus of the Law itself. By the moral law he meant the Decalogue, which he defined as "the true and eternal rule of righteousness" for all men and nations "who wish to conform their lives to God's will."[46] Concerning the moral law, Calvin developed five themes in the *Institutes* that are mirrored in the sermons.

First, the moral law must be understood in relation to the natural law which historically and psychologically precedes it. The moral law is nothing less than a witness to the natural law which God has engraved upon the consciences of men.[47] Since the fall, men's consciences are tainted, but enough of the natural law is recoverable to hold men accountable before God.

[44]*CO* 1.27–55.

[45]See *Institution de la Religion Chrestienne,* ed. Jacques Pannier, Les Textes Français (4 vols.: Paris: Societe Les Belles Lettres, 1936–1939). (Hereafter cited as Pannier, ed., vol., and p.) Pannier presents the 1541 French translation of the 1539 Latin edition. Cf. LCC translation. The latter is based on the text of the *Institutes* in the *Joannis Calvini Opera Selecta,* eds. Peter Barth and Wilhelm Niesel (Munich: Kaiser, 1928–1936), vols. 3–5; 2d ed. vol. 3 (1957); vol. 4 (1959). (Hereafter cited as *OS* bk., chap., and pt.) McNeill's edition incorporates certain superscript letters which indicate the five major editorial strata behind the LCC translation. See *LCC* 20.24. These superscript letters designate the preponderance of Calvin's work on the Law and Ten Commandments to date to the 1539 edition and in some cases to the 1536 edition.

[46]*OS* 4.20.15; *LCC* 21.1503. Cf. Pannier, ed., 4.217.

[47]See *OS* 4.20.16.

Second, Christ is the end of the Law. This is especially true of Calvin's understanding of the "ceremonial law," with its "figures" and "foreshadows" of the clearer revelation to be given in the gospel.[48] But the "shadowy" nature of Law is not limited to ceremonial law. The moral law is also proleptic; it points forward to the Christ and has its end in him.[49]

In the sermons, few themes receive as much attention as the "shadowy" nature of the Law whose end is Christ. But what Calvin stresses is the enduring and permanent worth of the moral law, whose authority is in no way mitigated by the shadowy nature of ceremonial law. As Calvin states in "The Thirteenth Sermon":

> Now in particular he wanted to write . . . [the Law] on two tablets of stone that it might endure, for it was not given [to last] for just a brief period [of time] as something transient. It is true that the ceremonies have ended, which is why the Law is called temporal, but what we must keep in mind is that this order, which was established among the ancient people to serve until the coming of our Lord Jesus Christ, has now been abolished and things have become perfect, indeed to the extent that we are no longer under the shadows and figures which prevailed then. In any event, the truth and substance of the Law were not [confined] to one age; they constitute something permanent which shall abide forever.[50]

Third, in the *Institutes* the moral law is characterized as containing both promise and despair. It offers salvation, but who can be obedient to the Law? Calvin likewise stresses this theme in the sermons, realizing that the demands of the Law are more than man can satisfy, but this is true only if men adhere to them for the purpose of securing their salvation.[51]

Fourth, the Law has three functions. All of these, as outlined by Calvin in the *Institutes,* appear in the sermons: 1) the Law reveals the righteousness of God while exposing and condemning unrighteousness; 2) it deters malefactors and restrains the unregenerate until the day of their salvation; and 3) it teaches Christians God's will for holy living and exhorts them to meditation and obedience.[52]

---

[48]See *OS* 2.8.28–33. These sections are pre-1559.
[49]See *OS* 2.7.11 and 2.
[50]*CO* 26.393.
[51]Calvin devotes considerable discussion to this problem in "The Sixteenth Sermon."
[52]See *OS* 2.7.6–12.

In the sermons, it is this third function that dominates. In fact, the first use does not effectively appear until Calvin's sermon on the last commandment.[53] Then it receives mention in the Fourteenth,[54] Fifteenth,[55] and Sixteenth[56] sermons. The second function is largely implied. It is the third use that empowers the series. From beginning to end, Calvin's primary purpose is to demonstrate how God's will for everyday life is revealed in the Ten Commandments; and not only revealed, but published to exhort and strengthen man's witness and confirm his life in obedience to God. In this respect, the third use of the law constitutes the critical foundation for all sixteen sermons.

Finally, Calvin notes that the law no longer has the power to bind men's consciences with a curse. The Law is still to be revered and obeyed, but out of a sense of freedom and not despair.[57]

> What does this mean? That we should not be borne down by an unending bondage, which would agonize our consciences with the fear of death. Meanwhile this always remains an unassailable fact: no part of the authority of the law is withdrawn without our having always to receive it with the same veneration and obedience.[58]

From the point of view of the sermons, it is the second half of this statement that prevails. The emphasis on liberty is not muted; Calvin's purpose in the sermons was not to hail the removal of the Law's curse, as Luther so powerfully did in his *Lectures on Galatians;* rather, it was to persuade men that God's Law is "the true and eternal rule of righteousness," even for Christian believers. The Decalogue is precisely this because it continues to call men from self-deception and self-reliance and confronts them with God's rule for their lives.

Equally important to the *Institutes* before 1555 was a body of principles to be kept in mind when reading, interpreting, and applying the Ten Commandments. In the definitive edition of 1559, Calvin discusses these in Book 2, chapter 8, sections 1–12, but,

---

[53]*CO* 26.373, 379, 382. See "The Twelfth Sermon."
[54]*CO* 26.397–98. See "The Fourteenth Sermon," n. 19.
[55]*CO* 26.409, 416–417. See "The Fifteenth Sermon," nn. 19, 27, 117.
[56]*CO* 26.425. See "The Sixteenth Sermon," n. 69.
[57]See *OS* 2.7.14–15. Cf. Pannier, ed. 1.296f.
[58]*OS* 2.7.15; *LCC* 20.363–64.

like the foregoing themes, they were already in print by 1539.[59] These principles are central. As a reading of the sermons will demonstrate, they incontestably governed Calvin's approach in the Decalogue series. All together there are at least eight such principles. (In the *Institutes*, Calvin only identifies three as principles, but the additional five may justly be inferred.)

The first stresses the sufficiency of God's will. God alone is God, man's Creator, Father, and Lord. Therefore man must eschew his own "mind's caprice" and cling to the mind of God. Thus there is no need to alter the Law to suit human wills or to regard it as a mere springboard for moral reflection.[60]

The second emphasizes that the God of the Decalogue is both a righteous and merciful God. Neither dimension can be forgotten.[61] On the one hand, God threatens men with judgment, but on the other, he always attracts them "by an amicable means."[62]

The third stresses that since the lawgiver is spiritual, the law must be spiritually interpreted.[63] Thus it is not murder alone that is prohibited in the sixth commandment, but anger and hate as well; not merely adultery in the seventh, but also lust and inordinate passion; not simply covetousness in the tenth, but greed, avarice, and deceit—whatever their form.[64]

The fourth principle underscores the need to understand each commandment's purpose.[65] It is the purpose of a commandment that provides the key that makes the commandment accessible and relevant beyond the mere repetition of its words.

The fifth has to do with Calvin's rule of opposites. When something is commended, then its opposite is condemned.[66]

The sixth focuses on the strong language of the Law. Why are only heinous crimes forbidden? Because the flesh strives to obfuscate sin and vitiate it of its foulness. Thus the Law contains harsh

---

[59]See the superscript letters in the *LCC* 20.367–79. McNeill identifies the preponderance of Calvin's prefatory remarks on the Ten Commandments as belonging to 1536 and 1539 strata.

[60]See *OS* 2.8.2.

[61]See *OS* 2.8.4.

[62]*CO* 26.417. See "The Fifteenth Sermon," n. 105.

[63]In the *Institutes* (2.8.6), Calvin designates this principle as his first.

[64]See *OS* 2.8.6; *LCC* 20.372.

[65]Calvin's second principle in the *Institutes* (2.8.8).

[66]See *OS* 2.8.8; *LCC* 20.375.

examples to elicit our disgust of all sin.[67] Or as Calvin explains it in "The Eighth Sermon," "God confronts us with the most detestable things in order that we might learn to guard against doing evil."[68]

The seventh principle emphasizes the two tables of the Law as foci of perfect righteousness.[69] Perfect righteousness involves adherence to both tables of the Law, never the playing of one against the other. It is a principle that guides Calvin throughout his series.

Finally, Calvin mentions the precept of love.[70] This means loving your neighbor as yourself and doing unto others as you would have them do unto you. Whenever in doubt about the meaning of a commandment, the "precept of love" will provide clear insight.

In addition, there are three other principles that appear in the sermons and exercise occasional control over Calvin's interpretation of the Law: 1) the image of God in man, 2) a text's natural sense, and 3) the principle of accommodation.

The first underscores man's bond with his fellowman. Men belong to one race and ancestry. This ought to mollify what they do.[71] As for the second, Calvin reminds his hearers that the "true and natural sense" of a passage must always prevail.[72] The third reminds men that God has accommodated himself to each age according to its capacity to receive him.[73] It is a principle Calvin never tires of reiterating throughout the series. He uses it to underscore two basic convictions. On the one hand, there is an infinite distance between God and man. Man can never hope to rise to God, nor can he know God as he is in himself. On the other hand, accommodation dramatizes God's goodness and grace, as it is precisely this God who does descend, speak, and provide man with the eternal Word that alone engenders life.[74]

---

[67]See *OS* 2.8.10; *LCC* 20.376.

[68]*CO* 26.323. See "The Eighth Sermon," n.13.

[69]Calvin's third principle in the *Institutes* (2.8.11).

[70]In Latin: "dilectionis praeceptum," *OS* 3.393; in French: "le precepte de dilection," Pannier ed. 1.276. See *OS* 2.8.55; *LCC* 20.418.

[71]*CO* 26.304, 325, 351. See the sixth, eighth, and tenth Sermons, nn. 84, 26, 33 respectively.

[72]See T. H. L. Parker, *Calvin's New Testament Commentaries* (London: SCM Press Ltd., 1971), p. 64.

[73]See *OS* 2.11.13; *LCC* 20.462–63.

[74]*CO* 26.248, 251; see "The Second Sermon," nn. 10, 21. See also H. Jackson Forstman's discussion of accommodation in his *Word and Spirit: Calvin's Doctrine of Biblical Authority* (Stanford: Stanford University Press, 1962), pp. 13f., 16, 55, 60, 107, 114, 115.

Far more could be said by way of theological background, but suffice it to note that the *Institutes* provide the theological foundation upon which the sermons rest.

A Homiletical Footnote

Calvin's homiletical aims, gifts, and style have been surveyed by many able scholars.[75] This Introduction can do little more than add a footnote, but the footnote the Decalogue sermons permit us to add is a tantalizing one.

The Swiss printer Conrad Badius supplies an interesting Preface to his 1557 edition of Calvin's sermons on the Ten Commandments that provides a powerful, contemporary assessment of Calvin's preaching. Writes Badius:

> Among the excellent gifts with which God has enriched his Church in all times, one of the most useful and necessary is that of Prophecy. It exists for the purpose of clearly understanding and purely expounding to God's people the holy Scripture according to its *vray et naturel sens* and of understanding how to apply it properly to one's own time and in accordance with those with whom one has to do.[76]

Of note here are the last several lines, emphasizing the necessity of applying the true and natural Word to "one's own time" and in a manner that is relevant for those involved. It is obvious that Badius thinks that Calvin has accomplished this well. In fact, Badius observes that most people prefer "golden orators" who mouth a mixture of pleasantries and "morally questionable stories of secular writers," all of which undermine piety. Therefore, to combat this abuse, as well as to penetrate the world still dominated by the Pope, Badius explains:

> I thought that I would bring to the people a great consolation, through the use of my art, by enabling them to behold that pasture which sustains us and in what simplicity, purity, truth, reverence, and zeal the Word of God is proclaimed to us by those whom the Lord Jesus has commissioned as Pastors over his flock in this country.[77]

[75]See the appropriate references in the Bibliography.

[76]See *Sermons de M. Iehan Calvin sur les dix commandemens de la Loy, donnée de Dieu par Moyse, autrement appelez le Decalogue: Recueillis sur le champ et mot à mot de ses predications, lors qu'il preschoit le Deuteronome, sans que depuis y ait este rie[n] adiouste ne diminue* (A Genève, De l'imprimerie de Conrad Badius. 1557), p. 2. (Hereafter cited as Calvin, *Sermons sur les dix commandemens*, 1557 ed., p.) Translation my own.

[77]Ibid., p. 3.

Badius goes on to point out "the difference between expounding the Word of God and babbling in the pulpit." For this reason he has selected Calvin's Decalogue sermons, taken down precisely as Calvin preached them, without any "polishing up." Finally, Badius explains why in particular he wants to publish these sermons. Most people interpret the commandments literally, but what Calvin has done is to expound them so effectively that they genuinely touch life "interiorly."[78] In other words, Calvin has fulfilled Badius' definition of prophecy and has thereby confronted his audience with the Word of God in the context of their "own time" with all of its ramifications. In Badius' view, this is preaching.[79]

Textual Information

The text used as the basis for this volume is that published in the *Calvini Opera* 26.236–432. The *Corpus Reformation* contains Calvin's entire series on the Book of Deuteronomy, of which the Decalogue sermons constitute but a small section.

In their "Notice Litteraire" to the Deuteronomy collection, the *CR* editors discuss three major publications of Deuteronomy sermons which they consulted in order to establish an adequate text: a 1567 edition, a 1562 edition, and a 1562 Wolfenbüttel edition. The 1567 edition provided the editors with a complete copy of Calvin's *Sermons on the Book of Deuteronomy*.[80] This copy was made available by the Bibliothèque de Genève. Its editor was Thomas Courteau and its place of publication, Geneva. The *CR* editors also refer to a publication of Deuteronomy sermons which included only an extract of the 1567 edition. This is the 1562 edition, containing Calvin's sixteen *Sermons on the Ten Commandments*.[81] Its editor was Francois Estienne; Geneva was also its place of publication. The Wolfenbüttel text was in a poor state of preservation, and thus its usefulness was limited.

The *CR* editors explain that they collated the 1567 and 1562

---

[78] Ibid., p. 4.
[79] For an extensive study of Calvin's homiletical aims and abilities, vis-a-vis the Decalogue sermons, see the translator's Introduction to his doctoral dissertation, listed in the Bibliography.
[80] See *CO* 25.577–78.
[81] Ibid., cols. 593–94.

editions. They preferred the former and considered it the more accurate and reliable. But in the end, they judged the two editions textually the same. Second, they dropped the Bible references at the head of each sermon, and third, deleted Calvin's closing prayers.

The section I have translated begins with the thirtieth sermon Calvin preached on Deuteronomy and concludes with the forty-fifth. These sermons correspond to the sixteen on the Ten Commandments, which comprised the 1562 edition.

Although I did not have access to the 1567 edition, a microfilm copy of a 1557 edition, published by Conrad Badius, was made available to me. This copy was obtained from the Houghton Library of Harvard University and is coded as FC5. C1394.557s, film 75-.[82]

Having studied this Badius edition closely and having compared it to the *CR* text, my overall conclusion is that the *CR* editors have established a reliable text. Variations exist between the 1557 Badius edition and the collated text of the *CR*, but these discrepancies are not of a detrimental character. If anything, the *CR* text is more complete and stylistically superior.[83]

I have sought to translate Calvin's French into good, strong, readable English. In the process, I have attempted to capture his mood and intention as much as what he "literally" said. Throughout this book my concern has been for accuracy in words and expressions, but in a manner that does justice to nuances of both languages.

In general, I have observed the following procedure:

1. translated all of Calvin's biblical references directly from the French text of the sermons;

2. translated major words and terms in a consistent manner, footnoting the text where I have used synonyms;

3. broken up many long and complicated sentences into shorter ones for the sake of clarity;

4. preserved Calvin's hierarchical style as effectively as possible, insofar as Calvin's sentences are logically interlinked by forceful connectives that develop his thought; and

5. related (by means of footnotes) major concepts, data, and

---

[82]See n. 76.
[83]For a complete discussion of textual comparisons, see the translator's dissertation, cited in the Bibliography, pp. 165–79 of the dissertation.

material appearing in the sermons to sections in the Introduction, the *Institutes*, and other Calvinist literature.

In order of their importance and usefulness, the following principal dictionaries and glossaries have guided me in this task.

Huguet, Edmond Eugene Auguste. *Dictionnaire de la langue française du seizième siècle.* 7 vols. Paris: Champion: Didier, 1925–1967.

Godefroy, Frédéric Eugène. *Dictionnaire de l'Ancienne Langue Française et de Tous Ses Dialects du IXe. au XVe. Siècle.* 10 vols. Paris: F. Vieweg; E. Bouillon, 1880–1902.

Benoit, Jean-Daniel, ed. "Glossaire." *Jean Calvin: Institution de la Religion Chres-tienne.* Centre de Recherches d'Historie des Religions de l'Université de Stras-bourg. 5 vols. Paris: Librairie Philosophique J. Vrin, 1957–63. Vol. 5, pp. 389–463.

The New Cassell's French Dictionary. Completely revised by Denis Girad, Gaston Dulong et als. New York: Funk and Wagnalls, 1968.

Lafaye, M. comp. *Dictionnaire des Synonymes de Langue Française.* Paris: Librairie de L. Hachette et Cie., 1858.

Chevallet, A. De. *Origine et Formation de la Langue Française.* 2d ed. 3 vols. Paris: J.-B. Dumonlin, Librairie, 1858.

Higman, Francis M., ed. "Glossary." *Jean Calvin, Three French Treatises.* Athlone Renaissance Library. London: The Athlone Press, 1970. pp. 169–71.

Pannier, Jacques, ed. "Glossaire." *Jean Calvin, Institution de la Religion Chrestienne.* Les Textes Francais. 4 vols. Paris: Societe Les Belles Lettres, 1936–39. Vol. 4, pp. 361–63.

This is an independent translation. The last translation of the Deuteronomy corpus was rendered by Arthur Golding in 1583.[84] Because Golding's translation made available Calvin's closing prayers, I have incorporated these in the footnotes at the end of each sermon. The greatest value of Golding's work, however, lies in the marginal citations of some of Calvin's biblical references.

Finally, I alone must assume full responsibility for all inac-curacies and ineptitude of expression. In the French the sermons often attain an eloquence that does not survive in the translation.

---

[84]The bibliographical information for the Golding translation is: *The Sermons of M. Iohn Calvin Upon the Fifth Booke of Moses called Deuteronomie:* Faithfully gathered word for word as he preached them in open Pulpet; Together with a preface of the Ministers of the Church of Geneva, and an admonishment made by the Deacons there. Also there are annexed two profitable Tables, the one containing the chiefe matters; the other the places of Scripture herein alledged. Translated out of French by Arthur Golding. At London, Printed by Henry Middleton for George Bishop. Anno Domini 1583. (Hereafter cited as *Sermons Upon the Fifth Book of Moses,* trans. Golding.)

Publications in English

Between 1579 and 1581 the *Sermons on the Ten Commandments* enjoyed no less than six printings in English.[85] The entire Deuteronomy series did not appear until 1583; it was reissued twice.[86] The major editions and their reissues are as follows:

Sermons of M. Iohn Caluine, vpon the X. Commandementes of the Lawe, geven of God by Moses, otherwise called the Decalogue. Gathered word for word, presently at his Sermons, when he preached on Deuteronomie . . . Translated out of Frenche into English, by I. H(armar). London (Thomas Dawson): for Iohn Harison, 1579.

Another issue. For G. Bishop, 1579.

Another issue. For T. Woodcocke, 1579.

Another issue. For G. Bishop, 1581.

Another issue. For T. Woodcocke, 1581.

Another issue. For I. Harison, 1581.

The sermons of M. Iohn Calvin vpon the fifth booke of Moses called Deuteronomie: faithfully gathered word for word as he preached them (by D. Raguenier) . . . *Together with a Preface of the ministers of the Church of Geneva.* . . . Translated out of French by Arthur Golding, London: H. Middleton for G. Bishop, 1583.

Another issue. For I. Harison, 1583.

Another issue. For T. Woodcocke, 1583.

[85] See British Museum: *General Catalogue of Printed Books to 1955, Compact Edition* (New York: Readex Microprint Corporation, 1967), vol. 4, pp. 96–97. Cf. also *The National Union Catalog Pre-1956 Imprints* (London: Balding & Mansell Ltd., 1970), vol. 91, pp. 294–95.

[86] Ibid.

John Calvin's Sermons on the Ten Commandments

Friday, June 7, 1555[1]

Sermon One[2]

Deuteronomy 4:44–5:3[3]

Recognizing how difficult it is for the world to be retained
under his subjection, God chose a people and willed to govern
them not simply for a limited period,[4] but continuously that they
might become sufficiently accustomed to his yoke[5]—which is how
he daily makes use of the same in his church. In fact, hearing
God's truth [proclaimed] only once ought to be enough. However,
we do not believe as promptly as we ought, for no sooner than we
begin we regress and ultimately forget what we have learned.

For this reason, (I say) God is not satisfied with a once-for-all

[1]N. in *CO:* "This sermon corresponds to the first in the 1562 collection, pp.
10–30, where nevertheless it is said to refer to Chapter 4:44–46 only." *CO* 26.235.

[2]The original title: "The Twelfth Sermon on Chapter 4:44–49 and Chapter
5:1–3" of Deuteronomy. *CO* 26.235.

[3]Cf. Calvin's development of this text in his *Commentaries on the Four Last Books of
Moses Arranged in Form of a Harmony,* trans. Charles William Bingham (4 vols.:
Grand Rapids: Wm. B. Eerdmans Publishing Company, 1950), vol. 1, pp. 338–41.
(Hereinafter cited as Comm. *Four Books of Moses,* vol. and p.) For the original Latin
text see *CO* 24.203–11.

[4]coup.

[5]ioug.

revelation concerning what is necessary for our salvation, but he recalls it to our memory and impresses it upon our hearts as much as possible. That is why, in this passage, Moses recounts that not only did he transmit[6] the law on Horeb, but after completing his wanderings of forty years or thereabouts, he again instructed the people. But as we have already discussed,[7] the important point is that throughout that time he never ceased to call to their attention what God had already commanded him to proclaim.

But the diligence we observe in Moses is not superfluous. When he says: *having come near the Jordan, having defeated Sihon King of the Amorites and Og King of Bashan his neighbor, he once again recalled to their memory the statutes and ordinances of God,*[8] he did so that the people might pause there and take advantage of the law and, as if they had not been sufficiently taught, at least learn the truth of God while resting there. That is what Moses meant in this passage. For he particularly mentions *the Law, the Testimonies, the Statutes, and the Ordinances,*[9] in order to explain better (as we have already touched on earlier), that God, far from only half-teaching his people, or proposing an obscure, deficient, or imperfect doctrine, included in the law all that was good and useful. So that if the people had accepted it, there would have been no need to inquire further, for on the whole they were already being led by the law. That is the point. For what they were being taught was as fully doctrine as the law.

Next are the *testimonies*. In essence they mean the same thing as if God had declared that when he makes a covenant with men and enumerates it article by article, he neither omits nor forgets anything essential to that mutual covenant which he made when it pleased him to adopt us for his people and his church and to lead us to God. Everything which concerns this spiritual union between himself and us is included under this word *testimony*. They are the articles. For when a covenant is made, what is appropriate for each party is laid down. We see then how God solemnly affirmed[10] here that the law contained a sufficient doctrine, on condition that men adhere to it. The statutes and the ordinances come next.

---

[6]baillé-donné.
[7]In reference to preceding sermons preached on Deuteronomy.
[8]A conflation of Deut. 4:46–47.
[9]Deut. 4:45.
[10]protesté-affirmé.

Now it is admirable that God goes to such pains to teach us and further declares that he omits nothing. Nevertheless our minds are so fickle that we always covet something better than what we can find in the Word of God. This diabolic curiosity has forever reigned in the world. And even today we see that wherever one turns one cannot come to the end of this accursed cupidity—that men always desire to be wiser than God intends. And why? [For] although we cannot pretend when his Word is preached to us that he might not have declared to us all that was good,[11] we wriggle, however, and always want excessively more than God has shown us. Therefore whenever such a vice is detected among us, so much the more is it imperative that we remember the warning which is contained here: for it informs us that if we wish to allow God to be our master, then we shall discover in his school all perfect wisdom. For the law exists precisely to make us prudent.

Then further it contains (as we have said) articles whose purpose is to unite us to our God. And *that*[12] constitutes our happiness and glory. And then it shows us the rule for right living;[13] for it is no longer a question of searching for what God approves, as we have both the statutes and ordinances. Therefore we well know and are all persuaded that our life will be pleasing to God when we do not exceed the limits which he has assigned us. But if we add anything to it at all, we must not suppose that God will approve of that as an ordinance or as a good thing. For he has not neglected anything that is necessary and useful.

These two points are well worth noting. For their purpose is to recommend as highly as possible that doctrine which is proclaimed to us every day in the name of God. Therefore seeing that it is a perfect wisdom, ought we not apply our entire capacity to it and secure it? When we see that God does not cease, but daily continues to teach us, should we not from our side also be attentive and diligent to profit under him? And if at first we are not as successful as we ought to be, throughout the rest of our life should we not strive to understand the will of God better until such time as we are liberated from all ignorance—which will only be after we have left this world and not before?

Moses did well. It is certain that today he should serve us as

---

[11]"Car nous ne pouvons pas porter envie, quant sa parole nous est preschee, qu'il ne nous ait declaré tout ce qui estoit bon." *CO* 26.236.

[12]Italics my own.

[13]Cf. *Institutes* 2.7.12; 2.8.1.

both a rule and example. For he did not at all act rashly.[14] Thus God established him as a mirror to all prophets and to all who are responsible for teaching in the church of God. Let us therefore perceive that God did not merely intend for us to receive his truth only on one day, as if one lesson were adequate for us; rather, what we have heard is reiterated for us in order that it might dwell in us and become so rooted in us that we are no longer able to plead the excuse: "O I have not yet been that well informed!"

God, then, on his part is always ready in order that we might not err, unless we do so knowingly or by deliberate malice.

Now the *temple of Peor* is specifically mentioned here as an object which diverted the people toward superstitions, and yet it was also a remedy in which God often urged them through his Word not to participate[15] in pagan idolatries. Nevertheless it is true that a severe chastisement has befallen those who of necessity keep their attention fixed on an idol's temple.

It was as if God has despised them in order to say: "I have called you to possess a land which has been dedicated to my service. There you would have seen nothing that would have made you take offense. For my sanctuary would have been set up in your midst, I would have been purely worshiped according to my law, the land would not have been profaned by ancient superstitions, for all that would have been razed. One would have had everything except to reecho my praises. Now you are here in a corner of a country where you gaze on an idol's temple, where there are sordid abominations. Therefore since you have not been worthy to enter the land that I have promised you, it is a fitting vengeance that you are conscious of your sins."

That is, then, how God willed to punish his people when they abandoned him to dwell near the temple of Peor. And today when we mingle with idolaters, and are conscious of the offenses which they commit and how they pervert all religion, let us be aware that God punishes us through such idolatry[16] and that he at least humbles us because of our sins. Furthermore we must grieve, not only for the offenses which unbelievers commit, but knowing well that we are not worthy until all the world is reformed and there is unanimity and harmony in religion, until God is purely worshiped by all; until then we are not worthy of beholding that country.

---

[14]"Car il ne s'est point fait aussi á la vollee." *CO* 26.237.
[15]melast-se méla.
[16]par ce moyen-la.

Therefore let us consider as sin the tendency to be attracted to any superstitions.[17]

But whatever the case, God did not forget to provide a sufficient cure for the people of Israel. For when the law had been taught by Moses, it was as if God had separated his own from the wretchedly blind[18] who were becoming exhausted and even misled by their superstitions.

Now from this we need to observe that although the world was perverted and steeped in confusions, and although everything was full of errors and corruptions, nevertheless, we have the Word of God to guide us, for it must strengthen us in order to defy[19] all the superstitions of idolaters. And if after God has given us his Word we are so full of vanity as to decline such aid, then we have no further excuse. For as I have already said, this must be a rather effective bridle for us provided God declares his will to us.

Indeed, though all the world should pull against the grain, and some follow a whim, and others champion a specious religion, nonetheless, once we have heard the voice of God and have perceived his will, all that must be regarded as frivolous. Thus, let us learn to take pride in this reliable and infallible doctrine that we might retreat from all worthless opinions, from all errors, and whatever the devil might forge as well as men invent in the world. That is what we must cling to when Moses mentions the temple of Peor.

Now in addition he adds that *this was after the two Kings, Og King of Bashan and Sihon King of the Amorites, who lived at Heshbon, had been defeated.*[20] For this circumstance is mentioned for the purpose of holding the people accountable lest they should be disobedient to God.

Now we know that according to the favors God bestows on us, we ought to be that much more stimulated by his love and his fear. God is revealed as liberal toward us, and ought that not attract us toward him even more? For when a mortal man is obligated to us because of a certain benefice, he would be held in disregard if he did not acknowledge the benefit which we afforded him. How much less then an excuse has a man toward the

[17]"Ainse selon que les superstitions nous sont prochaines, et que nous sommes contraints d'en voir les marques, ou d'en ouyr quelque chose: que nous imputions cela à nos pechez." *CO* 26.238.

[18]les povres aveugles.

[19]despiter-defier.

[20]See Deut. 4:46–47.

living God! Let us keep in mind therefore that Moses expressly mentions these two defeated kings in order to help the people fully fathom that they [the defeats] are in fact two excellent victories [of God]. Hereby, whenever we have resolved to make an attack against the interdictions of our God, we have been valiantly repulsed, there has been no virtue in us, and our enemies have been like hornets whose sting puts out our eyes.[21] Such is the similitude contained in this passage.

Moreover, these were two strong and robust kings who were defeated—not that it cost us anything—whom God delivered into our hands. Who was the cause of these two victories? Was it not God who directs and governs all things? Seeing then that he has had compassion on us and has begun to accomplish the promise which he made to our fathers, of which we have already received a good proof, is it not truly appropriate that we take the trouble to yield ourselves to our God and totally be subject to him? Should we not put ourselves back in his hand, which he has so forcibly made known because of his love for us?

That, I contend, is what Moses understood by this passage which recounts the defeat of Sihon and Og. It was to expose the ingratitude of the people, unless they peaceably subject themselves to the service of God to whom they were so much indebted.

Now we ought also to apply this doctrine to our usage. For whenever we are aware of any idleness in ourselves, any indifference, any rebellion, anything that arouses[22] our flesh, or whenever we do not relate[23] to God out of joy,[24] or with as much excitement as is expected, let us begin to enumerate the benefits which we have received from him: "Poor creature, how lax you are not to adhere to your God when he has revealed[25] his will to you! Consider what you take from him. Consider the benefits which he has distributed until now." Therefore let each one of us examine how much we are indebted to him to the end that we might be that much more motivated to serve him. And in general let us recognize that not only has he created us, but having ransomed us by the blood of our Lord Jesus Christ—as he delivered the people from the country of Egypt—he has drawn us to him-

---

[21] " . . . comme des mouches quespes qui nous sont venus crever les yeus, . . . " CO 26.239.

[22] se rebecque-se révolte.

[23] aspirer.

[24] si alaigre.

[25] declairé-manifesté.

self by his grace and given us the doctrine of the gospel, thus taking us under his protection, the effect of which he demonstrates to us everyday.

Moreover, how often have we received aid and succor in our infirmities? Should we not have been overwhelmed a thousand times by Satan if our God had not extended his hand to assist us? We would have all been overcome. Not only would we have been smothered with temptations, but we would have been engulfed without the succor which I have described. And at the same time our Lord does not cease daily to confirm us in his grace. For our part then, as our text prescribes, let us be advised to take advantage of the opportunity to serve him more ardently.

Now following this Moses adds that he spoke to the people of Israel, saying, *Hear the Law which the Lord has proclaimed to you, in order to learn it and to observe it.*[26] Once again[27] Moses includes the preface which we have already seen, i.e., that the law of God is not given solely for men to hear it that they might be aware of its contents; rather, it is given that we might be reformed and that God may approve of the subjection which we render him. In short, we see that the doctrine of God results[28] in practice and that it is incumbent on us to demonstrate in reality that we have not been taught it without avail.

Now Moses says in the first place, *Hear the Law which I proclaim to your ears in order to learn it.* It's as if he were saying that God has no intention for the doctrine which is preached to us in his name and by his authority to fall to the ground; rather it is imperative that we carefully receive it and devote our study to it. For whose fault is it if we so poorly benefit from God's Word when we are so preoccupied with the things of this world? And is it not so because we come to the sermon and read the holy Scripture as if it were only a matter of duty? We still do not endeavor to perform the Law as it was intended in order to observe correctly what has been said to us. Therefore let us be advised to be good and diligent students, while God acts graciously to instruct us by his Word.

Furthermore, Moses emphasizes the text: *that he has proclaimed to your ears.* It is true that this manner of speaking could be harsh in our language, but it means that God does not speak an obscure or alien tongue to us. Rather, he privately declares to us all that is

[26]Deut. 5:1.
[27]derechef-de nouveau.
[28]gist.

required. Thus, in this manner he descends to us in order that we might have a simple declaration of his will. In the light of this, what excuse can hold up if his Word is lost, or if it is bent,[29] or if we do not use it to our advantage?

It is true that as long as we are dull and ignorant, we shall always find a great deal of obscurity in the Word of God, that it will be too high and too profound for us. But to whom should this fault be attributed? For let us note that all who complain[30] that the Word of God is an unknown language to them are censured[31] as liars. They do God wrong and blaspheme him, since they deny and despise the grace which Moses affirms was given to the people when the law was proclaimed. For at that time it is said that God spoke to the ears of the people by the mouth of Moses. Thus it is true that the doctrine which they received must equally have been intimately given; but today we have no reason to point out this subtlety as an excuse for not understanding fairly what is contained in the holy Scripture. For God is fairly near and speaks rather simply to us. Indeed, he does not let go of us, unless our ears are deaf to him. And even then we should note that he does not rest until we are ready to benefit from his teaching.

Nevertheless, we must return to what we read, *that the Law must be kept and followed by all.*[32] For if we will only consent to the Word of God and bear witness to it, that it is good, true, and holy, God will side with us. What is at issue then? God, who wishes to test whether he will be master or not! For this is the rule of our life: that we should not merely inquire about what he says to us, but that we should renounce our own desires and attachments, and we should ask for nothing except to please him and be governed by him and his justice. When we have done that, that will be a sufficient proof that God has attained the superiority which he merits. But until we come to that point, we shall never be able to profit from his teachings. Therefore let those who hear the Word of God always keep in mind this phrase "to do." Why? Because it is God who exercises the grace that we might be taught. And for what purpose? Not that we might listen for him to say: "That is well said," or "That is good," but to the end that our life might be reformed, and that, insofar as his rule is both good and reliable,

---

[29]s'escoule-se fléchit.
[30]se pleignent.
[31]redarguez-blâmés.
[32]Deut. 5:1.

we might no longer err as we have done in the past. Indeed, the unfortunate still ignore that they are wandering from the right path, for they are not at all taught as we. Nevertheless, his teaching ought serve our mortification in order that God might dominate us and we might be subject to him.

That in short is what Moses meant when he assures the people in this preface that he set forth the law, not that they might hear it, or have their ears wafted by it, but that they might both keep and receive it.

Next, he quotes the following statement in order to confirm it: *For God made a covenant with the people on the mountains of Horeb,*[33] the better to bring them to fear and obey him forever.[34] For if God only demanded his due, we should still be required to cling to him and to confine ourselves to his commandments. Moreover, when it pleases him by his infinite goodness to enter into a common treaty, and when he mutually binds himself to us without having to do so, when he enumerates that treaty article by article, when he chooses to be our father and savior, when he receives us as his flock and his inheritance, let us abide under his protection, filled with its eternal life for us. When all of those things are done, is it proper that our hearts become mollified even if they were at one time stone? When creatures see that the living God humbles himself to that extent, that he wills to enter into covenant that he might say: "Let us consider our situation. It is true that there is an infinite distance between you and me and that I should be able to command of you whatever seems good to me without having anything in common with you, for you are not worthy to approach me and have any dealings with whoever can command of you what he wills, with no further declarations to you except: 'That is what I will and conceive.' But behold, I set aside my right. I come here to present myself to you as your guide and savior. I want to govern you. You are like my little family. And if you are satisfied with my Word, I will be your King. Furthermore, do not think that the covenant which I made with your fathers was intended to take anything from you. For I have no need, nor am I indigent in anything. And what could you do for me anyway? But I procure your well-being and your salvation. Therefore, on my part, I am prepared to enter into covenant, article by article, and to pledge myself to you."

[33]Deut. 5:2.
[34]Reading with Golding, *Sermons Upon the Fifth Book of Moses,* p. 179.

When the living God humbles himself to that extent, I beg of you, should we not be more than ingrates if we did not humble ourselves before him and abstain[35] from all pride and arrogance? For it is not without cause that Moses speaks here of the covenant which God made with his people, primarily that his goodness and grace might be known.

Now if that took place in the time of the law, today there is an even better reason. For our Lord not only made a covenant with the Jews on that one occasion, but when he sent his unique Son, he revealed himself as our father and savior more amply than he had ever done and in an unsurpassably gentle and conciliatory manner,[36] as if he had divulged his most intimate feelings.[37] Accordingly, God has given us his heart in the person of our Lord Jesus Christ who so intimately communicates with us that he no longer calls us his servants but his friends.[38]

[Therefore] I beg of you, has the devil not bewitched us if we are not moved to submit everything to him, surrendering ourselves and all our feelings? Thus if we are conscious of any malice in ourselves which prevents us from serving God, or of any laziness, or if we are so asleep in the world that we cannot be awakened to magnify God, let us remember this covenant which the Lord made with us.

Now following this Moses adds: *It was not with our fathers that the Lord made the covenant, but with us,*[39] with those of us who are living today. This text can be understood in a twofold sense. On the one hand, it can be interpreted as a comparison which Moses makes in order to explain that the people who were living then could have been far more motivated to serve God, since they had received more grace than their fathers. To this end he speaks in Exodus: "I did not make myself known to your fathers by this name."[40] Speaking to Moses, God says that he did not reveal himself as God to Abraham, Isaac, and Jacob as he has to Moses. This means that the people should now have been alert, because God was revealing himself in an extraordinary way. On the other hand, this passage can be interpreted to mean that God did not make such a cov-

---

[35]deporter-abstenir.

[36]"... et d'une façon tant douce et amiable que rien plus:..." *CO* 26.242.

[37]"... que c'est autant comme s'il nous avoit ici desployé ses entrailles." *CO* 26.242.

[38]See John 15:15.

[39]Deut. 5:3.

[40]Exod. 6:3.

enant with our fathers. It is true that God spoke to his servants Abraham, Isaac, and Jacob and that they were sufficiently instructed. Particularly in the eighteenth chapter of Genesis it is said: "Shall I conceal from my servant Abraham what I intend to do now with Sodom and Gomorrah? For I know that he will instruct his family in my decrees, in my ordinances, in my judgments and laws."[41] There is Abraham, then, who sufficiently taught his family not simply in a meager way, but in judgments, statutes, and ordinances. In brief, it means that Abraham had the law of God engraved upon his heart. Moreover, it was a favor not to be despised when God sent his Law in two tables and willed that they contain a permanent instruction for his people. All this has been adequately testified for us.

That is what we should be able to reap from this passage when, in essence, Moses says[42] to the people: "My friends, perceive the good which God bestows upon us today, which he did not make available to our fathers, for he did not transmit a written law to them as he did to us, nor did he illuminate those things for them in detail. It is true that he sufficiently instructed them in whatever was necessary for their salvation. But the fact that he has descended to us constitutes a higher degree [of revelation] than ever attained, which should impel us all the more to draw near to him." Such is Moses' intention, if we interpret the passage in that way. Likewise, today whoever wishes may say that God has not dealt with our fathers as with us. Our Lord Jesus Christ said as much to his disciples: "Many Kings and Prophets desired to see the things which are preached to you; nevertheless, they did not have their wish."[43] In the same way, God, by his infinite mercy, willed to prefer us to the patriarchs and prophets, as it is also said that prophets were of greater service to our time than to their own.[44] Such words should encourage[45] us to come to him and to devote everything to his teaching.

Nevertheless, when everything is taken into consideration—although what we have just reviewed is inestimably useful and Scripture abounds with similar exhortations—when we ponder[46] his words, Moses perceived that God did not at all make his cov-

[41] An apparent paraphrased conflation of Gen. 18:17, 19.
[42] allegue-cite.
[43] See Luke 10:24.
[44] I Peter 1:12.
[45] enseignez.
[46] poisé-pesé or examiné.

enant with those who heard the law the first day that it was published, that is to say, not solely with them, but with those who survived them, who succeeded their trespass. Thus, ultimately Moses wanted to emphasize that the law, far from being mortal, or given only for the lifetime of those who first heard it, was a doctrine which was meant to keep its vigor and authority forever.

The Lord our God, he says, did not make the covenant with our fathers; that is to say, he did not merely will to have our fathers for his people, he did not bind himself to them so that his law would only be valid for forty or fifty years, but he also made a covenant with us and with those who were not even born when the law was published. Therefore you who were not at Mt. Horeb, you who did not see the fire on the mountain, may you nevertheless be assured that your God has nonetheless adopted you and that he has made a covenant in which you have been included. Therefore it is appropriate for you to observe his law, since it has been established to be permanent, to endure age after age, and to be preached until the end of the world.

That is Moses' true and natural sense.[47] And we can draw a favorable lesson from it; namely, that although we were not present at the beginning when the gospel was proclaimed and have not seen what was recounted to us from the law, nevertheless the work of God has not lost its authority. Why? It is true that when God chose Moses[48] that that was a special favor which he bestowed on the people who were living then. Nevertheless, the authority of our law must not be deprecated, for it contains the truth of God which abides forever, which never varies, and which does not perish[49] in the manner of men. It is said that men are like a flower, or like grass that is immediately withered and dry,[50] but the truth of God is always permanent.

Now this truth which is neither changing nor variable is contained in the law. It is true that the law with regard to its ceremonies has been abolished, but with regard to its substance and doctrine which it contains, it always has virtue; it never decays. Thus let us note that although we did not live in the time of Moses, that does not mean that we can scorn the remonstrances which he made and which are contained in the law. Why? Because

---

[47]See "Introduction," n. 72.
[48]suscité Moyse.
[49]caduque-qui n'est point passée.
[50]Ps. 90:5–6.

he was speaking to us; he was not simply speaking to that multitude which was assembled on the mountain of Horeb. In general, he was speaking to the whole world.

If that is said about the law, how much more ought it be said about the gospel! For, as we have said, the law, with regard to its shadows and figures, is dead in decadence, but in the gospel there is nothing comparable. Here our Lord makes his new and eternal testament, a covenant which endures from age to age. What is fitting then when the gospel is preached? That we understand that the Son of God has come into the world, not solely to teach those with whom he conversed when he was a mortal man, but he called the world to salvation and purchased for God his father those to whom the commissioned apostles' voice went out across the world to the end that those who had never heard his voice might become participants in his doctrine. Today we must receive that same doctrine as if Jesus Christ were still in our midst, as if the apostles were still speaking with their own mouth. That, I say, is what we have to retain from this passage.

Moreover, we must not make any change in the church of God, nor give any attention to innovations in his Word, knowing that he wishes for there always to be an even pace and tenor. For inasmuch as he gave his gospel and established a certain régime of time for both his apostles and the primitive church, it is necessary for that to occur and for us to stop there. If we go beyond that, it's as much as if we choose to make the Word of God mortal and corruptible with ourselves. Therefore let us realize that although the world is unsteady, subject to revolutions everyday, and that some of us are too frequently haunted by opinions, we should not suggest, however, that we have the liberty to do one thing today and another tomorrow. Why? Because God did not make his covenant with our fathers, but with us who are living today. In the meantime, insofar as we are in the world, let us recognize that God governs us here, that he shows us the road in order that we might not be errant pilgrims who ramble about from pillar to post, led by our appetites, but that we might be led as if by his hand.

In the final analysis, when Moses says: *We who are all living today,*[51] it is in order to point out that men during their lifetime must not forge any new law for themselves; they must not have

[51]Deut. 5:3.

one law for today and another for tomorrow. Why? Because life is [contained] in the law of God which ought to be sufficient for us. Therefore let us profit from it alone.

Moreover, there is no doubt that Moses upbraids the people for their ingratitude, unless they dedicate their life to the service of God. It's as if he said: "Why do we live? Is it not because our Lord put us in this world? And since the life he has given us is from him, should we not dedicate it to his service? Should it not all be consecrated to his will?"

That is the reproach which Moses levels here at those who go astray, who do not seek the Word of God. Nevertheless, if it is necessary for us to keep what we have reviewed, it is for the purpose of knowing that we do not have an "overnight law,"[52] but a doctrine in which we must be confirmed as long as we live. For once we have received what is contained in the holy Scripture, let us make it our study in order to profit from it and to advance in it, so much so that until God removes us from this world, we shall always believe in it, knowing that he wishes to hold us in his covenant, that on his part he will neither be disloyal nor inconsistent, but he will be firm in his resolve.

If this is the case, let us do the same; and as long as we shall live, let us have no other consideration than to adhere to him, as he has pointed it out to us by his Word. It is not necessary for us to pretend to unite ourselves to God by our fantasies, but as he accordingly draws near us, let us come to him, and having come to him, let us advise ourselves to stay here.

That is what we need to learn from this passage in order to be inclined to receive the instruction which will be given hereafter from the law of God and his commandments.[53]

---

[52]"... une doctrine de trois iours:..." CO 26.246.

[53]Golding's translation concludes this sermon with the following exhortation: "Nowe let us kneele downe in the presence of our good GOD with acknowledgement of our faultes, praying him to make us feele them better than we have done, so as our whole seeking may bee to submit our selves unto him, and hee may vouchsafe to reach us his hand, not suffering us to bee any more given to our owne fancies and affections, but that wee may magnify his goodnesse which he useth towardes us, and fare the better by it by yielding him the obedience that hee deserveth: specially because hee hath vouchsafed to bring us his lawe and declare it to us, and hath not only shewed us the way how to live well, but also vouchsafed to adopt us to bee his children, and to shewe himselfe to bee our father and Saviour for our Lorde Jesus Christes sake. That it may please him to graint this grace not only to us, but also to all people. Etc." *Sermons Upon the Fifth Book of Moses*, trans. Golding, pp. 181–82. Cf. Calvin, *Sermons sur les dix commandemens*, 1557 ed., p. 18.

Wednesday, June 12, 1555[1]

Sermon Two[2]

Deuteronomy 5:4–7[3]

We have seen by the preceding that Moses worked diligently in order to make the people conscious of the majesty which God's Word contains, to the end that it might be received with all reverence.[4] For although men vehemently reaffirm their will to obey God (for nature also compels them to that end), they are still unable to submit to it; nevertheless, it is the true proof for knowing whether or not we are subject to God. But such is the rebellious nature of the world. And although men confess that it is necessary to receive the Word of God without resistance, nevertheless with great trouble will we find one out of a hundred who submits in

[1]N. in *CO:* "This sermon corresponds to the second in the 1562 collection, pp. 31–49, where nevertheless it is said to refer to Chapter 5:1–4." *CO* 26.247.

[2]The original title: "The First Sermon on Chapter 5:4–7." *CO* 26.247.

[3]Cf. Calvin's discussion of the First Commandment in his Comm. *Four Books of Moses*, vol. 1, pp. 341–42, 417–19; *CO* 24.211, 261–62. Also see the *Catechism, CO* 6.54. Cf. also the *Institutes* 2.8.13–16.

[4]The word *reverence* is used to translate *crainte* here. For Calvin the law inexorably elicits our "fear" of God as much as our "love" and "reverence." See *Institutes* 2.8.2.

good earnest to accord it the authority which it merits. And why is that? Because we do not apprehend at all the majesty of God which is revealed here.·

That is why Moses, not without cause, so often admonished those we have discussed that the Word of God must be of such a majesty toward us that all creatures tremble under it. And now again[5] he adds a confirmation to this subject in saying: *that God spoke to the people face to face on the mountain, out of the midst of the fire.*[6] It's as if he were saying: "Now you have no cause for doubting whether the doctrine which I proclaim to you is of God or man. For it has been so much and more approved: God has revealed himself to you by visible and well-known signs so that you ought to be conscious that it is he who has spoken." Now we see Moses' intention.

However, before we leave the subject, one ought to be able to ask a question here. Since it is said that God spoke face to face, and in light of the fact that men cannot comprehend his infinite glory, with what eyes can we contemplate the essence of God? We are so feeble that if God only sends us a little ray of his light, we would be totally dazzled and confused. And besides, we know what is said: that we cannot see God face to face until we have been renewed, which will not be until the last day. For now (says Saint Paul), we see in a mirror only, in part and in obscurities.[7] Further, it is said in another passage that the gospel today presents us with the majesty of God in such a way that we are able to see it. But the law has been obscured and has had a veil over it, preventing the fathers from having known God in such a way and as intimately as we know [him] today.[8] But all of that is held in very good understanding. For when we make a comparison of the law with the gospel, it is certain that one will find what Paul says is true. For God is not revealed in such familiarity as he reveals himself to us by means of our Lord Jesus Christ who is his living image.

Today, then, the great treasures of wisdom are opened before us; we know that God calls us to his kingdom of heaven and that he shows us that he accepts us as his children and heirs. That was not the case in the time of the law. Nevertheless, although today

[5]derechef-de nouveau.
[6]Deut. 5:4.
[7]I Cor. 13:12.
[8]II Cor. 3:12–18.

we have such an intimate knowledge, and such a personal one at that, what we have just cited continues true, that we see only in part. Why? Because we are not yet participants in the glory of God, thus we cannot approach him; rather, it is necessary for him to reveal himself to us according to our rudeness[9] and infirmity. The fact remains that since the beginning of the world when God appeared to mortal men, it was not in order to reveal himself as he was, but according to men's ability to support him. We must always keep this in mind: that God was not known by the Fathers. And today he does not appear to us in his essence. Rather he accommodates himself to us. That being the case, it is necessary for him to descend according to our capacity in order to make us sense his presence with us.[10]

At all events it is not without cause that Moses says here: *that he spoke face to face.*[11] For he means that the people did not have a conjecture for doubting, or for imagining only some opinion, but they had an infallible testimony, such that they could conclude: Here is God who has truly communicated himself to us that our faith need no longer be uncertain. And the doctrine which is proclaimed to us in his name need no longer be disputed as to whether or not it merits reception. Why? Because God has given a certain mark which cannot deceive us nor leave us in doubt that it proceeds from him. Thus we now see Moses' meaning. In any event, we may gather a good lesson from it. For if God does not reveal himself to us in as lofty a manner as our ambition requires, remember that it is for our profit and salvation that he does so. For if we but consider our infirmity, that should humble the audacity to which our nature is always soliciting us. For we would like to inquire into the secrets of God without end or measure. And why? Because we do not understand our own limits?[12] Nevertheless, let us magnify the goodness of our God, seeing that it pleased him to have regard for both us and our rudeness and that he is satisfied to hide his glory from us in order that we might not be overwhelmed by it.

For (as we have already said) we are not able to support it being as fragile as we are. However, know that there is no longer any

[9]rudesse-ignorance or rudeness.
[10]See "Introduction," n. 74.
[11]*Face to face.* Cf. Calvin's discussion of this phrase in his Comm. *Four Books of Moses,* vol. 1, pp. 341f; *CO* 24.211. The phrase confirms God's authorship of the law.
[12]faculte.

excuse when God shall have given us some evident sign of his presence except that we render to him the respect which he is due. Let us not expect God to come in his inestimable glory, for the skies to burst asunder, for all the angels of paradise to appear to us. But when our Lord reveals to us that it is he who speaks, let that suffice for us. Let us humble ourselves immediately. For if under these circumstances we still wish to be sluggish, he will blame us for having turned our back on him since he has shown his face to us.

Now it is true that in another place it is said to us that men cannot see the face of God without perishing, but although Moses had this revelation which is mentioned in Numbers,[13] that God was as familiar to him as a friend, the fact remains that it is said that he did not see him except for his back. Still its purpose is ever to show us that we must not presume to approach God as long as we are surrounded by our flesh, that we must not think to rise that high. For if the angels of paradise themselves under the figure of Seraphim hide their eyes when God reveals himself, what does this mean for us who only grovel here on earth? In any event, this is what God condemns in our ingratitude when we have not willed to contemplate his face and when the signs which reveal his presence to us are not considered sufficient.

Above all let us keep in mind here that it is as much a question of our subjection to the gospel as to the law. For it is in the gospel that God principally wills to be known of men in order that they may worship him, simply receiving all that proceeds from his mouth. To what end then shall we apply this sentence of Moses? That when the Scripture is put before us, and one preaches it to us and expounds it for us, or when we read it, that this preface might humble us to the end that we exalt God in all reverence and not attempt to dispute his Word, but tremble under it as it is pointed out in the prophet Isaiah.[14] For all that is contained in Holy Scripture is so well attested to us that we can say that God spoke to men as if he were revealing himself in a visible manner.

Still Moses adds: *that he was between the two as an intermediary between God and men, because the people were afraid and did not dare climb the mountain.*[15] Moses' meaning here is that although the law was

---

[13]N. in *CO:* "The 1562 edition reads more correctly—in Exod. (33:11, 23)." *CO* 26.249.

[14]Isa. 66:2, 5.

[15]Deut. 5:5.

carried by a mortal man, that should not detract from its authority. For that is due to the people's imperfection; it is the result of their vice. And it is a passage well-worth noting. For we are always looking for subterfuges in order to condone disrespect for the Word of God. True, we will not overtly pretend this, but the fact remains that this malice will be found in almost all the world; that we are comfortable when we can find some pretext for saying: "O I do not know if this Word is of God; I do not know if it is addressed to me; I do not know under what conditions." That is how the world always seeks to exempt itself from the obedience of the Word of God; and this excuse is by far too common when we say: "Yes, it is true that God must surely be obeyed, but in the meantime it is men like ourselves who preach. And it is necessary that their doctrine be received as if they were men who had come from heaven."

It seems to many people that that kind of thinking is sufficient to justify their continual rebellion against God, or in any event it does not restrain[16] them significantly to subject themselves to him and his Word.[17]

Now we have a response here whose purpose is to put an end to all[18] that: namely, that God when he sends his Word by the hand of men does so as a consequence of their vice and infirmity. Nevertheless he does not neglect to provide some mark of his glory to the end that his Word is easily recognized as celestial. For when we regularly inquire into it, we see that God approves it so much and more. So then it is not solely for the ancient Fathers that Moses spoke, but his admonition is addressed to us. Its purpose is to help us see that although men are made messengers in order to preach the Word of God, that does not detract from its majesty. And certainly we misunderstood our fragility when we hunger for God to perform miracles everyday and do not even understand what is fitting for us. As for miracles, there have been enough of them to ratify the truth of both the law and the gospel to those of us who have a full certainty about them. Nevertheless, today it is appropriate that God should send us people similar to ourselves to whom he commits the task of teaching us in his name and in his stead as he gently allures us and all humanity to himself.[19] After

---

[16]chaille.
[17]Calvin may well have had the Perrinists and his Bernese opponents in mind.
[18]pour . . . coupper broche.
[19]Calvin frequently emphasizes God's gentleness in accommodating himself to men. See the *Institutes* 2.8.4, 14.

all, do you think we could actually stand before his presence if he were to appear as he truly is? Alas! We would be totally consumed. If God were to speak in his force, we know what is said: the very rocks and mountains would melt.[20] And we who are so utterly weak, could we subsist before such a force without it destroying us?

Let us note then that when God ordained for his Word to be preached to us and made available in writing, he was accommodating himself to our weakness and was treating us as if he were a mortal man in order that we might not be frightened in coming to him, but that we might be drawn to him in all gentleness.[21] Moreover, consider the honor he bestows upon us when it pleases him to choose from among us people of no valor who nevertheless represent his person and speak to us in his Name. For what more could he assign to the angels of paradise? Could he give them a more honorable charge and office? In the fact that he deigns to fashion men into such a noble and excellent vessel[22] as to carry his Word, he reveals how great his goodness is toward us, that it is more than paternal.

Now in addition he tests our humility. For if he thundered from heaven, if he appeared to us visibly, if the angels descended, it would hardly be a thing of astonishment if men believed his Word. But when both the great and the small receive the decree[23] which he has instituted in his church: that we should obey his Word when it is preached, that is the means by which our faith is tested. Nevertheless, let us always return to this: that God has sufficiently revealed himself to men, so much so that we shall have no occasion to put his Word in doubt and dispute what has happened. For his will for us is more than certain on condition that we are not unwilling to receive the signs which have been given to us concerning it.

Thus you see what we have to cling to in Moses' passage when he says that the people did not dare climb the mountain because of the terror they perceived. And although today we would not refuse it if God were to speak to us, yet when everything is taken into consideration, it would be of no profit to us. Therefore let us

---

[20]An allusion to Ps. 97:5; Isa. 64:1, 3; Mic. 1:4.
[21]See n. 10 above.
[22]chose.
[23]ordre.

understand that God's use of the medium of men must not diminish at all the certainty of our faith.

In consequence it is said that God taught the people saying: "I
am the Lord your God, who rescued you from the land of Egypt.
You shall have no other God before me."[24] Here, in order to hold
the people of Israel in check, God shows them that the knowledge
which they have must separate them from all superstitions. For if
the pagans had idols and were misled by their errors and fantasies, we should not be astonished. Let us understand that it
comes from man himself. We are so inclined toward vanity that it
is a pity. It is hardly necessary for us to go to school in order to
learn to be deceived, for in this respect each of us is rather a
skilled teacher.[25] Briefly, we always tend toward evil, even under
the species of good, so that in place of serving God, there is
nothing in us but corruption and idolatry.

And so the pagans had their diverse superstitions, for each one
could conjure a god according to his post, and in the meanwhile
the living God was abandoned by all. And why? Because he was
not so gracious as to reveal himself to all the world. And so men
became stupid, but it was the fault of [their] teaching. In any
event, this does not excuse them, for they are still guilty before
God. Moreover, the source of idolatry came from the ingratitude
and malice of men who abandoned God on their own accord. But
when the world became decadent[26] (as I have already discussed),
the poor pagans wandered like blind men, for they had no light to
show them the way to salvation.

Now unless they hold to the law which God has given them, he
here accuses the people of Israel of rebellion. How is that? *I am the
Lord your God.* When he says, "I am the Lord," it is in order to
exclude all the gods which have been invented by men. It's as if he
said: "There is only one sole deity, and that will be found in me.
Thus it follows that those who have known me, who turn aside to
serve their idols, have no excuse, provided, to their knowledge,
they have not renounced the living God."

Now when he adds *that he is the God of this people,* his purpose is
to show that he was adequately revealed. It's as if he said: "I have
separated you from all the rest of men. You see how the others
rave. But this is due to the fact that they have neither guidance

[24]Deut. 5:6–7.
[25]grand docteur.
[26]abastardi.

nor direction.[27] But I have chosen you for my people and I have revealed[28] myself to you. Moreover, since I am your God, cling therefore to me, or you will have even less of an excuse than the pagans. For if that were the case your punishment would of necessity be double, a hundred times more heavy,[29] seeing that you would have corrupted the faith you promised me and would have broken the covenant which I made with you."

He cites[30] still further the grace which he bestowed upon the people, saying, *when he took them out of the land of Egypt, out of the house of bondage.*[31] By this he means that he has truly bound them to himself so that the people cannot revolt against him without meriting further punishment. For seeing that they shall have forgotten the redemption by which they were redeemed, their ingratitude will be double. For since they were purchased by the hand of God, it was imperative that they give themselves in service to him who was their Redeemer.

And in particular he calls Egypt "the House of Bondage" in order that the people thoroughly remember the condition under which they had existed there.[32] For we see how those who had sighed and cried when oppressed by such violence and tyranny as we read in Exodus, that no sooner than God had delivered them, they asked to return. And from whence did this proceed? Is it not from the fact that they no longer remembered the oppression which they suffered and the fact that the devil blinded their eyes in order that the grace of God might not be esteemed by them as it deserves? That is the reason why Moses entitles the land of Egypt: "The House of Bondage." In the end the commandment is added: *that the people shall have no other gods before him whom they must hold as their God.*[33]

Now let us apply all of this doctrine to our usage. In the first place, when he says, *I am the Lord,* let us truly learn to grasp the weight of these words: that since the majesty of God has appeared to us, we conceive of no other deity. For God cannot allow any rival.[34] If the sun obscures the light of the stars, is it not reasona-

---

[27]adresse.
[28]baillé.
[29]griefue.
[30]allegue-cite.
[31]Deut. 5:6.
[32]Cf. the *Institutes* 2.8.15.
[33]Deut. 5:7.
[34]"Car Dieu ne peut souffria d'autre compagnon." *CO* 26.253.

ble that when God reveals himself we should each worship him
and that what formerly appeared as glory seems as nothing now?
That is why it is said in the Prophets that when the Lord shall
reign, there will be no other light than his own; that even the sun
will be obscured, the moon will be turned into darkness.[35] That is
in order to show us that when we mingle with God any fantasies
off the top of our head, we diminish all rights that belong to him.
For he cannot bear any rival. It is necessary then that this word of
the Lord disarm in us all fantasies in order that we do not take
any further license to conceive of this or that. Let us be content
simply to have one sole God and let him suffice.

That is also why it is said that when our Lord Jesus shall have
set up and established his seat in the world that the idols of Egypt
will tumble.[36] Now this passage also belongs to us. For, in the
same way, Moses was saying to the people of old: "You have the
Lord who has appeared to you, it is imperative then that all idols
be driven from your midst." Furthermore, since God has revealed
himself to us in the person of his unique Son, it is equally imperative that all idols be swept away.

Now we know that this country of Egypt, above all the others of
the world, had been crammed full of idols. Therefore, inasmuch
as they were formerly plunged in lies and darkness, surrounded
by an infinite number of idols, all that has to be swept away when
God reveals that he is the Lord. Still when he is called *our God*, its
purpose is to win us over to himself in such a way that his majesty
might be known by us in an amiable way. For if God only spoke in
his eternity and essence we would often be confused. True, that
would be a fitting condemnation for all daydreaming, but in any
event it would hardly serve for our instruction and benefit. Rather
it is necessary that God, having revealed himself to us as the only
one we ought to worship and to whom we ought do homage,
should come in a gentle and intimate manner,[37] in order that we
might be able to accept him as our Father and as our master,
recognizing that he wishes to abide with us in order that we might
adhere to him. This is what the title means which is claimed in this
passage, saying: "I am not solely the Lord who has come to startle
you, but, at the same time, I am your God. I have chosen you for
myself. It is my will that you be my inheritance."

[35]See Ezek. 13:7, 10.
[36]See Isa. 19:1.
[37]See the *Institutes* 2.8.4.

Now, then, we see why he authorizes his law: in order that we might receive it in all fear and humility.[38] Nevertheless he wishes for us to accept it as friendly, in order that we might taste it and take pleasure in submitting ourselves to it and permit ourselves to be governed by it according to the doctrine which it contains. And thus, in sum, all excuse is taken away from us when today we do not do homage to our God, denouncing all superstitions and whatever is contrary to his service. Why? Because he must draw to himself by means of these titles which he attributes to himself which are to be held in awę by us. When he speaks to us of his dominion, which is over us, and when he refers to himself as our God, that ought to make us aware[39] of his paternal goodness. We thus see that there remains nothing else except to hearken to what is revealed to us in the law of God and simply to hold to it.

And that is why he reproaches the people of Israel, for they neither feared him nor loved him. "If I am your God and your master, where is your fear? And if I am your father, where is your love?" says the prophet Malachi.[40] There is no doubt that the prophet has in mind what is covered here by Moses. For when God calls himself the Lord, it is in order that we might honor him with the reverence which he is due. When he calls himself the God of the people, his purpose is to win them by friendship and to show them that since he has elected them, it is quite reasonable for them to entrust everything in his hands.

Now if this was the case under the law, today even more so he belongs to us. For although God in the person of his unique Son willed to be emptied,[41] nevertheless he has always retained his glory, and his emptying has never diminished any of his eminence mentioned here.[42] The humiliation of our Lord Jesus Christ is an infallible testimony of the mercy of our God, but whatever the case, this must not lead us to scorn. For God willed to win us over to his infinite glory that he might be worshiped by us when he descended. It is with good reason then that he reproaches us today, for unless we fear him and love him, we, too, in every respect, are inexcusable. For he reveals himself as our God and our master. Where then is our fear when we do not take account of

---

[38]See n. 4 above.
[39]gouster.
[40]Mal. 1:6.
[41]aneanti.
[42]See Phil. 2:7–8.

what he commands, when we are unyielding to his threats[43] to the point that we dismiss them, when we always continue to practice our evil deeds, although he reveals himself as our judge and calls us to account for the fact that we are only making a mockery of ourselves? Where is that awe which is due our God? For if he were a mortal creature, we would fear him more than we do the living God who has complete mastery over us. Moreover it is not enough that we fear God in a servile manner, as if we were being forced; rather, it is imperative that love be joined with it. For that is why he is called our Father. In fact we ought to note that when he revealed himself as the God of Israel, under that term he meant that he would also be our savior. "Thou art our God," (says Habakkuk), "and we cannot perish."[44] Therefore let us earnestly retain these titles, seeing that they belong to us; that is to say, since the majesty of God is shining in our Lord Jesus Christ,[45] they ought to benefit our instruction today.

Now, nevertheless, we ought also to note what he adds about the grace which he has bestowed upon his people. "I brought you," he says, "out of the land of Egypt."[46] It is true that God here especially willed to bind the people of Israel to himself above all nations. For that is why he has specifically mentioned the redemption which he has made. But when God speaks we ought to think of all the benefits by means of which he has bound us to himself, which are infinite and inestimable. But at all events we must test them according to our ability and we must apply our full understanding to them; and insofar as we fail,[47] we must strive that much harder to know them, at least those which can instruct us in the fear and in the love of our God.

But does God speak in this way? Well, in the first place we must consider that it is he who has created and formed us; thus we are his. That is a benefit which is already well refined.[48] And although each one of us should strive full-strength to serve God, how should we be able to reward him as we should for putting us in this world and feeding us? Moreover, when we thoroughly contemplate the testimonies which he renders us of his love, seeing

---

[43]For Calvin's discussion of the threats and promises which accompany the law, see the *Institutes* 2.8.4. Cf. Comm. *Four Books of Moses*, vol. 2, pp. 110; *CO* 24.378.
[44]Hab. 1:12.
[45]See I Tim. 3:16.
[46]Deut. 5:6.
[47]deffaillons.
[48]exquis-raffiné.

that he has created the world because of us, that he has destined and consecrated everything to our usage, that he has implanted his image in us to the end that we might be immortal, that he has prepared[49] for us a better inheritance than this decrepit life— when we see all this, would we not be more than stupid if we failed to be enraptured with an ardent desire to worship our God and to devote ourselves and everything to him?

But in addition to this, it is necessary for us to make an investigation of all the benefits which God has bestowed on us, the common as well as the particular. In fact it would even be proper for us to confess with David: "Lord, when I think of your goodness, my spirit is plunged into the abyss; their number make my hair stand on end," as he speaks of it in Psalm 40.[50] Moreover, once we have acknowledged in general how indebted we are to our God, let each one in his privacy think also of the benefits that he has received from the hand of God. For in the passage where it was said of old to the people of Israel: "I have brought you out of the land of Egypt," let us understand from what it is that our Lord has delivered us when he willed to include us in his house and his church. For we are children of Adam, miserable in nature, heirs of death, possessors only of sin, and in consequence it is fitting that we should be execrable to our God. Let men please themselves and glorify themselves as much as they want; if such is their origin, here is their nobility: they are slaves of Satan; they have an abyss of sin and corruption within themselves; they only have the wrath[51] and malediction of God upon their heads. In brief, being banished from the kingdom of heaven, they are abandoned to all misfortune. But our Lord has delivered us from that by the hand of his Son. He did not solely send us a Moses, as he did to the people of old; rather he did not spare his unique Son, but handed him over to death for us. Therefore being purchased with so dear and inestimable a price—such as the sacred blood of the Son of God—ought we not totally surrender ourselves to him?

Besides, when it is said that Egypt is a house of bondage, I pray you, doesn't that mean that when the devil holds us in his grasp and under his tyranny that we have no means of escaping from death, that we are cut off from all hope of salvation, and that God

---

[49]appresté-préparé.
[50]Allusion to Ps. 40:2, 11–12.
[51]l'ire.

is against us? When we are exempt from all that, where can a more excellent redemption be found than what is spoken of here by Moses? And thus in the place where it was said to the people of old: "Your God has delivered you from the land of Egypt," now it is said that we are not our own. [Indeed] as Saint Paul explains in the fourteenth chapter of Romans and again in the seventh chapter of the First Letter to the Corinthians: "We are not our own." It is no longer fitting that the faithful are given the liberty to do whatever seems good to them and that each one follow his own appetite. Why? The Lord Jesus is dead and is risen[52] in order to rule over both the living and the dead. Thus there is ample justification for Jesus Christ to be Lord of both life and death,[53] since he did not spare himself when our redemption and salvation were in question. Moreover, beyond this, the Son of God has offered himself for our salvation. Let us understand then today that by means of the gospel he makes us participants of that benefit, for he gathers us to himself in order that we might be his flock.

Now it is true that he is the Lamb without spot who has taken away the sin of the world; he offered himself in order to reconcile men to God. But the fact remains that we see many people who are abandoned and to whom the door is closed, as God does not bestow on them this grace to illumine them in faith as he has with us.[54] And thus let us carefully note that since the gospel has been announced to us, and contains the testimony that the Son of God wishes to make valid in us this redemption which he has accomplished once and for all,[55] and that he wishes for us to rejoice in such a benefit, then our ingratitude will be that much more wretched unless we make the effort to surrender ourselves to our God who binds us to himself.

If unbelievers behave like runaway horses,[56] if they overflow with superstitions and dissipate their life, indeed it is because they have no bridle; God has not retained them as his servants. In the papacy we see the horrible confusion that is present there; nevertheless neither is there any doctrine which might redirect men toward God, rather it serves for alienating them from him. And we see that the devil has truly gained a foothold, that all is full of

---

[52]ressuscité.
[53]The order in the text is "death and life."
[54]This is the first appearance of any reference to Calvin's doctrine of predestination in the series.
[55]une fois.
[56]"font des chevaux eschappez."

fraud and illusions, and that the living God is forsaken. It is a horrible confusion.

But for our part, when God reclaims us for himself, are we not all the more strictly obligated fully to unite ourselves with him, to hold ourselves under the obedience of the doctrine which is proclaimed to us in his name? And thus let us learn to hold ourselves truly to our God, to renounce anything that we might be able to forge in our head. For we no longer have to falter this way or that, or be troubled by anything whatever, for there is one sole God who wishes to possess us, who does not want his honor sullied by having it transferred to creatures, and who watches over us in order that we might realize that it is he alone whom we must invoke and in whose succor and grace our refuge lies.

And finally, since he wishes to have and hold us in his house, let us walk as in his presence and in his sight, indeed, in such a way that we worship him as our only God, not solely in ceremonies, or in external affirmation, but in our heart, since we know his service is spiritual. In brief, let him possess our bodies and souls, in order that he might be glorified in all and by all.[57]

---

[57]Golding's translation concludes this sermon with the following prayer: "Now let us kneele downe in the presence of our good God with acknowledgement of our faultes, praying him to make us feele them better, that it may leade us to true repentance to be mortified more and more, so as our wicked lustes may be cut off, and we bee wholy given to feare and honour him: & that forasmuch as wee can not serve him thoroughly as he deserveth, so long as we be hild downe under the infirmities of our flesh: it may please him to uphold us, untill hee have clothed us with his own righteousness. And so let us all say, Almighty God, etc." *Sermons Upon the Fifth Book of Moses,* trans. Golding, p. 187. Cf. Calvin, *Sermons sur les dix commandemens,* 1557 ed., p. 31.

Sermon Three[2]

Deuteronomy 5:8–10[3]

Because men are so inclined to corrupt the worship of God by malicious superstitions, it is expedient for God to threaten them in order that they might be retained as by force, or otherwise their vanity will carry them away[4] to the extent that they will imagine of God all that is contrary to his majesty. And this is a notable point which is emphasized here,[5] one we have already touched on. For since the people of Israel knew the living God, it almost seems unnecessary for him to prohibit them from making any images for themselves, but due to our wretched inclination, it was necessary for this prohibition to be added with rigorous force if we were to see it. And it is also to our benefit that such was done. For this vice is rooted in the depths of our bones. But God shows us

[1]N. in CO: "This sermon corresponds to the third in the 1562 collection pp. 50–72." CO 26.258.

[2]The original title: "The Second Sermon on Chapter 5:8–10." CO 26.258.

[3]Cf. Calvin's use of this same text in his Comm. *Four Books of Moses*, vol. 2, pp. 106–15; CO 24.375–81. See also the *Institutes* 2.8.17–21, and the *Catechism*, CO 6.56, 58, 60.

[4]transportera-entraînera.

[5]que cestuy ci.

that he will not allow any idolatry and that we ought to be shocked[6] by such a menace, as there is no one[7] among us who does not invent idols in infinite number. And that is the means by which the honor of the living God is swept into our imaginations. Let us carefully note then that we are accused[8] here of having a perverse and evil nature, one which always draws us toward superstitions, and that it is necessary for us to be pulled back in a violent manner. For on our own accord we would never be able to worship God in true purity, we would not even conceive of him or of what is properly his.

At the same time we also see to what end our "good intentions"[9] serve. For if there is anything which men are able to excuse in themselves, which they attempt[10] to do so well, it is their proclivity to conceive of idols. And why do men do it except to worship God, to be incited to a greater devotion, and to have a greater certainty that God will grant their requests? Such are they then who attempt to hide behind this pretext[11] of "good intentions"; but on the contrary we see that God despises them; we see that he pronounces a horrible sentence of condemnation on all who allow themselves to be governed by their [own] opinion.[12] They would say, of course (and such is the case), that they mean to worship God. But how? He does not at all accept such worship. Rather he despises it and considers it detestable. And with good reason. For as we have previously shown, his majesty is reduced to a travesty[13] when we attempt to represent him by means of any visible image.

Thus we are instructed in this passage not to undertake what might seem good to us. And above all, when it is a matter of worshiping God, we are not to give any attention whatever to our imagination. But we are to follow in all simplicity what he has ordained by his Word, without adding anything to it at all. For as soon as we fall away from that, however slightly, whatever case we might cite,[14] and try to justify ourselves, God will surely punish us. For it is hardly a frivolous threat when it is said: *For he is a God of*

---

[6]navrez-blessés.
[7]il n'y a celuy-il n'y a personne.
[8]redarguez-blâmés.
[9]Playful sarcasm on Calvin's part.
[10]cuident-cherchent.
[11]couleur-prétexte.
[12]cuider-opinion.
[13]desguisee.
[14]alleguions-citerions.

zeal and wrath, who visits the iniquity of the Fathers upon their children.[15] There are then two points[16] which we need to emphasize in this passage. The one is that as long as we are given over to a nature which is prone to idolatry, this threat of God will always command our attention lest we attempt to mix anything with his Word, or invent some idolatry, for God should be purely worshiped by us according to his nature and not according to our imagination. That is one point. The other is that we should know that it is unnecessary to parade our "good intentions" as a coverup for what we have invented, indeed; but on the contrary we should know that the principal service which God requires is obedience.

Now let us come to the words that are written[17] here: God says in the first place: *I am the Lord your God* (notice the emphasis on *might*),[18] or still better, *God-Almighty.* Here again he puts himself in opposition to idols. For we have already seen that in order to correct superstitions, he confronted them in his majesty. Now in order to remove all excuse from men, God manifested himself at least[19] on one occasion to all [the people]. Nevertheless, seeing that we do not know the true end of religion, nor are even able to discern who is the true God, it is hardly a matter of surprise[20] if our senses digress,[21] or if we ramble about without any sense of direction, and are only misled. But against this, once[22] God has revealed himself to us and we have understood his truth, that is reason enough for all our daydreaming to cease and for us to abide[23] by what we have understood. For this cause God reiterates this statement that he revealed himself to the people of Israel and chose them for himself and even wishes to govern [them] by means of the law which is now [being] proclaimed.

---

[15]Deut. 5:9.
[16]Cf. Calvin's twofold division of the entire commandment in the *Institutes* 2.8.17: "The commandment has two parts. The first restrains our license from daring to subject God, who is incomprehensible, to our sense perceptions, or to represent him by any form. The second part forbids us to worship any images in the name of religion."*LCC* 20.383f. Cf. also Calvin's Comm. *Four Books of Moses*, vol. 2, pp. 108f; *CO* 24.376.
[17]couchez-écrits.
[18]voire, *fort.* See the *Institutes* 2.8.18. In the latter Calvin suggests that the name of God is derived from "might." Cf. also his Comm. *Four Books of Moses*, vol. 2, p. 110; *CO* 24.378–79.
[19]I have added the "at least" to highlight Calvin's emphasis.
[20]s' . . . esbahir-s' . . . etonner.
[21]extravaguent-sortent de la route.
[22]une fois.
[23]que nous demeurions arrestez.

Now in particular he is called *a jealous God, and God of wrath.*[24] For this word in our text means both. And even though he is called God here, nevertheless the name he uses suggests force. For when he is called *jealous*, without a doubt it simply means that he will not permit his honor to be violated. And if anyone should take away what properly belongs to him in order to confer it upon creatures, he most certainly will not be so patient as to tolerate such a sacrilege. And therefore though the honor of God, which is befitting to him, may no longer be precious[25] to us, that does not mean that it must be equally disregarded by him. In the end we will see that it is not forgotten by him and that he wishes to maintain his glory as emphasized throughout holy Scripture.

The truth is [that] if we had one grain of intelligence, we would be zealous for the honor of our God, so much so that it would be entirely unnecessary for anyone to solicit us to that end. We should even be engaged in fulfilling what is written in the Psalm: that his zeal should devour us, that we should be engulfed by it; and should we see anyone casting opprobrium against his majesty, or vilifying it, of necessity we would feel a burning fire within us. But observe! We are so careful to maintain our own honor, yet whenever the world abandons itself to idolatry, we allow the honor of God to be trampled under foot, to be the butt of jokes, to be mocked, or worse still, torn to shreds. Thus since we do not do as we ought, it is necessary for our Lord to show us (as soon as he has reproached us for our cowardice and unthankfulness) that if we are still idle and nonchalant, he will not permit us to possess such zeal as we ought for maintaining his honor. When he has been oppressed by men in that way, he will seek vengeance.

Now in order for us to understand that God, who is jealous of his honor, more than has the capacity to punish idolaters, he takes this name for God (as we have already touched on) which implies force. Moreover, the two words[26] must be joined together. For Moses meant what is better explained by the prophet Nahum, when he says: "The Lord is a jealous God, a God of vengeance; a God who punishes all who have sinned against him and who keeps watch on his enemies, a God who comes in the whirlwind and tempest."[27] The prophet utilizes this word: that God is jealous,

---

[24] Calvin barely alludes to this text in the *Institutes* 2.8.18; however, he discusses God's "wrath" in a variety of places. See the "Subject Index," *LCC* 21.1713.

[25] recommandé-précieux.

[26] The two words to be held together are "jealous" and "wrath."

[27] An allusion to Nah. 1:2–3.

which is to say that he forgets nothing, his eyes are not closed when we show contempt for him, rather he notes it; for everything is registered before him, and one day he will weigh it all.[28] But once he has developed this theme, that God intends to maintain his honor, he shows at the same time that he has the wherewithal and is armed with the strength to punish his enemies, that they cannot escape from his hand. That is why he speaks of the whirlwind and the tempest; that is why he speaks of vengeance. And even if God were momentarily to close his eyes,[29] or were to relax his vigil against his enemies, in due time they would realize with whom they had to deal and that they had provoked the living God. That is one theme.

The other stresses that he is equally powerful enough to execute his zeal, that he is not at all like mortal men who are offended and angry when anyone dishonors them, or causes them an injury, but who do not have the means to act as they would like. God is not like that, for he is armed with the ability[30] to confound all his enemies. Now it is true that we must not imagine God possessing human faculties[31] such as we observe in men who bustle[32] about. There is no wrath[33] in God. But because we cannot comprehend God as he is, he has to accommodate himself to our ignorance. Thus whenever the Scripture speaks of "anger," "wrath," and "indignation,"[34] it isn't that God is subject to these, or that he in any way resembles us, or is violent; [on the contrary] he always abides in his [own] state and, as Saint James uses the simile to demonstrate, there can be no change in his essence, there is not even the slightest "shadow" in him.[35] Nevertheless, because we cannot comprehend the judgments and threats of God unless we use the words "wrath," "anger," and "indignation,"[36] for that reason the holy Scripture employs them. And let us also principally note that God has revealed in this passage that it is a dreadful thing to fall into his hands. And above all when we have perverted the purity of his service by our evil inventions and have willed to attempt what our minds conspire, let us be conscious of

[28]". . . et qu'il faut qu'il vienne à conte." *CO* 26.260.
[29]dissimule-ferme les yeux sur.
[30]vertu.
[31]affections.
[32]s'esmeuvent-se remuent.
[33]courroux.
[34]". . . d'ire, de courroux, et d'indignation . . . " *CO* 26.261.
[35]See James 1:17.
[36]". . . de Courroux, d'Ire, d'Indignation: . . . " *CO* 26.261.

with whom we have to deal, that he is an exceedingly powerful master for us to make sport of him in such a way.

Nevertheless God is not simply satisfied with threatening those who have turned aside from his law through their idolatries, that is, it isn't enough for him to say that he will punish each of them, but he extends his vengeance to their posterity. *I am*, he says, *the jealous God who punishes the iniquity of the fathers upon the children to the third and fourth generation.*[37] On the surface this seems completely incompatible with the justice of God—for him to punish children for their fathers' and mothers' sins; and even beyond that common sense recoils from it. We see what the prophet Ezekiel said about it: that whoever shall have sinned shall bear his own payment, and that the son shall bear the iniquity of the father no more than the father that of the son.[38] Our passage then would appear to be uncultivated and harsh and even in defiance of justice and equity in God. For sin entails its wage, that is death for whoever commits it. Thus why should the innocent die? Besides, if that reason were still not sufficient, there is the testimony of the holy Scripture that God reveals that he will not punish innocent children for their fathers' sins.[39] And he even rebukes the Jews because of this blasphemy which appeared on their lips which they had already made into a proverb: "Our fathers have eaten sour grapes and our teeth have been set on edge."[40] What they meant by it was: "It isn't for faults which we have committed that God treats us with such severity, for we have lived as we ought, but he punishes us for the sins of our fathers."[41] That is how the Jews murmur against God. But he promises that such a blasphemy will no longer reign.

But when all of that is carefully considered, there is no aversion. For in the text from Ezekiel, God meant nothing other than [the fact] that those who are punished by him cannot cite their innocence; they cannot say that he is wrong in being so stern with them, for when the matter is carefully examined they will each on their own account be found to be guilty.[42] I still say that they had

[37]Deut. 5:9. See Calvin's discussion of this text in the *Institutes* 2.8.18–21. Cf. also his Comm. *Four Books of Moses*, vol. 2, pp. 111–12; *CO* 24.379–80.
[38]A reference to Ezek. 18:19–20. See also Calvin's treatment of this verse in his Comm. *Four Books of Moses*, vol. 2, pp. 113–14; *CO* 24.380–81.
[39]Ezek. 18:19.
[40]Isa. 31:29.
[41]Calvin elaborates this passage more fully in the *Institutes* 2.8.20.
[42]Beginning with this sentence and continuing through the next eight paragraphs something of the controversy with Zébédée, Lange and the Bernese offi-

only to come from their mother's womb, that it was entirely unnecessary for them to have committed public grievous faults. For
what is our race? What is the nature we bear if it isn't totally evil?
Thus children are already sinners condemned before God while
still in their mother's womb. One may not yet perceive their evil,
but the fact remains that their nature is vicious and perverse; they
possess a hidden seed and because of this original sin which comes
from Adam upon all human beings, they already stand in condemnation.

Now since little children are not exempt from the anger and
curse of God, it is certain that if he punishes them it is not without
cause and that we may always be assured that he has only pre-
ceeded equitably as a good judge. By a still stronger reason, those
who are already grown cannot be said to be innocent, but we shall
find them much more culpable. And thus with regard to Ezekiel it
is entirely clear that God does not punish innocent children because of their fathers [sins], rather the fault equally lies in them.

Furthermore, when he says *that he punishes the iniquity of the
fathers on the children*, [43] let us note how this is done and this difficulty should be even better resolved. In the first place we know
that God owes us nothing and, if he acts kindly toward us, it's
because of his pure grace and not because he has to. Nevertheless,
if he wishes to be stern toward us, he can leave us all in condemnation as we now are. Let God only withdraw his mercy and that
will establish God judge over all the world. Let that happen and
we are lost. There is no remedy. And great and small, fathers and
children, without exception (I say), we would be damned if God
did not remove the curse which entraps us, which behold he does
out of his generous liberality without being required to do so.

Seeing then that God can utterly ruin and destroy us, if it
pleases him to use his goodness and clemency toward some, to call
them to himself, and to rescue them from their abyss, what fault
can anyone find with that? [44] Why reproach him for that? Why
should we raise our eyebrows [45] if he has pity on his creatures?
And although he does not use an equal standard toward all, nevertheless it is necessary to keep our mouth closed. Indeed, it is

cials is mirrored in Calvin's review of his doctrine of predestination. These paragraphs constitute some of the clearest examples of how the events of 1555 are
reflected in Calvin's series.

[43] Deut. 5:9.

[44] Keep in mind Calvin's struggles with the Bernese officials and his opponents:
Zébédée, Lange, Bolsec, and others. See n. 42 above.

[45] " . . . que nostre oeil soit malin, . . . " *CO* 26.262.

even necessary for us to open it to confess that what he does is within reason and equitable, even though it might transcend our grasp. For we do not always understand why in fact God decrees what he does for men. But it is proper for our curiosity[46] to be abated and for us to learn to worship God in his judgments when they are too lofty and secret for us. But whatever the case, let this general rule stand: that God could have left us in our perdition where we were if that had seemed good to him, and by the same token everyone would have perished. But because it pleased God to show himself as pitiable and benign, not toward everyone but toward a part, that is what distinguishes some from the others. But nevertheless he leaves those who seem good to him in their malediction, as they were born.

Now if we ask, "Why is God merciful toward some and stern toward others?" it is true that the first cause is unknown to us and is not open to inquiry. Why? Because it is essential here that our senses be constrained[47] and captivated and that we confess that God has the freedom to choose those who seem good to him and to reject the rest. But whatever the case, he makes this promise to the faithful: that he will have pity on their children, and, as he has already begun to show them his mercy, he will continue to do so until the thousandth generation. We now see that there are several reasons why God has pity on some rather than on the others. And in contrast, he threatens the unbelievers and will not only curse them but also their race and those who are descended from their line.

Now we come to God's mercy and punishment. It isn't that he blesses the children of believers with riches, health, and similar things, or that he causes them to prosper with respect to the world. That isn't the greatest blessing of God, nor is that the perspective from which be begins. Rather he blesses them when he governs them through his Holy Spirit, gives them the mark of adoption of his children, and corrects and purges them of their iniquities in order to restore[48] them to his image. That is the mercy which God bestows upon the children of the faithful: that he does not permit them to remain in their corruption and malice, but reforms them and governs them more and more and even causes them to prosper in this world until the highest level of

---

[46]cacquet-curiosité.
[47]serrez.
[48]reformer.

mercy is reached, which is when he draws them into his kingdom and into eternal life.

On the other hand, when he punishes the iniquities of the fathers upon the children, he leaves a race such as it is. [For example], take a reprobate, or a hater of God, or a hypocrite, or an unbeliever and his children. God does not recognize them so to speak; he takes them for strangers; he does not include them at all in the number of his own; he will not deign to reveal himself to them as their father; he thus leaves them abandoned to the possession of Satan. And thus when they are destitute of God's Spirit, what can become of them but evil and that they increasingly provoke his anger? Now does our Lord punish them without cause? Will they be able to say they are innocent? Of course not! For there is already enough sin in them. Thus we see much better that what God declared by Ezekiel is true, that is, that whoever sins shall bear his own payment, such as he deserves, and that the innocent will not be punished because of the iniquitous and the transgressor. Nevertheless we also see that it is not without cause that he has revealed that he will punish the iniquity of the fathers upon the children. And why is that? It is his nature not to bestow grace on the children of evildoers and unbelievers, or especially those who are contemptuous of his Word, or hypocrites who abuse his name. It is within God's liberty to withdraw his Spirit from their entire posterity. And when their children are thus alienated from God, what do they retain but Adam's corruption? There is nothing in them but sin and corruption, nevertheless it is more than fitting that they should be God's enemies. Thus that is how he justly punishes them. And lest they sue for exemption from his hand by saying that he was wrong and cruel toward them, it is [more] fitting for every mouth to be closed.

It is true that we will never be able to satisfy rebels, for as we see there are some who rise up against God with such audacity that they make the noble and the sober ashamed.[49] But let us leave these dogs to yelp while we glorify our God in all humility, knowing that it is for the least that he has this authority and this right: to be gracious to those to whom it seems good to him. And by this means it is necessary for us to conclude that if God withdraws his Spirit from the offspring of the wicked, one cannot accuse him of cruelty. For they are punishable when they are thus forsaken by

---

[49]In all likelihood a direct allusion to Zébédée and the others. See n. 42 above.

him and are not governed by his Holy Spirit. Therefore let us note carefully that this sentence does not clash with that of Ezekiel's. And now let us return to Moses' meaning.

Undoubtedly he did not intend to impress upon us here a fear of God greater than if he had simply said, "God will punish you if you corrupt his service, change anything in religion, or imagine him under any figure; do not think that you will escape his vengeance, for he cannot permit his honor to be annihilated in such a way." Men are so stubborn[50] and sluggish that if Moses had simply said that, then they might not have been sufficiently aroused[51] by fear. But Moses presses on. God, he says, will not only punish you personally, but he will extend his vengeance to your offspring, and not simply to your children, but he will pursue to the very end; for you will constantly feel his anger like a burning fire; even after your death people will see the marks of your iniquity. God will dismiss you to ignominy; indeed it would be fitting if you were hanged. Although you should be ground into the earth, if the vengeance of God pursues you in that way, may your sins be recalled[52] from age to age, that people may know that you were rebellious against him who showed you so much grace, that at least you might have become like the sheep of his flock, governed by him according to his Word. Therefore let us at least learn to be no longer stupid when God awakens us in this way.

It is true that if God should indicate his anger by so much as a word, or by several outward signs, we would be filled with fear and terror. But because we are so slow to expect anything,[53] at least when God explains that after we have suffered he will still prosecute his vengeance on all our offspring and that, following our trespass, all who proceed from us shall necessarily be condemned, when God speaks in this way, [at least] let us be more attentive to walk in his fear and to redirect ourselves toward him in order that we might not provoke his anger, since it is so terrible. That is how we can benefit from this passage.

Now he writes *of those who hate him.*[54] In this phrase he includes all transgressors of the law. If we ask, "Does this mean that all who turn aside from obedience to God necessarily hate him?" the an-

---

[50]durs.
[51]esmeus-remués.
[52]ramenteus-rappellés.
[53]durs à l'esperon. This phrase might also be translated: "difficult to stimulate." See Huguet, vol. 3, p. 671.
[54]Deut. 5:9.

swer is yes, for this passage indicates as much, not because they appear to, but because it is true. And we must not base that on our judgment, for God alone is a competent judge to make that decision. And because men, when they devote themselves to evil deeds, neither say nor think in their hearts that they hate God, it is essential for this vice to be exposed. It is true that hypocrites pretend that it is the love of God that makes them look good, and in fact there will be found some seed in them, but it is a degenerate[55] and vicious seed; the fact remains that this hate for God neither appears in hypocrites nor even in those who lead a reckless and profligate life. But in any event it is true, even though we may not be able to recognize it. For what all malefactors would like is for there to be no judge, or order, or police in the world;[56] therefore all who do not recognize themselves as subject to God (lo, to their good fortune) express contempt for him and would be content to see him pulled down from heaven. That is rather manifest[57] in those who are totally misdirected.[58] When men lay aside the reins on all iniquity, they can no longer bear any correction; still less are they docile. If anyone bothers them they grind their teeth; they give a free rein to their rage;[59] they are like madmen against God. Therefore this hatred of God is rather notable in those who relegate to themselves a shocking license to do evil, who are carried away with and steeped in their iniquities.

Moreover, it is true that we do not perceive it in those who still possess some fear and who are troubled when one speaks to them about God and his judgment. But the fact remains that there is already some hatred of God in them. It is true that they do not believe[60] in him; but God sees with much greater clarity than we, and, though we do not recognize these things, he notices them. We must always return to what Saint John says: "that God is greater than our consciences,"[61] which is to say that although our consciences bear witness against our faults, God does not remain immovable. And thus in sum let us remember that all who do not align themselves under God's obedience and who do not humble themselves under his majesty in order to worship and honor him,

[55]bastarde-dégénérée.
[56]Possibly an allusion to the Perrinist struggles and the May 16 riot.
[57]patent-béant.
[58]pervertis-détournés.
[59]se tempestent-donnent libre cours à leur colère.
[60]cuident-croient.
[61]I John 3:20.

all these hate him, although in fact they may not show it at first and we cannot even discern it.

That is also why when God speaks of those who keep his commandments, that he begins with love. He says: *That he will be merciful to a thousand generations of those who love him.*[62] And why? For it is impossible for us to desire to honor God and to be subject to him without having sensed this love of which he speaks here. And this can serve as a profitable teaching, as we shall afterwards see, that Moses wishing to give a summary of the law says: "What does your God ask of you Israel except that you love him with all your heart and adhere to him?" We can never know, I say, what it is to observe the law of God and live by it unless we begin with this love. And why? Because God wants willing submission.[63] He does not solely want us to worship him out of servile fear. Rather he wants us to come to him with a sincere and cheerful heart, so much so that we take pleasure in honoring him. And that cannot be done unless we love him. Thus let us note that the beginning of obedience, as well as its source, foundation, and root, is this love of God; that we would not attempt to come to him unless we found in him our deepest pleasure.[64] Furthermore let us recognize that that is our true blessedness, and that we cannot ask for more than it be governed according to his will, and to be in conformity with it.

Moreover, let us note that this love cannot exist until we have tasted the goodness of our God. For as long as we conceive of God as being opposed to us, of necessity we will flee from him. Therefore do we wish to love him? Do we wish to be reformed by being obedient to him that we might receive all of our pleasure in his service? Then we must realize that he is our Father and Savior, that he only wants to be favorable to us. Thus once we have tasted his mutual love which he reserves for us, then we will be motivated to love him as our Father. For if this love is in us, then there will be no doubt that we will obey him and that his law will rule in our thoughts, our affections, and in all our members. For as we have already said, what is the cause of our being rebellious against God if it isn't our hatred of him? Whereas, on the contrary, the love of God will direct us to serve him and to submit to his justice

---

[62] Deut. 5:10. Cf. Calvin's treatment of this text in the *Institutes* 2.8.21.
[63] services volontaires.
[64] plaisir singulier.

to the extent that we will see a conformity and harmony between the law of God and all our desires and affections.[65]

Still in order to understand this better, let us consider who God is. For he does not wish to be known according to our nature; and when we hear his name mentioned, it isn't enough to attribute this title of "God" to him, rather he wants to be known as he truly is; that is to say, as just, [and] good, that he is the perfection and fountain of all wisdom, of all virtue, of all integrity and righteousness. Thus once we begin to conceive of God as he truly is, that is, in his justice, integrity, and righteousness, we will only want to accommodate ourselves to him. On the other hand, when we love evil and are enveloped by it, of necessity we will hate God. And why? [Now] it isn't a question here of his naked essence[66]; we must not think of God as an idol; we must comprehend him in his justice and righteousness. Thus when we hate what is in God, that is to say, his righteousness and his integrity, of necessity we hate him too; for he cannot disclaim himself; he cannot disguise himself; he cannot transfigure himself into our guise; he remains forever himself.[67] Therefore as I have already touched on, all who love God are solely concerned with being obedient to his law and with keeping his commandments. For these things are inseparably united. That is what we must grasp in this passage.

Now from this we are warned to have a greater horror than we have ever had of all rebellion and offenses, for it is no small matter to be declared an enemy of God and to make war with him. For since we cannot lift ourselves to him, or turn aside from him, or reject his yoke, let us not be convicted of being his enemies or of having openly made war against him. Would that not be a detestable thing?[68] Therefore let us learn to hold our sins and vices in horror, since these charge us with being enemies of God and require him to show himself adverse to our party. And furthermore we are also admonished to come to God with a pure and sincere affection. For it is not enough to restrain our feet and our

[65]See Calvin's treatment of this theme in the *Institutes* 2.8.17. Cf. Comm. *Four Books of Moses*, vol. 2, p. 107; *CO* 24.376. Calvin's emphasis in the Comm. lies in the necessity of knowing who God is in order to render him correct worship, for since God is Spirit, then our worship of him is spiritual and cannot be tied to physical objects. See also *Institutes* 2.8.6.

[66]une essence nue.

[67]semblable à soy.

[68]Remember that on June 3, Ami Perrin and four others were "convicted" and sentenced to death for their part in the May 16 tumult.

hands and our eyes from doing evil, rather the heart must lead the way and God be worshiped by us in true affection. And that affection must not be constrained, but it must proceed from a true love of God.

Thus, in the first place, when we sincerely want to observe the law, we must recognize that God is a good and favorable father toward us to the end that we might be led[69] by his mutual love. Furthermore, let us not deceive ourselves by confessing that we love God unless that is reflected in our total life. For when the love of God is spoken here, Moses adds that *those who love him also keep his commandments.*[70] Thus it is necessary for our life to conform to this pattern in order to certify whether we love or hate God.

Moreover, it is not without cause that God, making a comparison here between his anger and vengeance against his mercy, says *that he will punish those who hate him to the third and fourth generations and that he will be gracious to those who love him to a thousand generations.*[71] Now by that he shows what is still better explained in other texts of Scripture, that he is slow to anger, inclined toward mercy, patient, and that, if his anger burns for a minute, his lovingkindness is for life and permanent. Thus there you have the true character of God; that he only wants to draw men in all gentleness and does so through his goodness. When he punishes them it is almost[72] against his nature. Not that it is any more improper for God to punish than it is for him to be gracious, but he wishes to show us that his goodness is much greater, and, in brief, that he is not harsh; rather he only wants to open his heart to us if we will [but] permit him. In fact, he wills to be known as good and merciful;[73] and it is in that that his glory principally shines.

Therefore let us carefully note that it is not without cause that Moses has assigned here a thousand generations to the lovingkindness of God and that he has confined his anger and vengeance to three or four generations. It's as if he were saying: "It is true that our Lord will not permit superstitions to go unpunished; when you pervert his worship and honor, enjoying yourselves after your reveries, you will be conscious of their punishment and

---

[69] resolus.
[70] Deut. 5:10.
[71] Deut. 5:9–10.
[72] quasi.
[73] pitoyable.

even your children after you. For when the fire of his indignation is kindled against you, it will not be extinguished as quickly as you think. Nevertheless he will not cease being merciful. And his steadfast love will always be greater than his wrath."[74] And in fact, not only by means of the threat which we have heard has God willed to hold the world in the right religion that it might not be obsessed with idols and grotesque figures, but he has also willed by means of the promise, which is contained here, to attract us. And if we accord him the love and reverence which we owe him, he prefers to win us by his goodness rather than to hold us by threats.[75]

And that is why he says: "My children, do not expect me to punish you. True, if you provoke me I will not permit you to sport with me in that way, but at the same time after you have aroused my anger, I still prefer to attract and lure you by loving-kindness. Therefore I declare to you that if you abide purely and entirely in my obedience, I will continue to deal graciously with you for a thousand generations. That is how conscious your children will be of me in spite of your trespass." That is what we must glean from this text.

And moreover, in conclusion, let us note that it is not without reason that God uses this word loving-kindness,[76] which could possibly mean a reward and service which he will pay. He could have easily said: "I will recognize the service of those who have honored and worshiped me, who have loved me and observed my law; I will show them that the service by means of which they have honored me is not a lost effort." God could have said that. Instead he said: I will show them loving-kindness. And how is that? If we serve God, does it not seem fair that he should reward us? Rather he shows that it isn't because he was obligated to do so or due to merits that he is gracious to those who have honored him and followed his commandments, but because he chooses to exercise loving-kindness.

Now this word loving-kindness serves to deflate all human pride, so much so that men cannot glorify in their words as if they merited a reward. Rather let us perceive that [what] God intended to mean by it is that when we serve him we still have need of

[74]ire.
[75]On the function which promises and threats serve in the law, see the *Institutes* 2.7.4.
[76]Misericorde.

his support as well as need of his forgiveness of our vices and weaknesses.

Those are the two points which we must note in this text. The one[77] is that, although we may worship God in all purity, if he rewards us it isn't because of something he owes us. For in fact, from whence is the capacity to worship him derived if it isn't from his pure grace? What therefore does he owe us? Even more,[78] when it pleases him to examine us in his sternness, we will all be found to be guilty before him. Therefore what God rewards us, when we have served him, comes from his pure goodness and not because he is in any way obligated. But more than that, it is imperative for him to forgive us our sins and to support us: I say even in those things we do well. Therefore let us understand that God reveals himself as benign and generous toward us because he indeed wishes to support us in our weaknesses, making us taste his loving-kindness, precisely at that point where he could have made us conscious of his sternness. For we must realize that without this loving-kindness we would have all been lost; even had we attempted to obey him, we would have been found guilty had he not used this goodness of which he speaks. Therefore if we want to be assured of our salvation, it is his loving-kindness that must constitute our refuge.[79]

---

[77]Calvin will not cite a second point per se.

[78]This seems to begin the second point Calvin wishes to make.

[79]Golding's translation concludes this sermon with the following exhortation and prayer: "Nowe let us kneele down in the presence of our good God with acknowledgement of our sinnes, praying him to make us feele them better than wee have done, that it may leade us to true repentance, so as being taught to feare him, wee may stande in such awe, that as soone as he threateneth us with his wrath, wee may conceive the power that is in him, to the ende that being humbled in ourselves, wee may have recourse to his fatherly goodnesse, not doubting but that when hee hath once begunne to shewe himselfe a father and Saviour toward us, he will continue so stil yea even after our decease, so that wee shrinke not from him through our owne naughtinesse and disobedience. That it may please him to graunt this grace, not onely to us, but also to all people and nations of the earth, Etc." *Sermons Upon the Fifth Book of Moses,* trans. by Golding, p. 193. Cf. Calvin, *Sermons sur les dix commandemens,* 1557 ed., p. 46.

Wednesday, June 19, 1555[1]

Sermon Four[2]

Deuteronomy 5:11[3]

If we were well-advised we would not need to be taught to act reverently toward God, for nature ought to bring us to that end.[4] For [after all] what reason are we created in this world? Why do we live here if it isn't for the purpose of paying homage to him from whom we received every good and to apply ourselves to glorify his majesty? That is the end and whole sum of this life. Nevertheless instead of honoring our God and applying ourselves to that end, it appears that we have conspired the very opposite. For some would like to see all memory of God blotted out; others despise and make light of him; still others blatantly[5] blaspheme

---

[1]N. in *CO:* "This sermon corresponds to the fourth in the 1562 collection, pp. 72–94." *CO* 26.270.

[2]The original title: "The Third Sermon on Chapter 5:11." *CO* 26.270.

[3]See also Calvin's discussion of the Third Commandment in the *Institutes* 2.8.22–27; Comm. *Four Books of Moses*, vol. 2, pp. 408–10; *CO* 24.559–61; *Catechism, CO* 6.60, 62.

[4]Cf. *Institutes* 2.8.1.

[5]à plein gosier.

81

him: all to the extent that we sufficiently show that we do not know why we live and enjoy life.

Now because our life is marked by such vice, God wants to remedy it and show us that at least we must refrain from abusing his holy name, for that is how we profane him. And that is why he has commanded *that his name shall not be taken in vain.*[6] By these words he means that we must carefully recognize the proper and lawful usage of his name. It is true that we are not worthy under any circumstance to take the name of the Lord in our mouth, for we need to consider what the prophet Isaiah said in the sixth chapter: "Lord, my lips are unclean and I live in the midst of a people who are totally unclean."[7] Seeing then that we possess only infection and filth in ourselves, it is certain that we cannot make use of God's name except for the fact that God still wants us to use his name on condition that we glorify him. Therefore let us take careful note when it is said *that we may not take the* name of God in vain, that our Lord holds us responsible[8] for our ingratitude unless we know how to use his name as he has permitted us and follow the rule which is contained in his Word: which is the lawful means for being able to use the name of God.

Nevertheless, in order that this might be more clearly understood, we must observe that God in this text[9] has decided to show us [the nature of] that majesty which is contained in his name in order that we might use it in our speech with complete reverence and honor.[10] It is from this point of view then that he regards this matter of the oath,[11] particularly where swearing is involved. [In addition] we see how our Lord loves us, inasmuch as he lends[12] us his name in order that we might be able to communicate with our neighbors. [Furthermore] should there be any difficulty or difference between us, it becomes possible to settle[13] matters by this

---

[6]Deut. 5:11.

[7]Isa. 6:5.

[8]redargue-blâme.

[9]sous une espece.

[10]Cf. *Institutes* 2.8.22: "The purpose of this commandment is: God wills that we hallow the majesty of his name. Therefore, it means in brief that we are not to profane his name by treating it contemptuously and irreverently."

[11]Calvin nowhere clearly defines what he means by "the oath" in this sermon. However, as early as his 1539 edition of the *Institutes* he did. "In the first place, we must state what an oath is. It is calling God as witness to confirm the truth of our word." *Institutes* 2.8.23.

[12]preste.

[13]vuider-vider.

means; that is, if we are uncertain or are in doubt over any matter, the name of God can be introduced as a mediator in order to remove any scruple[s]. In this way, wherever such confirmation exists, matters become more certain. Is it not an inestimable goodness [then] that our God so stoops toward us and permits us to use his name? And why does he do it? It is certain that the majesty of God is so precious that it ought not to be humbled to that extent, but he wants so much to accommodate himself toward us, that our shamefulness is even greater if we profane the name of God in our oaths. And that happens not only when we perjure ourselves, but whenever we take the name of God in vain,[14] or do not think to speak warily, especially if the subject with which we are dealing deserves to be carefully confirmed. Therefore when we proceed in such a heedless manner, that is how the name of God is profaned.

It is true that God considers[15] it a kind of service whenever any one swears[16] by his name; not that he will be bound to us by it, rather the very contrary. For as I have already mentioned, we must sense in this matter how God bears with us seeing that he permits us to use his name; likewise in swearing we confess that God has total superiority over us. Whoever is inferior swears by his sovereign, says the apostle to the Hebrews.[17] And even if we know to what end the oath tends, it still only applies[18] to the sole majesty of God. For we like to ratify both secret things and matters which have no proof between men. But this is not possible for any creature to do. Only God can do that as it is he who searches our hearts to the very bottom. For it is not without cause that he claims for himself this title of truth.

Thus we see that in swearing we do homage to God. [For] we confess that he is our judge and that it is to him that we must have recourse with regard to doubtful and hidden things, since his office is glorified by such means. Moreover [in swearing we affirm] that he will maintain the truth since that belongs to his honor. That is why God considers it a type of service when men swear by his name, provided the oaths are not superfluous.[19]

[14]à la vollee-sans réfléchir.
[15]repute-considère.
[16]iure. Cf. Comm. *Four Books of Moses,* vol. 2, p. 408; *CO* 24.559. There Calvin writes: " . . . to swear by God's name is a species or part of religious worship. . . . "
[17]Heb. 6:16.
[18]convenir-s'accorder.
[19]See Calvin's discussion of "false" and "idle" oaths in the *Institutes* 2.8.24–25.

Thereby we see that the fault of those who perjure themselves, or who swear rashly, is so much the more aggravated, for it is in violation of God's service and destroys the latter in us.

As for those who perjure themselves, not only are they guilty of having taken the name of God in vain and of falsely abusing it, but they are traitors[20] and forgers. What greater outrage could we commit against God than to annihilate his truth? For there is nothing which more appropriately belongs to him; it would be as if we should will to topple him from his throne and even deprive him of all his divine honor and glory. And that happens whenever anyone turns[21] his truth into a lie. Whoever does so perjures himself, that is to say, whoever takes the name of God in evil conscience in order to strengthen[22] his lies or to deceive or alter[23] things certainly blasphemes in doing so.

Now in particular I say if we wish "to alter things." Why? Many condone it under the pretext[24] that it is difficult to be accused[25] of perjury before men. And why? They are so noble[26] and so portray[27] their situation that it appears that they do not perjure themselves. But God does not accept such subtleties. Therefore we must not suppose that we are finished with him or are free of him when we have employed such circuits and subterfuges. Thus in effect we finally see that all who take the name of God, other than in sincerity[28] and simplicity, blaspheme him. Let that constitute one point.

Now those who swear without purpose and without thinking clearly demonstrate that they do not take account of God and only mock him.[29] It is true that they confess to the contrary; they will rather say that such is not their intention at all, but that is only hypocrisy. For consequences clearly reveal[30] that they have no reverence for God. When a mortal man is dear[31] to us, we do not take his name in vain; we would not want anyone to make fun[32] of

[20]traistres.
[21]covertit-tourne.
[22]pour donner couler.
[23]desguiser-altérer.
[24]sous ombre-sous prétexte.
[25]conveincus-confondus.
[26]"Ils tournent à l'entour du pot, ... " CO 26.272.
[27]fardent-peignent.
[28]rondeur.
[29]Cf. Institutes 2.8.25.
[30]l'effet monstre assez.
[31]recommandé-précieux.
[32]qu'on s'en gabbe.

his name. And if anyone were to gossip about him or mock him there would be a free-for-all.[33] We would hold such in opprobrium. And do we hope to enjoy more privilege than the living God? We are disgraceful beasts[34] and corrupt, and nevertheless we still want to be [held] in esteem and reputation while our God is dethroned. In such ways as this today we see that there is scarcely any religion in the world. Although many pretend to be Christians, nevertheless they have never been known to be such, nor to worship God, nor pay him homage, nor render him that service which is properly his. For how does the name of God fare?[35] Men cannot trade for a quart [of wine] without swearing. If the honor of God were esteemed by us, it is certain that we would abstain from such a superfluity of oaths; what is more, it would be regarded with horror. Yet today people not only make light of God's honor and when a man is accused of having so sworn, it appears to him that he has been done a great injustice. If anyone has undertaken something which does not serve to his advantage, he will be irritated[36] and angry with it and will bitterly complain. And if our zeal for God arouses our anger when his name is thus disrespected, then look out for the quarreling, the spitefulness, and grinding of teeth that will follow. But since the world has come into such possession of spite for God and has become callous toward him, it is a sign that people no longer know his majesty.

Moreover, although they justify it[37] under the pretext that it is the customary thing and that from custom law is derived, yet in fact God does reveal in the end that his name is dearer to him than men have held it, and that if we make it cheap we will dearly pay for it. Furthermore, in the end, it will be necessary for us to recognize that the earth on which we have lived has been defiled by us and that all of the benefits which we have received, and the fact that God has increased us by his hand, are matters for which we shall certainly have to account, seeing that we have not acknowledged him who was their author in order to honor him as he deserves.

Thus in the first place that is what we have to note in this passage: that God upholds us, and that he avails himself of such a

---

[33]". . . , qu'il soit là meslé parmi." CO 26.273.
[34]literally: "carrion and corruption."
[35]trotte.
[36]marri-irrité.
[37]". . . , combien qu'on se donne une license tant enorme. . . . " CO 26.273.

humanity toward us that he especially wishes that we make use of his name in lawful things, and that, based on this permission, we can sufficiently know that he is more than our Father. Nevertheless he admonishes us to be diligent enough to refrain from all harmful oaths. For with regard to perjury, as we have said, it is a shameful and execrable outrage which we inflict on him, seeing that his truth is changed into a lie; we are forgers through and through. Such is more than a mortal crime.

But it is not enough for us to be on guard against perjury; it is also imperative that our oaths be sober and that the name of God not be flipped[38] like an alms-coin[39] between us, but that necessity excuse us when we must employ it. For since we acknowledge in our oaths that God has total superiority over us, we ought to see thereby that oaths which involve creatures are wrong and proceed from superstition. Like in the papacy, one swears by Saint Anthony or by Saint John: it's the same as if they were swearing by idols. And why? For we must always come back to that sentence which I cited from the apostle,[40] that we acknowledge that God is our superior, lo, our sovereign, whenever we swear by his name. And that is also the reason why God swears to confirm us in his promises or to awaken us when he sees that we are obstinate and callous in our faults and that we are not afraid of his judgments. He swears. And by whom? By himself? He reserves this honor for himself, of which we will later treat in the sixth chapter of this book. And thus those who swear by creatures are idolaters. And that is why this matter is further mentioned [in conjunction] with superstitions, as the oath is considered a testimony which can mislead men since they are turned away from the purity of the law. It is necessary (says Jeremiah[41]) that pastors who have charge of leading people teach [them] to swear by the name of God, that is to say, that all [our] other oaths be set aside and that nothing else be introduced.

Moreover, as I have already said, when the name of God is mentioned let us note that not only are we forbidden to pronounce the word, but we must [also] have respect for its essence. God is not a sophist who makes use of frivolous subtleties toward us, rather he considers the deed itself. True, there may be some

---

[38]trotte.
[39]plotte.
[40]Heb. 6:16.
[41]Jer. 12:16; 5:7. See the *Institutes* 2.8.23 where these passages are also cited.

who do not expressly swear by the name of God, but they do not cease to be guilty or transgressors. For we must come back to what our Lord Jesus Christ says in the fifth chapter of Saint Matthew: "When you swear by heaven, is that not the throne of the living God? If you swear by his temple, is that not the seat of his Majesty?"[42] Thus if we believe[43] that we are not condemned when we have uttered the name of God [in that way], it is still an abuse; let us not be deceived about that, for the excuse is too puerile. And why? Does heaven not carry a mark of the majesty of God? Therefore his glory has been diminished. The same is true of the earth, which is his footstool, which Jesus Christ mentions in that passage which I have quoted.[44] Thus in short let us conclude that it is necessary to hold the name of God in such reverence that all our oaths may be banished[45] among us, unless necessity[46] requires it and God allows us to use his name.

Moreover, let us always follow this rule: to have the simplicity in our speech to say: "It is so," assuring ourselves that whatever is advantageous is evil and condemned by the law whenever we take the name of God in vain. And in fact we can also see that there is a twofold evil in all superfluous oaths and in those in which the name of God is not at all honored as it deserves. For if anyone thus carelessly uses it at random,[47] it is a sign that he hardly takes account of what he is saying. And then from whence does that proceed if it isn't from the fact that men are so lying and so full of fraud that when they speak to each other, no one can believe what the other says to him. Indeed it proceeds from perversity and malice. For when God gave us a tongue, it was in part for the purpose of communicating with one another, for it is like the messenger of the heart, for by means of it we express what we have conceived in our minds. Thus we see that superfluous oaths have proceeded from the disloyalty of men. And it is hardly necessary to inquire further, or to make an exhaustive study,[48] for we can

---

[42]Matt. 5:34–35.
[43]cuidons-croyons.
[44]See Calvin's elaboration of this text in the *Institutes* 2.8.26. He essentially establishes the same point.
[45]abbatus.
[46]In the *Institutes* 2.8.26 Calvin argues against the Anabaptists who condemn all oaths. "Now the eternal God not only permits oaths as a legitimate thing under the law . . . , but commands their use in case of necessity [Exod. 22:10–11]." *LCC* 2.391.
[47]"Car si on le fait ainsi voler à l'aventure: . . . " *CO* 26.275.
[48]long procez.

each testify to it. Whatever the case, let us learn to use [our tongue] in such sobriety as God commands. Thus let us not swear without purpose and unless we are required.

Further, to clarify it still more, it will seem to many people that it is immaterial when they swear by their faith. Nor is it true that the greater part swear by nothing, for they have no faith, no more than dogs; they have no conscience, nor religion. However this word *Faith* does not cease to be prized by God. For he considers it precious, and it is a sacred thing to him which cannot and must not be profaned, unless we wish to be guilty and incur the wrath[49] which is indicated here, as we shall see.

Therefore let us carefully note that it isn't enough not to have expressly declared, "By God!" but when one swears by his faith or derives a confirmation based on a mark of God's majesty, God's name is certainly profaned in that instance. And now what will be the fate of those who not only use spurious oaths for disguising their words and swearing without thinking, as if in mockery, but who defy[50] God by execrable blasphemies, sparing neither flesh, nor blood, nor death, nor anything? Are they held guilty only because they have simply abused the name of God? No! But because they have committed the most accursed opprobrium that can be done. [For I have in mind] our Lord Jesus Christ, the Lord of glory who emptied himself for a time, as Saint Paul[51] puts it. Now if there were no other reason than this, that he who being the fountain of life became a mortal man, who having charge over the angels of paradise took on the form of a servant in order to pour out his blood for our redemption and in the end suffered the punishment which we deserved—if there were no other reason than this, is it still necessary that today he should be rewarded by being reviled by the foul mouths of those who call themselves Christians?

For when they swear by his blood, or death, or his wounds, or whatever, are they not in fact crucifying the Son of God again and tearing him to pieces? And do they not deserve to be cut off from the church of God, behold, from the world, and no longer numbered among his creatures? Is that the reward from our hands that our Lord Jesus deserves for his act of abasement and humiliation? When God upbraids his people: "My people, what have I

---

[49]la menace.
[50]despitent-défient.
[51]Phil. 2:7.

done to you?" he says, "I brought you out of Egypt; I led you by the desert; I nurtured you in all kindness and humanity; I planted you in my inheritance that you might be like a vine which would yield me good fruit; I cultivated you and maintained you. Now must you [taste] like gall to me and only produce fruits which are bitter to me, as if to strangle me?"[52]

Now this applies to us today. For when the Son of God, who is ordained the judge of the world, shall come in the last day, he will be able to say to us: "What? You have carried my name, you have been baptized in memory and testimony that I was your Redeemer; I drew you out of the pit into which you had plunged. I delivered you from eternal death by means of the cruel death which I suffered. And for this cause I was made man. I submitted myself to the punishment of God my Father in order that you might benefit by my grace and way, and here is the reward which you have paid me, that I am torn to pieces by you, that I am thrown there in opprobrium, that the death which I endured for you is [held] in mockery, that my blood which is the washing and purging of your soul is trodden under foot, in brief that you have taken the occasion to blaspheme and vilify against me as if I were a poor detestable creature."

When the sovereign judge shall reproach us for this, I pray you, is it not for the purpose of overwhelming us and casting us into the bottom of the abyss? And nevertheless there are very few who think so. For if superfluous oaths were [held] today in great horror by men as they should be, they would not so readily allocate to themselves a license and audacity to persist in their perjuries as they do.

As for blasphemies, can we not see what they amount to? Nevertheless, we would like to be zealous for our honor and reputation even though the name of God is trampled under our feet. If one had spoken of someone's father [in that way] he would start a quarrel and take it to court, or many would even seek vengeance by their own hands and at what a cost. It would seem to them that they had an honest excuse for continuing their fathers' quarrel. [Yet] here is our sovereign Father who is offended in the same way, who not without cause is called the Lord of glory before whose Son every knee shall bow, as Saint Paul says in Philippians; he is mocked. One could not do worse by him than if he were to

[52]An allusion to Mic. 6:34.

spit in his face. Yet those who call themselves Christians and pretend to procure his honor blaspheme him with the greatest abhorrence. But whatever the case, as I have already said, our Lord will not cease to maintain his honor, as he says, when he sees that men are so profane as to deface his Majesty to the extent that they do. He makes a solemn oath that he will seek vengeance on them: "I am the Eternal One[53] (says the Lord); I will not give my honor to another."[54] For he does not will for his honor to be ascribed to idols; moreover it is certain that this applies even further, that is, that when men do falsely abuse his sacred name, they will feel how esteemed it is by him. Nevertheless let us not attempt such a thing, but let us learn to act reverently toward our God and toward him who possesses all sovereign majesty, that is to our Lord Jesus Christ, and that we learn at the same time to swear in such a way that it always confirms that we belong to him, that he is our Father, our creator, and our judge. That, in brief, is what we must glean from this passage.

But at the same time God's threat remains wherever we see the stupidity of men, for Satan has so bewitched them that they do not apprehend the wrath of God when it is set before them. *I will not hold him guiltless who takes my name in vain.*[55] That is God who is speaking. I beg of you, as I have said, should not the hair of those who blaspheme so shamefully stand on end? When anyone casually swears by his faith God arms himself and says: "No! Since you have not honored me you will be required to account for such a sacrilege." God cannot tolerate a single lie in us; if there is perjury, it is even worse. If anyone blasphemes, it is the extremity of all evil; it's as if we should openly scorn God, as if we should choose to attack God and wound him. Now if a person does not [seriously] consider this punishment which is prepared[56] for all who have thus adulterated the name of God, or who have dishonored him, is it not necessary to say that [here we find] a surly drunkenness and that men are insane and that Satan blinds them of everything? Alas, yes! And nevertheless it is so common a thing as hardly to matter. If a master were to say in his house: "I want to be obeyed, but above all there is still one thing I want done and will not suffer anyone to err therein, for if they do they will

---

[53]vivant.
[54]Isa. 42:8; 48:11.
[55]Deut. 5:11.
[56]apprestee-preparée.

eventually be caught and punished as they deserve." If there is anything to such a master's warning one cannot be too careful not to be somewhat afraid. Yet here is God who censures all who shall have transgressed his law in any article whatever: "Cursed is he who shall not have honored father and mother.[57] Cursed is he who shall have stolen. Cursed is he who shall have practiced lewdness and who shall not have done all the things which are contained in the law."[58] Surely there is a threat here against those who shall have abused the name of God. Herein he shows us that, although he wants his law to be observed in all and by all, and that our life should be regulated by it, nevertheless he still reserves this point here to himself and wants his name to be honored.

Now however if this threat is ignored, and we fail to heed it, and it does not impede our ardent sporting of God and his majesty, must we not conclude, as I have already mentioned, that the devil has captured us and that we are deprived of sense and reason? But if this threat does not awaken us today, then in the end we will surely realize that God did not publish [any] false teachings in it. Therefore let us learn to be touched to the quick when we see that our Lord is so strictly opposed and that he reveals himself as a party adverse to all who have abused his name. For will it cost us anymore to abstain from treacherous oaths as it does from inconsistencies and above all blasphemies? For the greatest excuse which those have who want to decrease their fault here is that they cannot refrain because of habit. But surely if each were to set before himself God as his judge, he would immediately forget oaths; and where it is a matter of using the name of God, one would not have to do so except with great simplicity. For if men sought out law they would find the majesty of God present there; they would contemplate him as judge when they call upon him for testimony. For we cannot use his name unless it is in accordance with what Saint Paul[59] says, that we should not use the name of God unless we do so with complete holiness.

Therefore this is precisely what ought to be done. But what is the actual case? As I have already said, our tongue overflows with contempt for the name of God no matter what men may say, even if they should strike [us].[60] For the remonstrances which are made

---

[57]Deut. 27:16.
[58]Further reference to Deut. 27:17–26.
[59]See II Tim. 2:19.
[60]"... que quelque chose qu'on crie, mesmes qu'on martelle quasi: ... " *CO* 26.278.

in the holy Scripture concerning this abuse of God's name are like great hammer-blows with which God strikes us, and nevertheless we continue to live as we always have and the name of God receives no further honor or majesty than it did before. Nevertheless, the fact remains that those who have any feeling and comprehension for the name of God must thoughtfully ponder what has been said here. Moreover, as I have pointed out, when we have been admonished by that which we have seen from the preceding, its purpose is that we might know that he who speaks is the eternal One, that he is our creator, and that it is he who has redeemed us, who has more than revealed himself to us as Father and Savior. Thus when that has been sufficiently implanted in our mind, it is certain that all oaths will be easily forgotten. But if we continue [to behave as we have], then what is said by the prophet Zechariah[61] will come to be true in our case, that is, that they will be conscious of him whom they have pierced, that is, of him whom they have offended. For although men flatter one another and only make light of their oaths and think that such will be easily pardoned, God will not let himself be offended and in the end will show that this is not the way which we ought to address ourselves to him.

Nevertheless, we have to note, that God apparently has willed to show, briefly, what reverence we ought to bear toward his name. It is true that oaths are particularly mentioned here, but at the same time this doctrine must be extended further: that when we think of God, or when he is mentioned to us, that we do so with complete reverence, that we be alert, not only in order to honor and esteem him above everyone and everything else, but in order to realize that we are in the presence of his inestimable glory, before which the angels tremble; and therefore that we who are poor creatures, who are more transient than all the rest,[62] ought at least pay homage to the sovereign majesty of our God when he is mentioned. That is a point we ought surely observe in this passage.

Now it is true that this doctrine in itself is easy enough, but it is obscure to us, because it is so poorly practiced. When we think of God, how many vain thoughts crowd our mind? It is true that our nature is inclined in this way, as we are all crammed with falsehood and there is nothing but darkness in us. But at the same

[61]Zech. 12:10.
[62]" . . . , si caduques que rien plus, . . . " *CO* 26.279.

time, if a man feeds himself on the evil and wicked imaginations
which he conceives against the honor of God, such readily demonstrates that he has conspired and plotted with the devil. For how
many are troubled when an evil imagination comes to mind,
something which they are convinced is wicked and against the
glory of God? How many attempt to repress it and crowd it out?
Rather they delight in it and bathe[63] in it. But once the mind is
thus polluted, that is to say, the intelligence of men spoiled, the
rest is easily corrupted. And that such is the case, consider how
men most commonly speak of God? What words do they use? It
seems that men only ask to be corrupted; hardly any leaven is
needed to leaven the whole lump, says Saint Paul[64] with regard to
this wicked proposal which depraves us and infects us with evil
vices.

Now the worst is when one speaks of God in a mocking manner.
For doesn't this mean that it is wrong to taunt God and make light
of him with words that are not only vain and frivolous but are also
shameful and detestable? Is it not a willful[65] violation of his
majesty? And nonetheless such is done and is so common that we
do not have to converse long in any group before discovering
scorn for God reflected there.[66] And can we not see from this that
we have never adequately worshiped him?[67] We may readily say
each day: "Hallowed be thy name" and do exactly the contrary.
Do we need any other sentence of condemnation than that? When
we come here to church, we confess with our tongue that we desire that the name of God be preserved in its honor; we say as
much at the table; each of us in rising or going to bed says the
same (I say those who are not entirely brutish, for there are some
who do not know what praying to God is).

But still regarding those who are honest enough to pray to God
and readily say with their mouth: "Hallowed be thy name," that
prayer has scarcely left the end of their tongue before there arises
a hypocritical oath in their mouth and they [begin to] parade the
name of God this way and that. And what is the result of such a
falsehood if it isn't the violation of God's majesty, like striking him
with a dagger, or slapping him in the face? And thus, as I have

---

[63]bagne-baigne.
[64]I Cor. 5:6.
[65]à nostre escient.
[66]"... qu'à grand peine sera-on en une compagnie à tenir longs propos, qu'il
n'y ait ie ne say quoy meslé où Dieu sera mesprisé." *CO* 26.280.
[67]"... que nous n'avons jamais seu que c'est de l'adorer?" *CO* 26.280.

said, we do not need any other judge to condemn us in our oaths than this declaration which we make when we ask God to maintain the holiness of his name and yet seek to destroy it as much as possible.

Now it is important for us to speak of God in complete reverence, even when we refer to his works. For example: when speaking of the weather, whether it is fair or rainy, we are nonetheless confronted by the marks of God's majesty. When he sends us bad weather he reveals himself as a judge to make us aware of his anger [in order] that we might examine our sins, grieve, and be led to repentance. If, instead of being humbled before God and displeased with having offended him, we are provoked, as we commonly see others filled with contempt, is it not fitting that this weather should last a long time? And so we do not flee back to our God; we do not ask him to forgive our sins. And such is the case in everything else. I cite[68] only one example to show you that when we have spoken of the works of God it is necessary either to be conscious of him as a Father in his goodness or to be conscious of him as a judge in his sternness. Thus when God does those things which are not acceptable to us, and which are contrary to our desire and wish, let us remember that he both chastises us and mortifies[69] our flesh in order that we might enter into knowledge of our sins for the purpose of condemning them and of being displeased with them.

If we do not glorify God in this way, we profane his holy name. And then, on the other hand, when God draws us gently as a benign and merciful father, it is in order that we might be led to him and that we should honor him that much more. And if our ingratitude is condemned for not honoring him from the first word which he has spoken, what will be [the case] when all these things are used against us, when God at some cost which he has risked for us shall have hardly won us to himself? Will he not have to show us in all and by all that we are contemptuous of his majesty and that we have trodden his works underfoot, that we have thrown up our snout like swine? I beg of you, will this not be a horrible condemnation if we are accused of that?

Now although God has stamped his mark upon all his works and ought to be known by us in both fair and foul weather, heat and cold, and in brief in every order of nature, yet, above all, he

[68]ameine-cite.
[69]nous matte-mortifie la chair.

has stamped his mark upon his Word. It is true that it is already an inexcusable crime when we do not acknowledge him for the benefits which he has bestowed on us. We take our life from him; it is in him that we live, as Saint Paul[70] says. If we do not think of God with respect to these benefits, that already constitutes too unreasonable[71] an ingratitude. But as I have already said, above all God has willed for his mark to be stamped upon his Word. All we have to do is contemplate heaven and earth and we shall see God everywhere. For what is the earth if it isn't a living image (as Saint Paul[72] says) in which God is revealed. Although he is invisible in his essence, he is still revealed there that we might worship him. But when we turn to the Holy Scripture we find there an image by means of which God more particularly reveals himself to us than he does in the sky or in the earth. Neither the sun nor the moon, albeit they give clarity to the world—reveal the majesty of God as much as the law, the prophets, and the gospel. Nevertheless, how we speak of them! And with what audacity! Today, I beg of you, do men not give themselves a license when they speak about the name of God in their imagination? And when they enter into dispute with the holy Scripture in the shadow of a mug of wine, in taverns, and by tables, do they humble themselves and acknowledge their ignorance and weakness and ask from God [the gift] of his holy Spirit in order that his secrets might be shared with us as it ought to be? No! Rather their discussions there are a mockery and expose that there is not only a dearth of religion in the world today but scarcely any [feeling of] need for it as well. We see that some make fun of the Holy Scripture; they reduce the Proverbs to a laughingstock; they do no more than deride it as if it served no purpose other than wax which anyone might disfigure and each one shape as seems best to him. Others launch into discussions on it, asking why is this and how do you account for that? And then when we come to the high mysteries of God, if anything bores us we are quite willing for all to be abolished. Now it's as much as if we hoped to overthrow God from heaven.

Therefore let us learn that above all God commends to us the honor and authority of his Word. It's as if he were saying that everything contained in the Holy Scripture ought to be received by us in complete humility, that we make ourselves docile to its

[70]See Acts 17:28.
[71]exhorbitante-deraisonnable.
[72]Rom. 1:30.

contents. Exactly! And although that might be contrary to our nature and we would prefer that God might have spoken in a more pleasing way to us, nevertheless let us render him the honor of bringing our entire being [to him] saying, "Lord, we are your disciples; we peaceably receive what it has pleased you to teach us, knowing that it is for our benefit and salvation." Without exception then let everything contained in Holy Scripture be received with reverence. And with regard to the holy mysteries of God, let us not evaluate them according to our understanding, but when things do not seem good and right to us, let us restrain ourselves; may God always have the center; may his Word enjoy complete freedom; and [especially] when we come to the sermon, may that always be impressed upon us.

That is how our God reveals himself. And he is seated as our judge. It is not a matter here of gambling against God, as we see reflected in several who come to the sermon. Indeed! They come poisoned in their heart against God and his Word and can only relate in total malice. They are even poisoned to the extent that they disgorge their blasphemies at table, or they will be found there when one has not spoken to their inclination.[73]

There you have the proper way to honor the name of God. Let us learn therefore that whether we are reading the Holy Scripture or one is preaching it, that we always hold the name of God in such majesty that we tremble when one speaks about it to us, above all when his Word is preached to us, as the prophet Isaiah[74] speaks of it. For that is how we shall declare, not only by mouth but in deed, that we are the true faithful. And God will also accept[75] us as his people and in the end will gather us into the inheritance of the kingdom of God.[76]

---

[73]This entire paragraph echoes something of Calvin's struggles with the Perrinists, issuing in the May 16 riot.

[74]See Isa. 66:2, 5.

[75]advouera-acceptera.

[76]Golding's translation concludes this sermon with the following exhortation: "Now let us kneele down in the presence of our good God with acknowledgement of our faults, praying him, not to impute those unto us which we have committed heretofore: but that it may please him so to reforme us to himselfe, as our whole seeking may be to honour him, and to give ourselves to his service, that he may dwell among us, and our Lord Jesus raigne over us, both by his holy spirit and by his woord. And so let us all say, Almighty God heavenly father, etc." *Sermons Upon the Fifth Book of Moses*, trans. Golding, p. 199. Cf. Calvin, *Sermons sur les dix commendemens*, 1557 ed., p. 61.

Thursday, June 20, 1555[1]

Sermon Five[2]

Deuteronomy 5:12–14[3]

After speaking about the correct form[4] of worshiping God,
about serving him and glorifying his name, without using it in
oaths or in other ways except to honor him, now mention is made
of the worship of God in accordance with what he requires in his
law, from the order which he has instituted, in order that the
faithful may practice it. The sabbath day[5] has been in part a
figurative way for showing that men cannot properly worship God
without dedicating themselves to him in such a way that they
separate themselves from the world.[6] Secondly, the sabbath day

---

[1]N. in *CO:* "This sermon corresponds to the fifth in the 1562 collection, pp.
94–117." *CO* 26.283.

[2]The original title: "The Fourth Sermon on Chapter 5:12–14." *CO* 26.283.

[3]See Calvin's development of the Fourth Commandment in the *Institutes*
2.8.28–34; Comm. *Four Books of Moses*, vol. 2, pp. 432–40; *CO* 24.575–81; *Catechism, CO* 6.62, 64, 66, 68.

[4]purement.

[5]literally: "day of rest."

[6]Throughout this sermon Calvin pleads for a self-emptying on the part of wor-
shipers in order that God may become the nexus of one's existence. More than
anything else, the sabbath serves to facilitate this purpose. See n. 40 below. "First,

has existed as a ceremony whose purpose was to assist the people
to assemble that they might hear the law, call upon the name of
God, and offer sacrifices and everything which concerns the
spiritual order.[7] Thus now we see the way in which the sabbath
day is presented. But that would not be easily understood without
distinction and if these two aspects were not studied in detail.

Therefore, we need to note that the sabbath day was a shadow[8]
under the law until the coming of our Lord Jesus Christ to represent that God requires men to rest from all their own works,
which is what I have been saying in a word: that we must mortify
our nature if we hope to be in conformity with our God. In any
event, Saint Paul stresses it, and in addition there are numerous
references to it in the New Testament. But it ought to suffice to
cite the more precise text, that is, in Colossians[9] where it is said
that we have the substance and the body of things which were
under the law, but we have them, he says, in Jesus Christ. And
therefore it was necessary for the ancient Fathers to participate in
this hope as much through the sabbath day as through other
ceremonies. But now that Christ[10] has been given to us, it is no
longer necessary for us to be limited by these obscurities.

It is true that the law is not altogether abolished, as it does not
fail to retain the substance and truth for us, but the obscurity has
been abolished with the coming of our Lord Jesus Christ. If we
ask how the ancient Fathers were aware of that, Moses has given
us a statement with regard to it as he has sufficiently shown in the
Book of Exodus.[11] For God, having proclaimed his law in the
twentieth chapter to Moses, discloses to him the end which it was
to serve and says that he has ordained the sabbath day as a reprieve[12] which the people of Israel were to keep holy unto him.
"It is (he says) the mark of my sanctification which I have instituted among you."[13] For when the Scripture speaks to us about

under the repose of the sabbath day the heavenly lawgiver meant to represent to
the people of Israel spiritual rest, in which believers ought to lay aside their own
works to allow God to work in them." *Institutes* 2.8.28; *LCC* 20.395.

[7]police. In the *Institutes* Calvin suggests three conditions under which this commandment is properly kept. The first two coincide with the two in this sermon, as
Calvin devoted two sermons to the Fourth Commandment. See the *Institutes* 2.8.28.

[8]On the role of the law as a shadow, see the *Institutes* 2.7.2ff.

[9]Col. 2:17.

[10]la chose.

[11]Exod. 20:10.

[12]une arre.

[13]Paraphrase of Exod. 20:11.

being sanctified before God, it means for us to separate ourselves from everything contrary to his service.[14] But now where will one find such purity? We are in the world and we know that in this world there is only perversity and malice, as Saint John says in his canonical Epistle.[15] But it is not necessary for men to go outside themselves to do battle against God and his justice, for as Saint Paul says in the eighth chapter of Romans,[16] all our senses and feelings are equally at enmity against God. When men let go of the reins on their thoughts, on their desires and wills, on all their cupidity, they overtly fight against God. We know what is said in the sixth chapter of Genesis,[17] that whatever man is capable of imagining is only evil continually, and that whatever man invents in himself and in his shop is only perverse and corrupt before God. Thus we see quite well that we cannot be sanctified before our God, that is to say, we cannot worship him in purity, unless we separate ourselves from opposing pollutions, or until what belongs to our nature is abolished.

Now it was necessary that all this be put in figures to the ancient fathers, seeing that Jesus Christ had not yet been fully revealed to them. But today, in Jesus Christ, we have the accomplishment and perfection of all those things. And to prove it, Saint Paul[18] says that the old man is crucified with him. When Saint Paul speaks in that manner about the old man, he means that [nature] which we have received from Adam. It is imperative that all that die and be annihilated, not the essence of our body or of our soul, but the malice which is in us, that blindness which makes us err, those evil desires which are totally rebellious against the justice of God—it is imperative that that (insofar as it has come from Adam) be abolished. And how is that done? It isn't done through our [own] industry, but we have acquired this right through our Lord Jesus Christ who died for us in order to blot out our sins that they might no longer be imputed against us. Because of his Holy Spirit we can renounce the world and even ourselves to the extent that our carnal affections no longer dominate us. And although we are full of rebellion, nevertheless the Spirit of God will rule over them and repress them and hold them in check. Moreover, it is also said

---

[14]See n. 6 above.
[15]See I John 2:15-17; 5:19.
[16]Rom. 8:7.
[17]Gen. 6:5.
[18]Rom. 6:6.

that we are resurrected with him,[19] which Saint Paul also stresses in that Colossian[20] passage which I have already cited.

But now this had not yet been manifested under the law. Thus it was necessary that the fathers who lived at that time have some aid, such as the sacrifices, in order to nurture them in the hope of the death of our Lord Jesus Christ, that they might understand that their sins were purged through the blood of the mediator. Likewise they had the sabbath day as a testimony that grace had been given to us to mortify all our thoughts and affections in order that God might live in us by means of his Holy Spirit.

Now we have a doorway for understanding what has been briefly touched on, that is, that the sabbath day was like a sign for representing what in fact has been accomplished by the coming of our Lord Jesus Christ. Let us also carefully note that the sabbath day extends to all the worship of God in order to show that men cannot purely honor him without renouncing themselves, or being separated from the pollutions of the world and of their own flesh. And that is also why he reproached the Jews through the prophet Ezekiel[21] for not having observed the sabbath day.

Now this was said to them in such a way as to indicate that they had violated the entire law in general. And not without justification. For whoever has defied the sabbath day has insofar as possible put under his feet the whole service of God. And if the sabbath day is not observed, all the other days lose their significance. For as mentioned in the prophet Isaiah,[22] it is crucial that men cast aside their own virtues, that they necessarily abstain[23] from them, or otherwise it is not the day of the Lord which he accepts or approves.[24] From this we see that no purpose is achieved in observing the ceremony alone. For indeed if the Jews had kept the ceremony, they would have gathered on the sabbath day without lifting a finger with regard to their household needs. Instead, they fed all their wicked ambitions and then put them into effect, which amounted to making fun of God, abusing his name, and depraving and corrupting every order he has instituted, for which he has accordingly reproached them. But the principal point was to consider the truth of the figure, that is, the spiritual service of

[19]Rom. 6:4-5, 8.
[20]See Col. 2:12, 13; 3:1.
[21]See Ezek. 20:21; 22:8; 32:38.
[22]See Isa. 58:13-14.
[23]s'en demettent-s'en privent.
[24]See n. 6 above.

God. Nevertheless it was necessary for the Jews to keep the ceremony which was commanded them. For God held them in this
harness; he was not content for them to possess the substance of
things, but at the same time he willed for them to have the
shadows until the coming of our Lord Jesus Christ. With that in
view we can understand what Saint Paul[25] says: that now we are
no longer subject to this ancient servitude of observing the sabbath day, for it is necessary for us to render this honor to Jesus
Christ, to content ourselves with what he himself has brought us
without any longer having what was exterior under the law.

Now we see how this observation is applicable[26] to us today. As
far as the ceremony goes (as I have said), that is in the past. The
crucial thing is for us to come to the substance, which means that
we must serve God well; we must learn to empty[27] ourselves of all
our will, of all our thoughts and affections. Why? Because when
we try[28] to be wise, imagining this or that as serving God, we
spoil[29] it all. The imperative thing is that we set aside our pru-
dence and listen to God speak, following neither our sense nor
our imagination. That is the beginning of how we ought to keep
the sabbath day: by disbelieving what seems good to us, for of
necessity we must rest. And how rest? By abiding in such a way
that our thoughts do not flutter about or invent first one thing
and then another.[30] It is necessary (I say) that we live in obedience
to our God. And when we are tempted by our appetites,[31] we
should recognize that these are so much at enmity against God
that all our affections are wicked and rebellious. Therefore it is
necessary that we still rest in this manner and that we place ourselves before God to the end that he alone may work in us, that he
alone may guide and govern us by his Holy Spirit. Therein we see
that God omitted nothing when he ordained the sabbath day.

Now since God went to such lengths, what greater doctrine of
perfect sanctity remains, seeing that we shall have what the Holy
Spirit has offered us? It is a matter of piously walking in the
obedience of our God. And how is that done? By our receiving his
simple Word and seeking to conform ourselves to his justice. Now

[25]See Col. 2:20.
[26]compete-est applicable à.
[27]See n. 6 above.
[28]voudrons.
[29]gasterons-ravagerons, dévasterons, pillerons. See Huguet, vol. 4, p. 276.
[30]ceci ne cela.
[31]appetisdésirs.

insofar as our nature is opposed to that, of necessity we must begin by this end: by denying ourselves.[32] When that has been done, shall we not possess what is required for serving God? But that is especially difficult. Thus let us see to it that we arouse ourselves when we hear that God commands us to keep the sabbath day, recognizing that this will not be [done] by our playing, but that he will have to force us to that end. For throughout our life, we shall benefit immensely if we have kept it, indeed have denied our nature and dedicated ourselves wholly to our God. Thus we ought to be inflamed that much more to keep spiritually this rest of the Lord, seeing that we are free from this servile subjection of the law and that God has granted us more privilege than he granted the fathers of old. For he is pleased that we should be dead in our old man that we might be renewed by the virtue of his Holy Spirit. We are no longer subject to this ceremony which was kept so narrowly under the law.[33]

Seeing that God deals with us so amicably, we are obligated that much more to consider the principal matter to the end that we might observe it correctly. Indeed! Moreover, it is not enough to allude to the fact that the ancient fathers possessed the ceremony in order to incite them, or that it served them as a hope, for we have far more than the external and visible sign since our Lord Jesus Christ has appeared to us, in whom all that was prefigured in shadows has been fulfilled. Therefore it is highly inappropriate for us to keep asking for those things which were under the law.

Thus you see how what was ordained here with regard to the sabbath has been fulfilled today, that is with respect to the truth of the figure which the fathers knew in shadow [form]. In fact, it is expedient that what has been commanded concerning the sabbath day should apply to all. For if we take the law of God in itself, we shall have a perpetual norm of justice.[34] And certainly under the ten commandments God willed to give us a norm that would abide forever. Therefore we must not imagine that what Moses has re-

---

[32]See Calvin's ch. on "Self Denial" in the *Institutes* 3.7.1–3.

[33]Cf. the *Institutes* 2.8.31: "But there is no doubt that by the Lord Jesus Christ's coming the ceremonial part of this commandment was abolished. For he himself is the truth, with whose presence all figures vanish; he is the body, at whose appearance the shadows are left behind. He is, I say, the true fulfillment of the Sabbath."

[34]Note Calvin's insistence on the permanent validity of the law. The fact that it served as a shadow, prefiguring all that Christ would fulfill, does not denigrate its capacity to serve as "a perpetual norm of justice." This is in harmony with Calvin's threefold use of the law; see the *Institutes* 2.7.6–12.

counted concerning the sabbath day is superfluous to us, not that the figure still lives on, but we have its truth. Moreover, that is why the apostle in the Epistle to the Hebrews,[35] the fourth chapter, applies what is said about the sabbath day to the instruction of Christians and the new church. For he shows that we must be conformed to our God in whom our full happiness and perfection reside, seeing that all of man's highest good lies[36] in what has been created in the image of God. What then is required now, seeing that this image has been effaced by sin, except that it be repaired? That is how we must take hold of our perfection: by conforming ourselves to our God and his will, by inquiring about his work to the end that we might do the same.

Therefore, in order to serve God better, let us understand that we have been commanded to restrain ourselves[37] with all our power that our thoughts, affections, and desires might be subdued and that God might reign in us and govern us by his Holy Spirit. Thus all hypocrites are only deceiving themselves.[38] For as long as their wicked lusts are hidden in their hearts, as long as they are full of envy, spite, ambition, cruelty, and fraud, it is certain that they can only violate the sabbath day. Therefore we can conclude that they are perverting the entire service of God similar to that which we have already cited in Ezekiel. Moreover, we read the same in Jeremiah.[39] And in fact that is why the ceremony was so rigid under the law. Do we really think that God has ever taken pleasure in men's idleness? Certainly not! Yet he punished those who had worked on the sabbath as harshly as those who had murdered a man.[40] It seems rather cruel for a man to die for

---

[35] Heb. 4:1–11.

[36] gist-action de jeter. See Huguet, vol. 4, p. 276.

[37] de mettre peine-s'efforcer de.

[38] "Et ainsi tous hypocrites auront beau se fader, et faire de belles mines." CO 26.288.

[39] See Jer. 17:24.

[40] See Num. 15:32, 35. In his Comm. Four Books of Moses, vol. 2, p. 434; CO 24.577; Calvin explains that God did not espouse "idleness" and "sloth" in ordering the sabbath. There is no virtue in the "simple cessation" of labor itself. Rather, on the sabbath man must desist from his own activity in order that God might work in him. This requires a willingness and an effort on man's part that is the farthest thing from "simple cessation" of labor. This note is sounded again in the following statement: "And certainly God took the seventh day for His own and hallowed it, when the creation of the world was finished, that He might keep His servants altogether free from every care, for the consideration of the beauty, excellence, and fitness of His works. There is indeed no moment which should be allowed to pass in which we are not attentive to the consideration of the wisdom, power,

chopping wood on the sabbath day, the same as if he had committed a murder. Yet God condemns to death whomever has cut wood on the sabbath. And why? Because all the service of God is included under this figure. The same applies[41] in Jeremiah[42] [where] it is said that they carried their burdens and drove carts[43] on the sabbath day. And why? It seems that God has singled out a frivolous and puerile thing, but he knows what this day of rest means. And when he had been scorned by the Jews in this way, it was like a sacrilege, for they demonstrated that the entire law meant nothing to them.

Thus to return to our own situation, seeing that today we do not have this rigid figure and that God has given us a great liberty, which has been acquired by us through the death and passion of our Lord Jesus Christ, let us learn to dedicate ourselves to him with solicitude,[44] and to recognize (as I have already touched on) that we shall have to labor hard in everything else, that it will amount to nothing unless our affections are held in check, unless we go to the trouble of renouncing all our thoughts and desires in such a way that only God governs us, and that we solemnly declare[45] that we ask only to rest in him. And for that reason God suggests himself as an example. For he was not content to command men to rest, but he showed the way. For after having created the world and all that it contains, he rested, not because he had to, or was in need of rest, rather its purpose was to invite us to contemplate his works that we might concentrate on them and nevertheless conform ourselves to him. Do we therefore wish to keep the spiritual rest? Everything, then, that is said about God desisting from his works also applies to us, for we must so conduct

goodness, and justice of God in His admirable creation and government of the world; but, since our minds are fickle, and apt therefore to be forgetful or distracted, God, in his indulgence providing against our infirmities, separates one day from the rest, and commands that it should be free from all earthly business and cares, so that nothing may stand in the way of that holy occupation. On this ground He did not merely wish that people should rest at home, but that they should meet in the sanctuary, there to engage themselves in prayer and sacrifices, and to make progress in religious knowledge through the interpretation of the Law. In this respect we have an equal necessity for the Sabbath with the ancient people, so that on one day we may be free and thus the better prepared to learn and to testify our faith." Ibid., p. 437; ibid., col. 579.

[41]voila purquoy.
[42]See Jer. 17:21-22, 28.
[43]charrie.
[44]See the *Institutes* 2.8.28.
[45]protester-affirmer solennellement.

ourselves as to cease doing whatever seems good to us and what our nature craves. If God's example does not motivate us, we only demonstrate that we really do not want anything [from him] and that by no means do we seek our happiness, but prefer to live by our own knowledge in our poverty and misery.

That then is the highest good of men, as I have said, that they adhere to and be joined to their God. Indeed, our Lord calls us to himself and shows us that we are unable to have a true union and sanctity with him unless we rest from our work. If we continue to hurry about and insist on being busybodies,[46] engaging in what seems best to us, we shall certainly sever the tie between God and ourselves, separate ourselves from him, and alienate ourselves from him as far as possible. And by doing so will people not be able to see that we are asking to be exposed as a prey to Satan and that he will mislead us and carry us away seeing that we shall no longer be under the protection of God? But what is the actual case? There are very few who think that way. We see the license which they all indulge. If you approach one of them and show him that he ought not pursue the way of his imagination, he will only reply: "I know how I need to behave."

Now one could not better despise God more openly than by such rebellion. It's as much as if someone should state that he does not want any superiority above us. It is true that men do not actually affirm that, but nevertheless it is so. For as I have said, there is no serving God until we begin at this point: to empty ourselves of our thoughts and affections.[47] Therefore when men want to be wise and trust in their own judgment, permit themselves to do whatever they find good, follow their affections and imaginations, and make no effort to repress them, but are even irritated when anyone tries to correct[48] them, it is a sign that they have never known what it was to serve God or what the principal point of the law was.

Therefore let us carefully note that when God cites himself as our example, his purpose is to invite us gently to keep the spiritual rest and ever think of ourselves (as I have already touched on) as being unhappy when we are forced to be separated from him. And here is the bond of this union: that we do not

[46]" . . . , et que nous vueillions remuer bras et iambes, . . . " *CO* 26.289.
[47]See n. 6 above.
[48]donter.

alienate ourselves from his religion and truth, but permit him to govern us.

Now it is possible to ask: why were the Jews commanded to rest solely on the seventh day? For we must not interpret this to mean that only one day a week we should renounce our thoughts and affections; rather we must continue in this attitude throughout our life.[49] In brief, it is a perpetual rest which God commands: one without any interval. Yet why did he choose only one day a week? It was in order to show us that when we have applied our best efforts to renounce our evil lusts, our pretenses, and whatever belongs to our nature, we shall still not fully attain to it until we are stripped of our flesh. It is true that it is necessary for the faithful throughout their life to keep the sabbath day, and to desist from their own wills and actions, and to endeavor to dedicate themselves to God in all humility in order to align themselves with him and to find peace in his obedience. It is crucial (I say) for us to proceed in that way, or otherwise all the service which we shall render to God will only be fictitious, and he will reject and reprove it.

Now at all events we cannot truly acquit ourselves by disavowing our affections, as there will always remain some fault. Saint Paul[50] certainly glorifies in the fact that as far as he is concerned the world is crucified to him and that he is crucified to the world, nevertheless he does not neglect to say that his flesh wars against the spirit and that there is never any accord. He even admits in the seventh chapter of Romans[51] that he has always felt in himself this repugnance, that he did not do the good that he willed, that is to say, that he did not accomplish it with an ardent affection, that he was not so resolute as to walk after God, as there was always some obstacle to impede him, for it seemed that he walked with a hobble instead of running with strength. Thus in the same way let us note that it is not without cause that God has ordained this seventh day of rest, indicating that we are unable, whether in a day or a month, to arrive at that perfection of holiness which he requires of us.[52] Why? Because even when we have struggled valiantly against the affections of our flesh and our evil thoughts,

---

[49]See Calvin's elaboration of this principle in the *Institutes* 2.8.30.
[50]See Gal. 6:14; 5:17.
[51]See Rom. 7:15, 19.
[52]Calvin develops this same note in a similar manner in the *Institutes* 2.8.30.

there will always be some residue until we are fully joined to God and he has gathered us into his heavenly Kingdom.

Until then there will always be some temptations in us, some troubles and anxiety, for we will keenly sense (I am referring to those who seek God) that we are still subject to many temptations, that we are conscious of many incentives by which we are drawn to this and that; and are these not enough of a retardation to impede spiritual rest? If a man were to rest in God as he ought, he would not conceive in his imagination of just anything to turn him from the right path. He would not possess evil affections or cupidity; all that would be far from him.

Thus when we concoct countless evil whims, Satan comes to assail us and to fill us with anxiety; when we have thought to do evil, there are things which jump about in us and which titillate us; although we hate the wrong, nevertheless by such temptations we are incited to pursue it. And as a result anyone can see that it is not an easy thing to be freed[53] from our wicked concupiscences to the extent that they no longer reign in us. Thus let us pursue this theme of celebrating the spiritual rest of God, because we shall not come to its end until the end of our life.

Now, in the light of this, we are admonished with respect to two things: the one is to be displeased with ourselves and always to grieve, although it seems to us that we have gone to great lengths to subject ourselves to our God; nevertheless, let us recognize that we are always on the road and that of necessity there is much that is required and commanded in the law that must be accomplished by us. It serves, accordingly, as a way of humbling us, seeing that God will always find so much more to command in us with respect to his service and the fact that we are nowhere near [fulfilling] the requirements of this spiritual rest. Now all of this provides us with an opportunity for our humiliation and sighing in true repentance; also, on the other hand, we must be that much more moved and excited to take advantage of the situation once we see [it]. How is that? It is true that God has granted me the grace to be willing to serve him, but how do I go about the latter? Alas, I am still far from attaining it. Thus once we grasp that, will it not make our own endeavor more imperative?[54] Thus in detesting the evil

---

[53]desveloppez-délivrer.
[54]". . . : que faut-il sinon s'efforcer?" CO 26.291.

which is in us, let'us be so much more inspired to profit continually in their rest, and to make progress in it, and for each of us daily to call ourself to account. Thus that is how God, after having given us an opportunity for humbling us throughout our life, shows us that we must be zealous to correct our vices and increasingly to mortify our flesh, that we might realize that it is not enough for our old man to be crucified in part, rather we must be entirely buried with Christ. For, as we have already cited, that is what Saint Paul says in his seventh chapter of Romans.[55] That is what is meant by the seventh day which is mentioned here.

Now we must come to the second point which emphasizes that the sabbath day was a [type of] civil order[56] for training the faithful in the service of God.[57] For that day was ordained in order that people might assemble themselves to hear the doctrine of the law preached, to participate[58] in the sacrifices, [and] to invoke the name of God. With respect to that, it applies as much to us as to the ancient people. For although the figurative aspect has been surpassed,[59] I affirm what Paul says in the Letter to the Colossians:[60] that nevertheless what is said of this order[61] still applies and has its usage. And what is this order? It is to assemble ourselves in the name of God. Indeed it is true that that must always be done, but because of our weakness, even because of our laziness, it is necessary for one day to be chosen. If we were as ardent in the service of God as we should be, it would not have been necessary to ordain one day of the week, for without a written law each would have assembled himself morning and evening in order that we might have become increasingly edified in the Word of God. And whereas we are so inclined toward evil that nothing is required to debauch us, that practice would still be necessary for us; thus we should have need of assembling ourselves every day in the name of God. But what is the actual case? We see with what great pain people assemble themselves on Sunday and how neces-

---

[55]See Rom. 7:40.
[56]police.
[57]Calvin's second point here corresponds with the second function of the Fourth Commandment as presented in the *Institutes* 2.8.28; *LCC* 20.395: "Secondly, he meant that there was to be a stated day for them to assemble to hear the law and perform the rites, or at least to devote it particularly to meditation upon his works, and thus through this remembrance to be trained in piety."
[58]communiquer-participer.
[59]" ... la figure soit cessee, ... " *CO* 26.291.
[60]See Col. 2:16–17.
[61]police.

sary it is to use force to retain a large part of the world. Thus
seeing such a weakness in ourselves, let us acknowledge that this
order[62] was not given solely to the Jews in order for them to have
a certain day on which they might assemble themselves, but at the
same time it applies to us.

Nevertheless, we have to note that there is more and that indeed it would be a meagre thing to have a rest regarding physical
activity[63] but not involving anything else. What is necessary then?
That we should strive toward a higher end than this rest here;
that we should desist from our works which are able to impede us
from meditating on the works of God, from calling upon his
name, and from our exercising his Word. If we turn Sunday into
a day for living it up,[64] for our sport and pleasure,[65] indeed how
will God be honored in that? Is it not a mockery and even a profanation of his name? But when shops are closed on Sunday, when
people do not travel in the usual way, its purpose is to provide
more leisure and liberty for attending to what God commands us
that we might be taught by his Word, that we might convene together in order to confess our faith, to invoke his name, [and] to
participate in the use of the sacraments. That is the end for which
this order must serve us.

Now let us consider whether those who call themselves Christians require of themselves what they should. There is a large
group which thinks that Sunday exists for the purpose of enabling
them to attend to their own affairs and who reserve this day for
that [purpose] as if there were no others throughout the week for
deliberating their business. For though the bell[66] tolls the sermon,
they seem only to have time for their own affairs and for one
thing and another. The rest glut[67] themselves and are shut up in
their houses because they do not dare display a manifest scorn on
the streets; in any case, Sunday is nothing more than a retreat for
them in which they stand aloof from the church of God.

---

[62] police.
[63] literally: "des mains et des pieds."
[64] "... à faire bonne chere, ... " *CO* 26.292.
[65] "... aller à l'esbat: ... " *CO* 26.292.
[66] E. W. Monter describes this bell in *Calvin's Geneva*. Its name was *La Clémence*.
It was on the North Tower of St. Pierre. On its base was a Gothic inscription: "I
praise the true God, I summon the people, I assemble the clergy, I weep for the
dead, I chase the plague away, I embellish feast days. My voice is the terror of all
devils," p. 13.
[67] gourmandent.

Now from the foregoing we see in what attitude[68] we hold all Christianity and the service of God. For what was given to us in order to help us approach God, we use as an occasion for alienating ourselves from him even more. And as a result we are led astray. We must recover it all. Is not such a diabolical malice in men? Would to God that we had to look hard for examples and that they were more rare. But as everything is profaned, we see that the majority hardly care about the usage of this day which has been instituted in order that we might withdraw from all earthly anxieties, from all business affairs, to the end that we might surrender everything to God.

Moreover, let us realize that it is not only for coming to the sermon that the day of Sunday is instituted, but in order that we might devote all the rest of time to praising God. Indeed! For although he nurtures us every day, nevertheless we do not sufficiently meditate on the favors he bestows on us in order to magnify them. It is true that it would be a poor thing if we did not think about the benefits of God except on Sunday, but on other days, seeing that we are so occupied with our affairs, we are not as much open to serve God as on a day which is totally dedicated to this. Thus we ought to observe Sunday as if from a tower in order that we might climb high upon it to contemplate the works of God from afar, in a way in which we are neither impeded by nor occupied with anything else, so that we might be able to extend all our senses to recognize the benefits and favors with which he has enlarged us. And when Sunday is able to help us practice that, that is to consider the works of God, then certainly once we have meditated on his works for a long time in order to know how to benefit from them, we will surrender to him all the rest of time. For this meditation will already have formed and polished us, [and] we shall be induced to thank our God on Monday and all the rest of the week. But when Sunday is spent not only in pastimes full of vanity, but in things which are entirely contrary to God, it seems that one has not at all celebrated Sunday [and] that God has been offended in many ways. Thus when people profane in this manner the holy order[69] which God has instituted to lead us to himself, why should they be astonished if all the rest of the week is degraded?

[68]affection.
[69]police.

Thus what is necessary? Let us recognize that it is not enough
for us to come to the sermon on Sunday in order to receive some
good doctrine and to invoke the name of God, but it is necessary
to ponder these things and to apply all our senses to understanding better the favors which God bestows upon us. And by this
means may we be moulded by that which costs us nothing,
[whether] on Monday or any other day of the week, to aspire to
our God. May we reduce to memory only what we have previously
known by [his] good leisure, that our minds may be delivered[70]
from all that hinders us and prevents us from recognizing the
works of God. Thus that is how we ought to observe today this
matter concerning the order.[71] We no longer have this figure and
shadow for the purpose of keeping a ceremony as rigid as it was
under the bondage of the law. Rather its purpose is to gather us
in order that according to our weakness we might be trained to
devote ourselves better to the service of God, that we might have
this day fully dedicated to him, to the end that we might be with-
drawn from the world and, as we have said, that it serve us for the
rest of our life.

Moreover, we have to note that on Sunday it is not enough for
each in his own way to think of God and his work, but it is essential for us to gather on that particular day in order to make a
public confession of our faith. In truth, as we have said, that
ought to be done every day, yet because of men's coarseness and
because of their nonchalance, it is necessary to have a special day
which should be totally dedicated to that end. It is true that we are
not limited to the seventh day. As indeed in fact we do not keep
the day which was commanded to the Jews.[72] For that was Satur-
day. But in order to demonstrate the liberty of Christians, the day
has been changed, seeing that Jesus Christ in his resurrection has
delivered us from all bondage of the law and has severed that
obligation.

That is why we have made this change in the day. But in any
event, we ought to observe this order of having some day of the
week, whether one or two. But all of that can be left up to the
liberty of Christians. Whatever the case, if a people is assembled
for having the common sacraments, for having public invocation

[70]desveloppez-délivrer.
[71]police.
[72]Calvin explains why Christians celebrate the sabbath on Sunday in the *Institutes* 2.8.38.

of the name of God, [or] for showing an accord and union of faith, it is proper to have a special day for that.[73] Thus it is not enough for each one to return to his house, whether it is for reading the holy Scriptures or for praying to God, rather it is a matter of coming in the company of the faithful, and of showing the concord which we have with all the body of the church, and of celebrating this order which our Lord has thus commanded. But what actually happens? We see the notorious profanation of the service of God. For (as I have already touched) are there not many who indeed wish to show that they only despise God and wish to be exempt from the common law? It is true that they will come five or six times a year to the sermon. And to do what? To make fun of God and of all his doctrine. It is true that they are the swine who come to foul the temple of God and who deserve instead to be in stables. It would be better if they would remain in their stinking holes; in short, it would be better if such rabble and disgusting[74] people were completely cut off from the temple of God rather than permitted to mingle with the company of the faithful. But still, how often they come! If the bell tolls long enough, you will see them take their seats. Thus that much more carefully must we see to it that we are induced to make such a confession of our faith that God may be honored by a common accord among us.

Furthermore, it is necessary for all superstitions to be abolished. For we see how in the papacy they have tried[75] to serve God by idleness. It is not in this way that we must celebrate the sabbath day. But in order to apply ourselves to its correct and lawful usage, it is necessary to realize (as we have already said) that our Lord only asks that this day be spent in hearing his Word, in offering common prayers, in confessing our faith, and in observing the sacraments. It is that to which we are called. Nevertheless we see how all of that has been corrupted and put into confusion in the papacy. For on the contrary, they have found days for honoring saints (male and female) and for creating idols. Moreover they have thought that it was necessary to serve in idleness. Seeing that the world is thus given over to corruption, so much the more must we indeed note this explanation[76] of the sabbath day, fol-

---

[73]See Acts 2:42; *Institutes* 2.8.32.
[74]poacres-povacres.
[75]on a cuidé-on a essayé.
[76]declaration-explication.

lowing the way in which it is developed by Moses. But that we might understand to what end our Lord commanded the ancient people, that it was a day of the week in which they were to rest, today, having understood that it was abolished with the coming of our Lord Jesus Christ, we have the spiritual rest that we might dedicate ourselves fully to God, renouncing all our senses [and] all our affections. In addition, we have the external order[77]—insofar as it applies to us—which exists for the purpose of enabling us to set aside our affairs and earthly business in order that, abstaining from everything else, we might meditate on the works of God and be trained to recognize the favors which God bestows on us. Furthermore, it inspires us to recognize the grace which he daily offers us in his Gospel that we might be conformed to it more and more. And when we have spent Sunday in praising and glorifying the name of God and in meditating on his works, then, throughout the rest of the week, we should show that we have benefited from it.[78]

[77]police.

[78]Golding's translation concludes the fifth sermon with the following exhortation and prayer: "Now let us kneele downe in the presence of our good GOD with acknowledgment of our faultes, praying him to make us feele them better than we have done. And forasmuch as wee can by no meanes serve him, until the forwardnesse that is in us be done away, and inasmuch as he hath tolde us that we shall not cease to fight against his righteousnesse, so long as wee give heede to our owne lusts and imaginations: it may please our good God to grant us such grace by the power of his holy Spirit, as wee may be fully fashioned lyke unto him that dyed and rose again for us to mortify us and to quicken us. So then let us beare the marke of our Lorde Jesus Christ even in renouncing ourselves, and let us so submit us to his will, as our whole seeking may bee to be fashioned lyke to his righteousness, that his laws may bee fulfilled in us even as it is spirituall, and wee be changed from flesh to spirit, to live under his obeisance. And because there is alwáyes so much in us to be mislyked: it may please the same good God to beare with our infirmities, until his rest be fully brought to passe in us, and that he have taken us up into his heavenly kingdome. That it may please him to graunt this grace not onely, etc." *Sermons Upon the Fifth Book of Moses,* trans. Golding, p. 205. Cf. Calvin, *Sermons sur les dix commandemens,* 1557 ed., p. 75.

Sermon Six[2]

Deuteronomy 5:13–15[3]

Yesterday we discussed how and why the commandment to keep the sabbath day[4] was given to the Jews: (in brief) it was said that it stood[5] as a symbol[6] for spiritual rest which the faithful had to observe[7] in order to worship God. Now insofar as our Lord Jesus Christ has brought us the fulfillment of that, we are no longer obligated to be limited by this shadow of the law, rather let us be satisfied that our old man has been[8] crucified in virtue of the passion and death of our Lord Jesus Christ in order that we might be renewed for the purpose of fully serving our God. But

[1]N. in *CO:* "This sermon corresponds to the sixth in the 1562 collection, pp. 117–140." *CO* 26.295.
[2]The original title: "The Fifth Sermon on Chapter 5:13–15." *CO* 26.295.
[3]See "The Fifth Sermon," n. 2.
[4]As noted earlier, Calvin refers to the sabbath day as "the day of rest"; le jour du repos.
[5]ç'esté.
[6]figure.
[7]faire.
[8]soit.

nevertheless we [still] have need of some order and guidance[9] in our midst.[10] Thus it is fitting that we should have a particular day for our assemblage in order that we might be confirmed in the doctrine of God and benefit from it everyday, that is to say, for the rest of our life: that we might also be well-trained to call upon his name [and] to make a confession of our faith.[11] And in the meantime the remainder of the day should be spent in considering the favors[12] which we receive all the time from God's hand in order that he might be glorified in them that much more.

But now we need to note what is said in Moses' text. *Thou shalt work six days,*[13] says the Lord. This must not be interpreted to mean that God commands us to work. Truly we are [already] born to that [end]. Moreover we know that God does not intend for us to be lazy living in this world[14]; for he has given men hands and feet; he has given them industry. And even before the fall,[15] it is said that Adam was placed in a garden in order to tend it. But the work in which men are now engaged[16] is a punishment for sin. For it is pointed out to them: "You will eat your bread by the sweat of your brow; it is a curse which has been placed on all human beings." For we are unworthy of hearing of this condition which [supposedly] belonged to our father,[17] that he could live a life of ease without harming himself. But still before sin had come into the world and we have been condemned by God to painful and forced work, men were already required to engage in some [type of] labor. And why? Because it is contrary to our nature to be like a block of useless wood. Therefore it is certain that we must apply ourselves to some [form of] labor all the days of our life. But the text does not simply command [us] to work six days. For in fact, under the law there were other solemn occasions whose purpose was not rest; there were feasts which certainly came in the middle of the week. But because their number was small, four days out of the year, God did not mention them here; he simply speaks of rest.

[9]police et ordre.
[10]Cf. Calvin's third function of the law, *Institutes* 2.7.12.
[11]This compares with the second purpose of the Fourth Commandment. See "The Fifth Sermon," n. 7.
[12]les graces.
[13]Deut. 5:13.
[14]See Calvin's Comm. *Four Books of Moses,* vol. 2, p. 434; *CO* 24.577: "Surely God has no delight in idleness and sloth, ... "
[15]le peché.
[16]prendront.
[17]Adam.

And when he says, "Thou shalt work six days," our Lord shows us that we must not begrudge giving and dedicating one specific day to him, seeing he has given us six for one.[18] It's as if he were saying: "Is it asking too much of you to choose one day which can be fully reserved for my service in order that you might do nothing else in it but read and practice my law, or at least hear the doctrine which can be preached to you, or come to the church in order that you might be confirmed there by the sacrifices which are offered in it, or to call upon my name and confess that you belong to the company of my people? Is it not fitting that you should do that, seeing that you have six entire free days for taking care of your needs and business affairs? Therefore, when I act with such humanity toward you, asking not for seven but only one day, does it not amount to unacceptable ingratitude when you invest[19] that time as if it were badly employed, or behave parsimoniously toward me over the seventh part of time? I give you all your life; the sun never shines on you but that you ought to be able to recognize my goodness and that I am a generous father toward you. For I cause[20] my sun to shine in order to give you light for your path, in order for each of you to pursue your needs. Therefore why shouldn't I have one day out of seven [in which] each person withdraws from his affairs in order that you might not be enveloped by such worldly solicitude so as to be unable to think of me?" Thus we now see that this statement about working six days was not given as a commandment, but it is rather a permission which God gives in order to reproach men for their ingratitude, unless, as he has indicated, they observe the sabbath day and keep it holy.

Now from this we need to glean a good and useful admonition, that when we are slow to obey God, it is helpful[21] to remember his gracious favors. For what could better stimulate our zeal for following what God commands than the thought that he does not treat us harshly nor excessively crowd us? For God could use a stern check if he pleased. He could restrain us by things so difficult that it would be impossible for us to break free of them. But he prefers to guide us as a father does his children. Seeing then that he so upholds us, shouldn't we be that much more motivated

[18]This identical note is sounded in Calvin's Comm. *Four Books of Moses*, vol. 2, p. 438; *CO* 24.579.
[19]pleignez.
[20]fay.
[21]faut.

to do what he commands us? Therefore whenever the commandments of God are difficult for us, or seem to be so, let us
realize that if he pressed us as much as he could, they would be
exceedingly more [difficult]. For if our Lord wanted to exercise
his authority to the fullest, we would be harrassed far more.
Therefore let us understand that he upholds us and utilizes an
infinitely paternal goodness [toward us].

In truth the law of God is impossible for us [to fulfill], let alone
keep with perfection, but when a person relying on his own
strength wants to acquit himself before God, he cannot lift a
finger nor have one single good idea as to how it should be
done.[22] In fact, we are so far from being ready[23] to obey God and
to do what his law contains, that all our thoughts and affections
are at enmity with God. If men were able on their own strength[24]
to fulfill the law, he would have said to them: "Work!" But on the
contrary he said: "Rest in order that God might work." Thus from
our perspective the law may well be impossible to do, but it is
possible for God to engrave it upon our hearts and to govern us
by his Holy Spirit, indeed, so much so that it will seem like a gentle and light burden to us, involving no hardship which we cannot
bear. Thus once men have carefully considered it, they will be
convinced that God upholds them like a father who is merciful
toward his children. Still let us learn not to be ungrateful and to
be exceedingly more motivated to worship our God, [especially] in
view of the fact that he does not command us [to do] things which
might seem too galling to us, or too painful, but he remembers
our frame. That is what we need to note in this passage where our
Lord reveals that he permits men [to enjoy] their comfort.

It is true, as was touched on yesterday, that we ought to be so
spiritual as to gather every day to call upon the name of God and
aim at a celestial life, forgetting all [our] earthly concerns. But
what actually happens? God sees that we are surrounded by our
flesh, that we creep upon the earth, that our weaknesses so dominate[25] us that we are unable to lead an angelic life. Thus God,
seeing such ignorance and debility in us, [and] having mercy because we cannot fully justify ourselves because of our current
condition,[26] releases us and does not at all display his utmost

---

[22]literally: "as to how to begin it."
[23]propres.
[24]vertu.
[25]transportent-entraînent.
[26]" . . . de ce qui seroit de nostre office, . . . " CO 26.298.

rigor. He even says that he will be satisfied if we will dedicate one day to him; especially will he be content if this day helps us throughout the rest of the week. And why? For (as I have said) he has not gone to the extremity, for he knew that we were too weak. Therefore seeing that he upholds us in this way and that he permits us to enjoy our comforts, so much the more are we cowardly, and shameless, and inexcusable, if we are not inspired to surrender ourselves to him.

Now at the same time it is said, *that neither shall [your] manservant, nor chambermaid, nor cattle, nor ass, nor beasts*[27] *work on the sabbath day, nor the stranger who is within your gates.*[28] As for the beasts, we might find it strange that God included them under the commandment to rest,[29] seeing that it is a high and holy[30] mystery as was discussed yesterday. But does it apply to cattle and asses? God says: "I gave you the sabbath day as a sign that I sanctify you, [and] that I am your God who reigns in your midst; that is something which is not common to all mortal men." For God does not extend that grace and privilege to pagans and unbelievers; he does not sanctify them. He speaks only to the people whom he has chosen as a heritage and whom he has adopted. Therefore insofar as the sabbath day is a sign that God has separated the faithful of his church from all the rest of the world, why is that extended to [cover] cattle and asses?

Now let us note that this [action] was not taken for the sake of dumb animals, but in order that men might have a reminder before their eyes in order to be that much more moved. Therefore this sacrament was not addressed to beasts which possess neither intelligence nor reason, but it is addressed to men who must keep it for their [own] benefit. We see that the sacrifices were made of dumb beasts; we know[31] that they engaged in elaborate preparations[32]; that they possessed vessels of gold and silver and similar things. And when all of that was sanctified, are we to suppose that God had put his Spirit into corruptible metals, into materials which had no conscience?[33] No! But all of that existed for men, as

[27]bestial-bêtes.
[28]Deut. 5:14. Calvin introduces this theme as the third purpose for which God gave the Fourth Commandment. "Thirdly, he resolved to give a day of rest to servants and those who are under the authority of others, in order that they should have some respite from toil." *Institutes* 2.8.28; *LCC* 20.395.
[29]l'observation du repos.
[30]celeste.
[31]nous voyons.
[32]appareil-preparatif, pompe.
[33]sentiment-conscience.

all creatures are made for our usage and benefit. [For] God is not the only one who benefits from them in this present and transient[34] life; rather in the course of it, he provides us with the marks of his grace in order that we might possess that many more means and aids for drawing us up to heaven. Thus when God willed for cattle and asses to be rested on the seventh day, it wasn't because he had made them participants in that spiritual rest which we discussed earlier,[35] but it was in order that the Jews, seeing their stables closed, might understand. And what were they to understand? [That] God sets in our midst before our eyes even dumb animals as a sign and visible sacrament. And their purpose is that, for our part, we might be that much more retained for God's service, knowing that we would be violating the entire law if we did not think of that which forms the principal point of all our life, which is, that we learn to denounce ourselves and no longer follow our [own] appetites, or reason, or wisdom. For our God should govern us. And we should become like dead creatures in order that he might live in us and we no longer pursue our own course which is so utterly corrupt. Accordingly, that is how God meant for the Jews to regard dumb brutes: as a visible sign which he had given them to the end that they might be that much more restrained and thereby admonished to keep the sabbath day in complete reverence.

We also see how God has always treated men according to their hardness[36] and has provided[37] them with remedies which were appropriate to them, seeing that they are not very inclined to come to him, before whom they might be so attracted. And that is [true] not only of the Jews, but equally of us. Therefore let us perceive the goodness of our God when we see that he neither forgets nor neglects anything at all that can heal our vices. And at the same time let us also understand the perversity which dominates[38] us in order that we [might] neither flatter nor ease up on the reins of our affections, seeing that we need to be constrained and that God gives us so many coaxing nudges,[39] as to stubborn horses. Therefore seeing that God goads us in this way, let us understand that it is not without cause that he does, but it is due

---

[34]caduque-qui passe.
[35]ci dessus.
[36]durté-dureté.
[37]proveus.
[38]literally: est en.
[39]coupe d'esperon.

to the fact that we are perverse and still rebellious. Therefore let us be displeased with all our affections and learn to become enslaved by nothing which might impede our following the course which God commands us. And furthermore, lest our nature resist this, let us be so captivated [by what God commands] that we may press on without ceasing until we are fully subdued[40] by our God. That is what we must emphasize in this passage beyond what will soon be said next with regard to slaves[41] and servants.

Now concerning the latter,[42] God reminds the Jews *that they had been slaves in the land of Egypt*[43] and that now they must humanely treat those who are under their powers. He says: *Your servant and your maid-servant shall rest.*[44] And for what reason? Because you were once in bondage. Certainly you would have liked for them to have given you some rest and relief; therefore it is imperative that now you show such a humanity toward those who are in your hand.

Now it certainly appears here that God may have ordered the sabbath day as [a form of] civil order,[45] [and] not as a spiritual one, as we earlier discussed,[46] it being done for [the sake of] charity. For he says: "When you were in bondage, didn't you want someone to give you some reprieve? Did you want to be harried all the time? Certainly not! Therefore it is crucial for you to be considerate of others." [Now that would mean that] this command isn't given for the service of God, but rather serves as a common charity which [we] ought to exercise toward our neighbors, no matter to what degree they might be inferior to us. But [on the contrary] insofar as this commandment is contained in the first table of the law, certainly this argument is only accessory.

I say the first table. For it is not without reason that God divided his law in this way, that is that he wrote it on two stones.[47] Had he willed, could he not have simply written it on one stone? Why then did he do it in two parts? It wasn't without reason.

---

[40]rangez-soumis.
[41]serfs.
[42]I have altered Calvin's sentence structure here in order to make a smoother, more readable, transition from the foregoing to the subsequent paragraph. In no way has this affected Calvin's intention or message.
[43]Deut. 5:15.
[44]Deut. 5:14.
[45]police.
[46]a este dit ci dessus.
[47]Calvin discusses the division of the Decalogue into two parts in the *Institutes* 2.8.11.

For there are two principal articles in the law of God: the one concerns what we owe him; the other what we owe our neighbors with whom we live.[48] Everything that concerns our life is grounded here. In the first place, knowing that we have a God to whom we belong, we ought to walk in his obedience. Then [knowing] that we owe[49] our life to him, we ought to do homage to him; [and] insofar as he has created us to a better hope and adopted us as his children, we ought to glorify him for such a goodness. Seeing [then] that he has purchased us through the blood of his Son that we might be totally his and has taken the trouble to retrieve us from the pollutions of the world in order that we might be his true sacrifices, let us call upon his name and put our refuge in him alone. Let us praise him for all his benefits. That is the first point of our life, that is the honor which we must render to our God. And secondly, seeing that he wishes to test[50] our obedience, there is also [the fact] that, when we live with men in complete integrity, we should not abandon ourselves to our own particular interests,[51] but we should undertake to help each other. Indeed, there should be a mutual honesty [between us], not simply for the purpose of abstaining from fraud, violence, and cruelty, but in order that our life might be sober and modest, and that we might not become profligate, shameless, and brutal. That is the second point of our life.

Now insofar as this is the case, that the commandment concerning the sabbath day is contained in the first table, it follows that it belongs to the spiritual service of God and that it is pointedly[52] not a question about the charity which we owe our neighbors. Why then is it mentioned here? It's as much as if our Lord were saying: "This superabundant day of rest will serve you in order that your servants and maid-servants may have respite with you." Not that this was the goal toward which God was tending, [for] it was not his principal aim for there to be one day a week in which people ceased to work in order to catch their breath and be

---

[48]conversans-vivants avec. Cf. *Institutes* 2.8.11: "God has so divided his law into two parts, which contain the whole of righteousness, as to assign the first part to those duties of religion which particularly concern the worship of his majesty; the second, to the duties of love that have to do with men."

[49]tenons.

[50]esprouver-prouver.

[51]profit.

[52]ne . . . point.

spared total exhaustion.[53] This was not the reason why God was motivated to ordain the sabbath day. It was in order that the faithful might understand that it is truly necessary to live in a holy way,[54] that they must rest from all their affections and desires, and that God must entirely work[55] in them. Besides, as the saying goes,[56] there is something here of an unexpected nature.[57] "Listen" (our Lord says), "remember that when you have this testimony in your midst, I am at work sanctifying you, and [when] you are trying to surrender yourself to me, consider that there is still one thing that will benefit you and that exists for your profit: that your family will not have to exhaust itself forever, for it is appropriate that your servants and maid-servants and your beasts enjoy some respite. Therefore you shall have that as [a kind of] superabundance."

Now we see why it is purposely mentioned here that the Jews were slaves in Egypt and that it is incumbent upon them to have respect for those who were held as captives under their hand. For Moses, [when] speaking of servants and chamber-maids, does not mean the same as is meant among us today. For, lo, servants were slaves whom one worked like cattle and asses; there existed such a harsh and inhumane condition that it was pitiful. Thus God shows that the Jewish people, [by] observing the sabbath day, will even gain profit and comfort for their family. "So far from" (he says) "being grieved over the fact that I have reserved one day out of every seven for myself, if you are not too cruel, and if you do not exercise tyranny against those who are in your power, that day" (he says) "is still to your benefit. If you should have no other consideration than this order,[58] that is, that on the sabbath day your servants enjoy rest, the commandment would serve you well.[59] But always be aware[60] that I have not simply ordered the commandment for your family, but in order that you might be advised concerning what I have shown you, that, when you are separated from unbelievers, you might be a royal sacrifice to me,

[53]ahanner-se fatiguer.
[54]sainctement.
[55]besongnast.
[56]qu'on appell.
[57]un bien survenant.
[58]police.
[59]". . . , cela vous y devrait induire: . . . " CO 26.302.
[60]cognoissez.

asking for nothing but to serve me with full integrity and pure conscience. When you hold that view, then you understand that this day can still provide you with some earthly gain; nevertheless, that is not what you ought to seek."[61] In sum, our Lord shows us here what Jesus Christ also proclaimed: that if we seek the kingdom of God, the rest will be added to us.[62] For it appears to us that if we aspire to a heavenly life, we shall die of hunger, that such will deprive us of all our pleasures[63]; in brief, when it comes to serving God, the devil always surfaces to solicit our disgust under the shadow and ruse that if we want to engage ourselves in God's service, we shall surely die of hunger, it will be a pity for us, [and] we shall have to take leave of the whole world.

Now it is true that we cannot serve God, that we may not be able to empty ourselves of our affections, and that we may not reject those earthly cares that press on us from every side, but nevertheless it is still necessary for us to lean[64] on this benediction which we are promised, that is, that when we seek the kingdom of God, we shall be blessed in transient things, that our Lord will have mercy on us and will give us all that he knows we need for this present life; only let us look to him for those things which we cannot acquire by our [own] industry. Thus you see what we are shown in this passage.

Now this counsel[65] must always serve us as a goad to induce us to follow what God commands us. For the primary thing which prevents us from regulating and submitting[66] our life in obedience to God is the conviction that being slaves[67] to ourselves is more to our advantage. Plus we always want to provide[68] for our own comforts, no matter what, and [enjoy] whatever belongs to the world. That is why men cannot follow God, but rather wander farther from him and pull in the opposite direction of his law, because it seems to them that in serving God they will not be able to do so to their advantage.

Now this is such a wretched, ungrateful response that it [only] aggravates their rebellion a hundred times more. What then must

---

[61]This entire argument was later redeveloped by Calvin in his Comm. *Four Books of Moses*, vol. 2, pp. 438–39; *CO* 24.580.
[62]Matt. 6:33.
[63]commoditez.
[64]reposer.
[65]sentence-avis, opinion.
[66]ranger-soumettre.
[67]adonnez à nous mesmes.
[68]provoir-pourvoir.

be done? Let us carefully note that we shall never be able to serve God with a free and easy heart, for we do not have that [kind of] resolve [that believes] that God foresees[69] our entire life and forgets none of it, as he explained to Joshua.[70] For the apostle in the Letter to the Hebrews applies this doctrine to all the faithful, especially to spare them too much anxiety. He says: "Your God will never abandon you; he will never forget you."[71] Now if we could only be persuaded just once that God watches over us and that he forsees[72] all our necessities, certainly we would not be so mired in our earthly concerns, we would not be led astray from serving him, we would not be prevented from meditating on the spiritual life, so much that we would pass through this world and make use of created things as if not to use them at all, because we would know that it is forever necessary to hold to more than this. Therefore, in brief, you see what we have to retain in this doctrine which our Lord points out. [For] although what he has commanded with respect to keeping the sabbath day is spiritual, nevertheless men will not fail to be conscious of their benefit, knowing that God will bless them when they rightly remember him and do not look everywhere for what they know serves their earthly comfort.

Now nevertheless we are admonished that if there are some who rule over others, they must not scorn their neighbors no matter how[73] inferior they may be to them. And this [provision] extends even further. For we must not only take into account[74] servants and chambermaids, but [also] the poor, and all who are not in authority or esteemed, all subjects who are not deemed worthy in the eyes of the world to be compared to us. For we know[75] how proud men are, for although we may have no occasion to be swelled, we are each covetous for some preeminence. Seeing then that such arrogance indwells us, that we each want to be elevated over our neighbors—in spite of any basis for it—what happens[76] when we are elevated? Look at those who are in the seat of justice. It almost appears to them that the world might be

---

[69]provoyera-préverra. Keep in mind Zébédée's attacks, aggravated by the actions of the Bernese magistrates.

[70]See Josh. 1:5.

[71]See Heb. 13:5.

[72]provoyera-préverra.

[73]combien que.

[74]exposer-expliquer.

[75]voyons.

[76]sera-ce.

their creation, except for the fact that God restrains them by his Holy Spirit and shows them that they must walk in all forbearance and must not oppress those who are under their charge. Rather they must fulfill a fatherly function[77] on their behalf, regarding their neighbors as their children, and still further, seeing that God honors them, they must walk in the greatest humility. [As for] those who proclaim the Word of God and have charge of leading others, how unfortunate they are[78] if they think that they ought to be exempt from the common ranks and [may] despise others. For it would be better if they broke their necks while mounting the pulpit than to be unwilling to be the first to walk after God and to live peaceably with their neighbors, demonstrating that they are the sheep of our Lord Jesus Christ's flock.

Now nonetheless it is true that the rich can certainly help the poor. When a man has servants and chambermaids working for him, he does not set his servant above himself at table, nor does he permit him to sleep in his bed. But in spite of any [right of] superiority which might exist, it is essential that we always arrive at this point: that we are united together in one flesh as we are all made in the image of God.[79] If we believe[80] that those who are descended of Adam's race are our flesh and our bone, ought that not make us subject[81] to humanity, though we behave like savage beasts toward each other? When the prophet Isaiah wants to persuade men of their inhumanity, he says: "You shall not despise your flesh."[82] That is how I must behold myself in a mirror, in light of how many human beings there are in the world. That is one point.

But there is still more: that is that the image of God is engraved in all men. Therefore not only do I despise my [own] flesh whenever I oppress anyone, but to my fullest capacity I violate the image of God. Therefore let us carefully note that God willed in this passage to point out to those who are in authority and who receive esteem, who are richer than others and who enjoy some degree of honor, that they must not abuse those who are under

---

[77]office de pere.
[78]A possible reference to Zébédée, Lange, Bolsec, and others.
[79]This is a central principle here and in the subsequent paragraph and one to which Calvin will return later when discussing the Sixth Commandment. See "The Eighth Sermon," n. 14.
[80]pensons.
[81]ranger-soumettre.
[82]Isa. 58:7.

their hand; they must not torment them beyond measure. They must always reflect[83] on the fact that we are all descended from Adam's race, that we possess a common nature, and that even the image of God is engraved on us.[84] That is what we have to note. Moreover, our Lord Jesus Christ has descended to earth[85] for the purpose of being entirely destroyed in order to condemn all pride and to show that there is no other means of serving God except in humility. That being the case, he has made us all members of his body, including slaves and those who are masters and superiors, without any distinction.

When we come to our Lord Jesus Christ and behold him, it is essential that we follow [his example]. Seeing that both the great and the small are members of his body and that he is our master,[86] that is reason enough for each [of us] to be conformed to his neighbors. And in addition, seeing that God has declared himself our father in more familiar terms than he did to those who lived under the law, may that inspire us to maintain fraternity among us. That again is what we have to glean from this text.

Now there is still one point with regard to what God institutes [as] a reminder[87] to the Jews: *that they were like poor slaves in the land of Egypt.*[88] Now we know that they were badly treated there with cruelty. But insofar as they sighed and groaned to God, and were heard, and behold wanted someone to help them, God declares that indeed they must also do the same. Now this contains a good lesson,[89] which is that when we think of ourselves, we will always be caught up in the need to perform our duty. And on the contrary, when we are cruel toward our neighbors, it's as much as if we are intoxicated with our comforts and do not think about our poverty and miseries. Whoever has been hungry and thirsty, [and] especially wanted someone to relieve his need, and sees a poor man, and thinks: "Now I have been in that condition and certainly wanted to be helped; indeed it seemed to me that people ought to have pitied me in order to help me." Whoever (I say) entertains thoughts like that upon seeing a poor man in need, must he not have a soft heart? But what [is the usual case]? When we are com-

---

[83]penser.
[84]See n. 79 above.
[85]ici bas.
[86]chef.
[87]memorial.
[88]Deut. 5:15.
[89]doctrine.

fortable, it is not a matter of our remembering our human poverty, rather we imagine that we are exempt from that and that we
are no longer part of the common class. And that is the reason
why we forget, and no longer have any compassion for our
neighbors, or for all that they endure. Therefore, seeing that we
are blindly in love with ourselves, and are content to be plunged
in our [own] delights, and hardly think of those who are suffering
and in want, so much the more do we need to hear[90] this passage
that our Lord may point out: "And who are you? Have you not
been in need yourself?"[91] And even if you should happen to get
angry[92] with them, does it ever occur to you that they are creatures made in the image of God? And if we insult them, why
should God have mercy on us?

Therefore let us practice this doctrine all our life. And as often
as we see people racked with misery, may this [thought] come to
mind: "Lo, have I not been in need as well as they?" And if right
now we were to be in such a state, would we not want to be
helped? Therefore insofar as this is true, is it right[93] for us to be
exempt from such a condition? The least we can do is to do unto
others as we would have them do unto us.[94] Our [own] nature
teaches us that. We don't have to go to school to learn that. Thus
we need no other trial to condemn us than what our Lord already
teaches us by experience. When we are guided by that thought,[95]
certainly we will be touched by humanity to aid those who are
indigent and in need. We will be moved to compassion, seeing
them suffer, so much so that if we have the means and capacity to
help and assist them, we will use it. Therefore you see what we
have to note in this passage when it is said that you were strangers
in the land of Egypt, therefore it is now proper for you to consider how to alleviate those who are in your hand, for when you
were a slave,[96] you certainly wanted someone to help you.

Now we come to those who were not [members] of the Jewish
people, but solely did business among them. Indeed, God also wills
for them to keep the sabbath day, even if God has not sanctified
them and even though this sign could not belong to them, as we

[90]bien noter.
[91]quelque fois.
[92]desborder.
[93]faut-il.
[94]Matt. 7:12.
[95]"Quand nous aurons cela, . . . " CO 26.306.
[96]serviteur.

have already said. Thus it seems that God profanes the sacrament when he makes it apply to unbelievers and to those who were not circumcised as a sign of the covenant, to those who possessed neither the law nor the promises. But we have to observe that what God says here about strangers always applies to the people whom he chose and adopted. For we know that if we permit conditions[97] [to exist] which are contrary to the service of God, even though some might say: "These people are not [members] of our group"; we may [still] be misled by their bad examples. [For] if one had permitted foreigners to work among the Jewish people, what would it have led to? The Jews would have traded with them and would have been profaned; there would have been no discretion on that day. For when opportunity[98] presents itself, we are easily led toward evil. And though it may not be a great occasion, our nature is so inclined toward evil that we are immediately led astray. Therefore what [good] does it serve if everyone is corrupted? Thus if one had given foreigners the liberty to work in the midst of the Jewish people, they might have been induced to corruption; each would have exempted himself and given himself the license to violate the sabbath day and not keep it. Therefore, in the same way that God willed for animals to rest, he ordered the same for foreigners in order that such an evil occasion might be avoided and this day be kept with the greatest reverence.

Now this [commandment] must serve us today.[99] For its purpose is to show us that vices must not be permitted in a people who make a Christian confession, so much so that they have to be punished even among those who are only passing through.[100] Why is that? When blasphemies are condemned among ourselves, if we were to hear a passer-by blaspheme, or make fun of God, and such should be endured and kept secret, would it not be a kind of profanation that would infect everything else if such blasphemies were upheld, or considered in vogue, and nothing were done to repress them? Yet it exists. [For] the truth is that blas-

---

[97]des choses.
[98]obiets-obstacles.
[99]maintenant.
[100]Possibly a reference to Michael Servetus who was "only passing through" Geneva when detected and arrested. The immediate context seems to suggest this. See Roland Bainton, *Hunted Heretic, The Life and Death of Michael Servetus, 1511–1553* (Boston: The Beacon Press, 1953), pp. 209–10. Bainton cites Calvin's letter in *CO* 8.460. Concerning the latter's attitude of Servetus's trial and fate, Bainton comments: "Nowhere does Calvin more clearly disclose himself as one of the last great figures of the Middle Ages," pp. 209f.

phemies are far from being punished as they should be in those who are not of our religion, in those who mix with us and make the Christian confession; [indeed] we see how they are tolerated much to our own confusion.

But in any event, if we permit papists and others just anything (for today the world is crammed full of despisers of God), if we permit them (I say) to slander the doctrine of the Gospel and to blaspheme the Name of God, it creates a corruption that lives on in such a way that it becomes increasingly difficult to cure. If we allow the debauched[101] and ruffians to influence us with their corrupt ways and bring into our midst more evil than we have, if we permit the profligate and corrupt to come here to practice their lewdness, will we not of necessity become debauched and totally corrupt with them?[102]

Therefore let us carefully note that our Lord wills to train his people in complete purity to the extent that those who profess to be Christian may not only abstain from evil, but insofar as possible, may equally refuse to tolerate it at all. For we must understand that the earth is profaned when the worship of God is contaminated here and his holy name is dishonored. The ground on which he wants us to live is polluted and cursed and nothing will make him come to us. In any event, when God gave this privilege to his children in order that they might remove[103] idolatry from the country in which they [were to] live, it is certain that if they failed they would provoke his anger and vengeance against themselves. [In the same way] today if we were to ask for the abominations of the papacy to be combined here with the pure worship of God and out of privilege were to grant a mass to the obstinate papists who would like to live here, thus providing them some corner in which they could perform their idolatries and superstitions, it would be like inviting God's anger against us and lighting the very fire of his vengeance. And why? Because since God has given those who hold the sword of justice in hand, who control the government in this life, the power to root out idolatries and these papal infections, then certainly if they were to maintain them, it would be like running God out in order to end his presence and reign in their midst.

---

[101]paillards-débauchés. "Paillards" may also mean "fornicators."
[102]A reference to the second use of the law.
[103]oster-ôter.

Therefore let us carefully note that it is not without cause that our Lord willed for the foreigners who were living in the midst of the people—though they were of a different faith and religion—to be forced to keep the seventh day. He willed it not on their behalf, nor for their instruction—for they were incapable of that—but in order to curtail any scandal that might corrupt the people and violate the worship of God that the land which he had given his servant Abraham as a heritage might be totally dedicated to him.

Now hereby we are not only admonished to be sanctified by the Word of God, but not to tolerate in our midst any commission of scandals and corruptions. For all of that must be put away from us. Besides, when our Lord wills for us to have such a zeal for maintaining his service that even those who have not professed to belong to his church are constrained to affiliate with and conform themselves to us when they are talking in our company, I beg of you, what excuse will we have if on our part we are not totally yielded to him and are not like mirrors for drawing and winning poor unbelievers to our God? For if we hope[104] to recover them when they have fallen and nevertheless they perceive in us similar and even worse vices, will they not be justified[105] in mocking all our remonstrances? Therefore seeing that foreigners have been prohibited from doing anything that is contrary to the worship of God, let us understand that we have been doubly commanded to walk in all solicitude and in such humility and sobriety that foreigners may be convinced that it is in good conscience and without hypocrisy[106] that we want God to be honored and that we cannot allow anyone to bring opprobrium to his majesty and glory.

Consequently that is what we have to emphasize in this text if today we want to keep what was commanded to the Jews, as by right in truth and substance it belongs to us. Thus in the same way that our Lord of old delivered his people from Egypt, so today he has delivered us from the pit of hell, and reclaimed us from eternal death, and the abyss of flames into which we have plunged in order to gather us into his heavenly kingdom, for he

---

[104]voulons.
[105]". . . n'airont-ils point occasion de. . . . " *CO* 26.308.
[106]feintise-hypocrisie.

has purchased us through the blood of his beloved Son, our Lord Jesus Christ.[107]

[107]Golding's translation concludes this sermon with the following admonition: "Nowe let us kneele down in the presence of our good God, with acknowledgment of our sinnes, praying him to make us feele them better than wee have done, to the ende that wee indevouring to refourme our selves more and more according to his righteousnesse, may fight daily against the lustes of our flesh, and shunne al that is against the pure service of our God, holding out in the same incounter till he have fully ridde us of it, and fashioned us againe after his owne image, according whereunto we were created at the first. That it may please him to graunt this grace, not onely to us but also to all people and nations of the earth, etc." *Sermons Upon the Fifth Book of Moses,* trans. Golding, p. 212. Cf. Calvin, *Sermons sur les dix commandemens,* 1557 ed., p. 91.

Sermon Seven[2]

Deuteronomy 5:16[3]

We have come to the second table of the law in which God shows us how we have to live[4] here together in harmony.[5] For as it has been discussed earlier, there are two principal things in our life: that we should worship God in purity, and secondly that we should deal[6] with men in complete integrity and honesty, rendering to each what is properly his.[7] Now inasmuch as the honor of God is more excellent than all that concerns men, it was appropriate that in the first and highest stage the rule was given for

---

[1]N. in *CO:* "This sermon corresponds to the seventh in the 1562 collection, pp. 140–61." *CO* 26.309.

[2]The original title: "The Sixth Sermon on Chapter 5:16." *CO* 26.309.

[3]Cf. also Calvin's discussion of the Sixth Commandment in the *Institutes* 2.8.35–38; Comm. *Four Books of Moses,* vol. 3, pp. 5–12, *CO* 24.601–6; *Catechism, CO* 6.68, 70. In addition, see Calvin's chapter on "Civil Government," *Institutes* 4.20.

[4]converser-habiter.

[5]The text simply reads: tous ensemble.

[6]communiquions.

[7]See "The Sixth Sermon," nn. 47 and 48. Calvin's chapter on "Christian Freedom" is also relevant to this sermon (*Institutes* 3.19). Writes Calvin: " . . . there is a

God to be honored as [indeed] we ought. That was dispensed with in the first table. Now God begins to explain[8] for us here how our life ought to be governed if we wish to serve him with respect to men.

Now we have already[9] explained[10] that God does not require any honor from us for any need he may have, or would such benefit him, [rather] it is for our good that he does it. Thus in this way he wills to test our obedience and the love which we bring him when he commands us to walk with our neighbors in all honesty and equity, and [commands] that we should live together in such communion and concord that we not live solely for ourselves, but work[11] together, and, according as each has the means and power to work effectively, compel and employ ourselves [to that end].[12] That is one test (I say) that God has taken in order to know whether we worship him with our heart. For we could put on a good show[13] and [participate in] ceremonies, but God would not be content with that. For this same reason our Lord Jesus Christ[14] says that the principal meaning of the law is justice, judgment, integrity, and faith; for such is the meaning of the word *faith*. Therefore when we live[15] among men without pretense,[16] when we are not given over to craftiness or malice, [and show] that we want to be of service to everyone and to uphold the good, then that is the essence of the law. However [the essence is] not that the worship of God might be forgotten because it is of less importance, but because it is impossible for men to act as they should toward their neighbors unless they are led by the fear of God.

Now let us discuss this commandment which was [just] read: that of *honoring* [our] *father and mother*.[17] Now although particular mention is made here of the father and the mother, there can be

twofold government in man: one aspect is spiritual, whereby the conscience is instructed in piety and in reverencing God; the second is political, whereby man is educated for the duties of humanity and citizenship that must be maintained among men": 3.19.15; *LCC* 20.847.

[8]declairer-expliquer.
[9]aussi.
[10]declairé-expliqué.
[11]communiquions.
[12]Cf. *Institutes* 2.8.11.
[13]faire beaucoup de belles mines.
[14]See Matt. 23:23.
[15]conversons-vivre.
[16]feintise-hypocrisie.
[17]Deut. 5:16.

no doubt about God's wanting to provide a general doctrine with respect to honoring all [forms of] authority.[18] That such is the case, we know that the law is a perfect norm in which there are no faults. Now if the law said nothing about other authorities, such as princes and magistrates and those who wield the sword of justice, if it said nothing about masters, it would contain errors. Thus we are forced to conclude in this text that God has commanded that all [persons] who enjoy any superior status are to be honored and obeyed. The advantage then is that all preeminence comes from God and forms an order which he has established, without which even the world cannot subsist.[19] For what would it be like if God had not taken this into consideration when he gave us a definite, holy form for upright[20] living? Nor must we find it strange that all of this is contained under one heading. For we have already discussed the fact that such can be observed in the law, whose advantage we shall yet see. Nor was it due to the fact that God could not speak more fully,[21] rather the better it serves to our benefit and instruction. For in spite of the fact that men crave to be seen as sharp and subtle, we know that they do not neglect to cover themselves with a shield of ignorance; [for] when we see that the law of God is about to crowd us, then we want an excuse to exempt ourselves from being under its subjection.

Now if the law of God was not suitable for teaching the most ignorant and stupid, many could cite that they are not scholars and have not been to school; thus it would appear that the law of God was not binding on them. But when we see that God has humbled himself to our ignorance and has spoken in the rough language[22] of our capacity, that removed every excuse from us and every pretext,[23] [so much so] that it is imperative for each [of us] to constrain[24] ourself and confess that nothing [shall] hinder

[18]superiorité. The *Catechism* summarizes best the central thesis that Calvin will develop in this sermon: "C: Though the words refer to father and mother only, we must understand all who are over us, since they have the same ground. M: What is the ground? C: This, that the Lord has raised them to a degree superior in honour. For there is no authority, either of parents, or princes, or governors of any kind, no empire and no honour, except by God's decree; for so it pleased him to order the world." *Catechism, LCC* 22.114; *CO* 6.68.

[19]See the *Institutes* 4.20.2 on the civil government as an integral order contributing to the world's peace and tranquility.

[20]bien.

[21]autre langage.

[22]grossierement.

[23]couppe la broche-ôte tout prétexte.

[24]se range-se contraint.

us [from doing God's will]: unless, of course, we are rebellious against God and do not want to bear his yoke.

That is why God included everything under one heading, in order to lead us like little children who are not capable of being taught in true perfection. In any event this is the true and natural sense[25] of the passage, as we shall soon see. For in this way God gave all the ten laws[26] which he lists; he also added exposition so that nothing would be obscure and we would not have to question or dispute what had been heard. Thus we see that God fully explained and pointed out that he not only wished for us to obey fathers and mothers, but all [our] superiors without exception.

In addition let us note that God spoke here about *honoring the father and mother* because he wanted to draw us [to himself] by the most suitable and proper means [according] to our nature. We know that men are so proud that they will not willingly bend their neck for anyone, [as] each thinks [himself] capable of being master. But the fact remains that it is difficult for men to humble themselves and to descend to the point that God might easily subdue[27] them, [that is] simply to obey those who have any authority over them. Therefore, God, seeing that subjection is such a contrary thing to our nature, set before us here [the figures of] father and mother, in order to attract us in a most amiable way.

Now it is quite a detestable thing, as well as contrary to nature, for a child not to acknowledge those through whom he came into the world, those who have fed and clothed him. Therefore when a child disowns[28] his father and his mother, he is a monster. Everyone will look upon him with disgust. And why? [Because] without God speaking a word, without our having any holy Scripture, or anyone preaching to us, nature already shows us that a child's duty toward his father and mother is one which cannot be broken.[29]

Thus we see our God's intention, for in putting before us [the figures of] father and mother, he willed to win us to himself in order that we might not be so cantankerous and might peaceably come to receive the yoke[30] he lays on us. And insofar as all authority which men possess comes from him, he speaks according

[25]See "Introduction," n. 72.
[26]parolles.
[27]rangez-soumis.
[28]mescognoist-mesconnaît.
[29]Cf. *Institutes* 2.8.35.
[30]subiection.

to the legitimate civil order:[31] [which means] that if we are careful to render him the homage which he is due, if each in his own place obeys those who are in authority over him, [if] each takes into account his own estate and condition, if children honor their fathers and mothers, if everyone honors those who sit in the seat of justice, and servants do the same toward their masters, in brief, there will be a beautiful harmony among us for our peace, according to the order[32] which our Lord has established, which is to be held inviolable by us.[33]

Moreover, when honor is spoken of here, it doesn't simply mean that children ought to make a display of affection[34] for their father[s] and mother[s], to tip their hat and make a bow,[35] for God does not care to be entertained in such a way. Honor means much more. It means for children to follow the advice of their fathers and mothers, for them to let themselves be guided by them, to take the trouble to fulfill their duty[36] to them: in brief, a child ought to understand that he is not at liberty with respect to his father and mother. In summation, that's what God meant by this word "Honor."[37] This being the case, we cannot have a better or more faithful expositor of the law than the Holy Spirit who spoke by the mouth of Moses, by all the prophets, and especially by Saint Paul. For we shall see hereafter that God made known the summary of this view, that is, that it is insufficient for children to nod their head toward or simply bow in front of their father[s] and mother[s], rather they must be subject to them and serve them to their fullest capacity. And [certainly] Paul[38] does not cite this point in order to exhort us to undertake some [kind of] formality; rather he says that children ought to be subject to their fathers and mothers. And he especially uses this word "subjection." Thus we see what is involved, as well as the natural sense of this passage.

Now let us return to what we have briefly discussed in order to benefit from it and reap [some] doctrine that might be useful to us. In the first place, seeing that God has given children their

---

[31]police.
[32]ordre.
[33]Cf. Calvin's summary of this same thesis in the *Institutes* 2.8.11, 35.
[34]caresse-démonstration d'affection.
[35]"..., qu'ils leur ostent le bonnet, et leur plient le genouil: ... " *CO* 26.311.
[36]devoir.
[37]In a similar manner, Calvin discusses the meaning of "honor" in his Comm. *Four Books of Moses*, vol. 3, pp. 6–7; *CO* 24.602–3.
[38]See Eph. 6:1; Col. 3:20.

fathers and mothers, let them understand that such is reason enough for them to obey them, or otherwise they reveal that they are contemptuous of God. And this rebellion which they flaunt[39] toward their superiors is not directed against men or animals, but is as much as if the majesty and glory of God were being trampled underfoot. Properly speaking, it is said that we only have one Father in heaven. And that is not only meant with regard to souls, but also with regard to bodies. Therefore this honor of being called Father properly belongs to God alone and can only apply to men when it pleases him to confer it on them. Seeing then that this title of Father is like a mark which God has engraved on men, we see that if children do not take their father and mother into consideration, they insult God. The same is true of those who disobey their princes and magistrates. And of servants who would like to confuse all orders and lord it about without them. And that is also why the pagans[40] associated the word *piety* with the honor we render father[s] and mother[s] and all who are in authority over us. *Piety,* properly speaking, is that reverence we owe God; but the pagans, although they were terribly blind, understood that God not only wants to be worshiped in his majesty, but when we are obedient to those who rule over us, in brief, he tests our obedience by this means.[41] Therefore, insofar as fathers and mothers, magistrates and all who exercise authority, are lieutenants of God and represent him, certainly if we despise and reject them, it's as much as if we should declare that we don't want to obey God.[42] Of course, one can argue the opposite; nevertheless it is true. If poor unbelievers understood that, and God permitted[43] such an attitude[44] among them, what excuse can we offer if we do not grasp it still better? When we hear that all parenthood comes from God, as Saint Paul[45] states it, and that we are restored to it through union with Jesus Christ, isn't that a far more express declaration [than theirs]? Must the pagans still be our teachers? But when those who call themselves Christians make [themselves]

[39]font.
[40]Calvin does not designate the specific classical author(s) he may have had in mind. However, in a related passage in the *Institutes* (4.20.9), the editor of the *LCC* (21.1495. n. 23) edition cites *Cicero* as a source.
[41]Cf. *Institutes* 4.20.23. "... the magistrate cannot be resisted without God being resisted at the same time,... "
[42]Ibid. Cf. *Institutes* 4.20.4–6.
[43]laissé.
[44]affection.
[45]See Eph. 3:15.

blind on this point, or cut off their ears in order not to understand what God has explained through the pagan mind,[46] how unfortunate they are and how much more horrible [their] condemnation! Therefore, in summary, let us carefully note that we cannot live together here unless this order which God has established is holily kept, that is,· unless we esteem and honor and obey all those who possess authority.[47] Without that, there would be one horrible confusion.

Therefore those who cannot submit themselves to the magistrates, who rebel against their fathers and mothers, who cannot bear the yoke of masters or mistresses, sufficiently show that they cannot join up[48] with anyone who doesn't reverse the complete order of nature and jumble heaven and earth, as people say. For that is the sole means by which God has willed to preserve the human race. In fact we see that he says that when he sends magistrates and princes, he not only causes men to fear them but even animals. That is how he puts it in Daniel.[49] And from that fact we are able to learn that those who oppose the civil order[50] which God has instituted, who strive to trouble everyone and reduce everything to confusion, are worse than brute beasts and deserve to be sent to their school. For our Lord, in order to shame men who are rational creatures, says that the fear of princes and magistrates ought to be extended to include dumb animals.[51] Therefore, as we have already explained, [can] we not see that the devil possesses everyone who cannot submit[52] in all modesty to the subjection which God has established and without which everything would perish and result in confusion in this world?

Nevertheless, if we are aware of any haughtiness in ourselves, and if it makes us ill to be subjects, let us fight against such pride and let the authority of God suffice to check us. For no matter how wild we might be, this [commandment] ought still enchain us (in a manner of speaking), hearing that God explains that he is not honored by us unless we render him homage through those whom he has established in his place and in whom he has engraved his image.

[46]les povres ignorans.
[47]superiorité.
[48]ne tient point.
[49]See Dan. 2:38; I Peter 2:13–14.
[50]police.
[51]"brute beasts."
[52]rangers-soumettre.

In brief, we see that charity begins by this end: that we should be humble and modest, and that no one should elevate himself in arrogance and presumption, and overrate himself, rather we should be ready to humble ourselves in order to submit to whatever pleases God. And that is also why Saint Paul[53] directs us toward charity when he expounds this commandment concerning the obedience of magistrates. For he shows that if we do not possess this gentleness in ourselves, to bend our neck when our Lord lays a yoke upon it, then we have no charity for our neighbors. If we crave for confusion and disorder,[54] and if superiors no longer receive respect, then everything may as well be up for plunder. It would be much better if each one [of us] lived apart and without company than to see the confusion that would arise if we were not to keep the civil order[55] which God has instituted.

Therefore, let us hold on to the fact that in order to live with our neighbors, we each have to correct this [tendency toward] arrogance and presumption and not retain it in our hearts, but we must learn to be humble and modest; we must realize[56] that it is [even] our responsibility to be subject[57] to the least, as Saint Paul[58] explains it. And in order to do that we must take account of our own worth. For that is what we abuse, for we would each like to enjoy a greater preeminence than God gives us. For we become blind in order not to see things in ourselves. And beyond that, we do not understand our [own] poverty and vices. Thus we each attempt[59] to be marvelous, or we are nothing. And then we are so inclined not to take account of our neighbors that we even despise all the virtues that God has put in them. And as a result so much malice and ingratitude ensue that we are incited toward pride, so much so that we each attribute to ourself more than is ours. And that is why we cannot submit ourselves as we should.

But instead of that, let us learn to do homage to God when we see that he has commanded us to be obedient to our supervisors; and then, let us understand that such as they are, they represent his will.[60] When a child has his father and mother, it is highly

---

[53]See Rom. 13:7.
[54]meslinge-mélange.
[55]police.
[56]sachions.
[57]ranger-soumettre.
[58]See Rom. 13:7.
[59]cuidera-essayera.
[60]"..., il vous les donne." CO 26.314.

inappropriate for him to say: "O there is my father. He is not at
all what he should be. I find fault with him." For he is still your
father. [And] it is imperative for the word to satisfy you, unless
you want to annihilate everything; unless you want to abolish the
order of nature. Either the order which God has instituted has no
value or effect, or you must honor your father such as he is. And
why [is that]? [Because] the one who has commanded you to
honor your father and mother has given you such a father as you
have. The same holds true for masters, princes, and superiors, for
as Saint Paul[61] and all the Scripture repeatedly demonstrates,[62]
they are not the products of chance; it is God who sends them.[63]
Above all we are also led to understand the providence of God
through experience, as well as the paternal care in which he holds
us when he institutes magistrates. Therefore let us learn to behold
the goodness of God in all who have authority over us in order to
submit ourselves to their obedience. That is what we want to
retain.

Now insofar as God has given us in one phrase and in one brief
summary the rule to obey all [our] superiors, let us mark that in so
doing he does not resign his right; he does not relinquish anything that is properly his. Therefore it is essential that God always
retain the sovereign position. And in fact, inasmuch as all parent-
age comes from him (as we have already cited in the passage in
Paul), let us note that when we obey father[s] and mother[s],
princes and magistrates, it's as if we were obeying officers of
God.[64] Therefore it is fitting that God should be honored over
and above all, indeed, to such an extent that the honor we render
to mortal men should not impede the service we must render to
God nor the homage we owe him, for we each ought to strive to
justify ourselves primarily before him. Indeed it would be something for a man to obey an officer and then spit in the face of the
judge or the prince. Where would that lead? The same is true
when we want to denude God of his preeminence and yet want to

[61]See Rom. 13:1; I Tim. 2:2; also I Peter 2:14.
[62]en est pleine.
[63]Cf. *Institutes* 4.20.4: " . . . it has not come about by human perversity that the
authority over all things on earth is in the hands of Kings and other rulers, but by
divine providence and holy ordinance."
[64]See the *Institutes* 4.20.23; *LCC* 21.1509–10, "The first duty of subjects toward
their magistrates is to think most honorably of their office, which they recognize as
a jurisdiction bestowed by God, and on that account to esteem and reverence them
as ministers and representatives of God."

obey men, for in the process we are not taking account of him who is above all. For that is contrary to nature, as the authority that belongs to men should in no way obscure God's glory. Therefore let us carefully mark that when we are commanded to be obedient to our superiors, the exception remains that nonetheless this [commandment] must not detract from any of those prerogatives which belong to God, which have already been treated in the first table. For we know that the service by [means of] which God is worshiped must precede everything else. And that is also why Saint Paul,[65] desirous to give us an exposition of this test, notably adds that it is "in the Lord" that children must obey their fathers and mothers. Besides we have said that this is the foundation upon which we must build[66] in order to be obedient, humble, and subject to our superiors, which is, to understand that God is represented in them. Now once we have removed the foundation, isn't it obvious that the entire edifice will slip[67] and come crashing down? Now in the same way, those who have no consideration for God remove the foundation of this doctrine; consequently, the procedure is too tricky and perverse.

Now this ought to warn those who are in authority, as much as it does their subjects. Thus if men and women have any children, they must understand that they should not unduly subject them, insofar as God rules over all. What must be done then? Let a father carefully instruct his children in the fear of the Lord and begin to show the way. Let the mother do the same. Let God receive his homage above the great and the small, the old and the young. Let magistrates labor to the end that God may be served and honored.[68] Let them maintain that goal in all that they do and with all their strength. Let them demonstrate that they are truly his officers seeing that he pays them the honor of being worthy to sit on the seat which is dedicated to his majesty [and] to carry the sword which is sacred to him. And insofar as he has elevated them to such dignity, of which they were unworthy, let them at least demonstrate that it is in his name that they have authority and that they are accountable to him. That is how princes must account for their duty.

Each must do the same in his home and in his family. Let those

---

[65] See Eph. 6:1.
[66] bastir-bâtir.
[67] trebusche-trébuche.
[68] Cf. *Institutes* 4.20.6.

on whom God has bestowed the fortune of having servants and chambermaids clearly remember[69] that there is a master over [us] all, and that he truly must be obeyed, and that his right must be preserved in its entirety. That is the instruction (I say), that must apply to all superiors, whatever their station, for they too are commanded to obey God. In addition, when fathers and mothers and magistrates want to elevate themselves against God, and elevate themselves in such tyranny that they usurp what properly belongs to God alone, and when they want to divert us from his obedience, that constitutes an exception which must not be obeyed.[70] Thus it is necessary for God to lead the procession and, afterwards, as the phrase goes, for creatures to follow in descending[71] order. And, in fact, that is the reason why modesty and humility are so often ill kept in the world, why children rise up against fathers and mothers and behave like wild beasts, why people are full of malice and rebellion, why servants are also full of disloyalty, and why you can never come[72] to the end of that sort of thing. It is a fitting punishment of God on all who have abused the dignity which he has given them. For we often see that princes do not rule in order to magnify the name of God or strive that he might be honored as he deserves, but on the contrary they prefer to set up idols and almost wrest God out of his throne in order to replace[73] him with themselves.[74]

We see [plenty of] that. Or at least we see princes ruling without restraint.[75] Thus it is right for God to avenge himself. For what zeal and affection do fathers and mothers have for instructing their children in the fear of God? It's all the same to them, provided they advance according to the world. It even seems that they want to rear them in complete impiety and in disrespect for God and his Word. Where fathers have been [like] wolves, they want to have wolfish [children]; where they have been old foxes, they want to have little sly devils; where they have been serpents, they want to have posterity after their kind. We know that. Therefore God is amply justified in avenging himself when creatures

[69]regardent bien.
[70]Cf. *Institutes* 8.20.32; *LCC* 21.1520: "If they command anything against him, let it go unesteemed."
[71]en ordre subalterne.
[72]chevir-venir à bout de.
[73]colloquer-placer.
[74]On "unjust magistrates" see the *Institutes* 4.20.24.
[75]à bride avalee-sans frein.

consequently forget who they are, and above all when men do not acknowledge that God has taken their hand in order to lift them up and bestow upon them a portion of his honor, albeit it is a lesser degree. We must always hold fast to that.

Nevertheless, isn't it the height of ingratitude[76] when a man in a position of authority and justice does not understand: "Who am I? I am [only] a poor earthworm and [yet] God wants me to carry his name for his sake, to exercise it with respect to the authority which he has given me." When a man doesn't understand that, isn't that the height of ingratitude? In the next place, when fathers fail to consider: "Behold, God is the unique father of the whole human race and yet he has attributed that highly honorable title to me. Isn't that a sufficient reason for me to be advised to render an account to him?" When masters and mistresses do not perceive: "We are no better than others and [yet] God has willed to honor us, not only by creating us in his image, but in addition by giving us a position which is above those who are subject to us." (I say) when people cannot grasp all of that, isn't it fitting to say that they have become entirely stupid?

Let us clearly note then that rebellions often proceed from such [thinking] as that, that those who are in authority have not understood their office which is that first of all they must procure homage for God and that people serve him and become subject to him.[77] Certainly children, the people, and servants will not be excused if the magistrates fail. We can see that God's vengeance is still just. But even more, we need to be motivated to follow what we have been shown, whether in this passage or throughout the holy Scripture, concerning what this commandment enjoins. Therefore, in brief, we are clearly warned that each shall have to account for himself in his own vocation and life.[78] And those on whom God has bestowed the honor of bearing the sword of justice and sitting in his seat, let them be carefully advised to rule in the name of God and see that he is worshiped and honored by all. And let them be like mirrors in order to set a good example. Let them hold their subjects in reasonable[79] check and in such order

---

[76] une ingratitude villaine.

[77] One of Calvin's central tenets is that the civil government and its magistrates are responsible for protecting the "outward worship of God." See the *Institutes* 4.20.2–3.

[78] estat.

[79] bonne.

that the Name of God is blessed and the mouth of every slanderer closed.[80] That is one point. [Further] let fathers and mothers take care to instruct their children well; let them teach them to recognize God as their only father. And with regard to their servants and chambermaids, let them teach them to serve in such a way that God is always the principal [end of their service]. May they not keep performing in the customary way. For it is all the same to men, provided their benefit and contentment are enhanced, though God is forgotten. Rather, may masters realize that it is essential for God to rule over them as well as over those who are their subjects. That is what is involved here with respect to those in authority.

Now for our part, let us be carefully warned that when we are rebellious against magistrates, and when we dare to elevate ourselves in opposition to the civil order, and when we attempt to ruin the order which God has established, we do not commit an outrage against creatures [alone], but it is God whom we assail. And what can we gain by making war against him? Are we able to emerge the stronger? No! Rather he will avenge himself with the greatest of ease,[81] and people will be completely stupified that he actually maintains what he has ordained by his mouth, indeed, with an admirable strength. So much then for this first point.

Next, let children be warned not to be presumptuous or fickle, or given to their desires,[82] but let them peaceably submit[83] to their fathers and mothers, knowing that they are fighting against God when they cannot submit to the yoke that our Lord places on them. Let servants and chambermaids realize that when they refuse to be subject to those whom they serve that God is offended by their action and that of necessity in the end they are guilty of not being willing to be governed by his hand.

Now therefore let us note that it is necessary for God to be honored first [and] for the the people genuinely[84] to obey their princes and magistrates, as the latter in no way detracts from any of God's prerogatives which he reserves for himself and of which he is worthy. For if princes want to lead us into evildoing and should try to overturn the pure doctrine of God, may God forbid

[80]See the duties of the magistrates, *Institutes* 4.20.4, 6, 9–10.
[81]sans coups ruer.
[82]appetis-désirs.
[83]se rangent-se soumettent.
[84]tellement.

their success in this endeavor. For too frequently we observe that this madness prevails[85] in many who would like [to see] religion twisted[86] to serve their gain, or who treat it like a wax figure and bend it to suit their will. Who are they anyway? They have lost all authority in revolting against him who possesses the highest sovereignty. Devils are required to bend their knee before God and our Lord Jesus Christ, yet here are mortal men who would like to usurp such power to the extent that the honor of God is overthrown and all his religion cast out. Therefore let us so learn to obey princes and fathers and mothers that God might retain his right in all integrity and that we might not be hindered from rendering him the homage which belongs to him, but insofar as we can without offending our conscience,[87] it is important for us to obey them peaceably. And although those in authority over us may not fulfill their duty, nevertheless children should still not misbehave, [even] when their fathers and mothers are too strict[88] and exercise too much control over them. It is true that fathers are forbidden to use cruelty against their children or even discourage them, nevertheless, although fathers may not have been properly counseled to rule their children gently, it still follows that children [should] bear that patiently. In brief, it is essential for us to endure all who have authority over us. That is what God intended to mean in this passage.

Now he also adds this promise: *In order that your days* (he says) *might be prolonged and that you might prosper in the land which the Lord your God gives you.*[89] Seeing that it is difficult for us to be humble, God has provided us a nudge[90] with his spurs saying, *Your God commands you to do it.*[91] And its purpose is to confirm the doctrine which we have already discussed, that is, that it is a frivolous and vain subterfuge to dispute whether those who enjoy a degree of honor above us deserve to be there, whether they take a sufficient account of their privilege, now that they have attained it. All of that must be cast aside. And why? For we ought to be content with what God has enjoined and completely acquiesce in his good

---

[85]est.
[86]se fleschist-se tourna.
[87]See n. 70 above; also Calvin's discussion on the freedom of the conscience, *Institutes* 3.19.14–16.
[88]aspres-exprès.
[89]Deut. 5:16.
[90]un coup d'esperon.
[91]Deut. 5:16.

pleasure. That is why, in particular, Moses adds here: *According as the Lord your God has commanded you.*[92] It's as if he were saying: "It is true that men always resist as much as they can. If people want to subjugate them, it will not be done willingly. And then there is their arrogance which is always soliciting them to want to be excessively elevated." Consequently there is no voluntary subjection such as God wants, rather you choose to be God's rebels (he says) when you engage in such disputes as: "Why should that person rule over me and why should I obey him, seeing that he is not better than I am?" If you harbor envy that way toward men, you only confront God who wants to know whether you will serve him or not. And if you do not receive his lieutenants when he sends them to you, that is a definite sign that you equally reject his yoke, and as a result his justice is violated and he feels insulted by you. And that such is the case, recognize [the fact] (says Moses) that children who rebel against their fathers and mothers readily cite first one thing and then another; that people who stir up trouble against their superiors have plenty of excuses. But it serves to no avail. The reason? Because God who has established positions[93] of authority in this world also intends for them to be kept. He has declared his will which cannot be retracted. Once God has made his decree,[94] it is no longer fitting to entertain the question as to what must be done, rather we ought to acquiesce and keep our mouths closed.

Now, nevertheless, in this commandment our Lord still acts out of his goodness, in order the better to win and hold us, to the end that we might obey our superiors. Such is the force of this promise. For as Saint Paul[95] says, this is the first commandment of the Law which contains a special promise. True, we have already seen earlier that God is merciful to a thousand generations of those who love him, [a note] that was added to the commandment in which God showed us that he wanted his service to be kept in all purity and that we should not fall back into idolatry or superstition. But that promise applies to the whole law, as we have seen. This promise here only applies to the commandment to obey [our] fathers and mothers. When we see that this is a sacrifice pleasing to God, that those who are in subjection should maintain

[92] Ibid.
[93] les superioritez.
[94] arrest.
[95] See Eph. 6:2.

that condition and not attempt to rebel or be wild, but should bend their neck in order to submit[96] themselves and should demonstrate that they truly want to obey God—[and] especially not refuse to be subject to those mortal men whom he has sent and established in his name—then there you have the purpose for which this promise was given. For God, seeing that we are hard to motivate,[97] willed to mollify our heart and willed to win us by gentleness and kindness,[98] in order that he might not hurt us or make it difficult for us to be obedient to our superiors. Now because the main point[99] cannot be totally resolved here, in summary we retain [the argument] that in order to serve God well, we have to subdue all pride and presumption in ourselves. [For] although by nature we possess this wretched tendency[100] to want to elevate ourselves—for ambition dominates the great and the small—nevertheless, in order for us to prepare to worship God, it is essential that such ambition be overcome. And why? Because the point at which we must begin true obedience is humility. For with respect to men, let us carefully mark that we cannot live in peace and concord unless those whom God has installed in office and dignity are obeyed, unless we receive them in God's Name, and unless we subjugate ourselves to them. Otherwise, everything is subverted[101] and we are worse [off] than wild beasts in the heart of the forest. Thus all who rebel against legitimate authority are both God and nature's enemies, as well as the enemies of the whole human race; they are monsters whom we ought to detest.

Now once we have demonstrated our obedience, being subject to those whom God has installed over us, let us equally realize[102] that we have an ample reason for humbling ourselves under him, and in such a way that he may be worshiped by us. [And] may we render him the homage which he is due, not in a ceremonial way only, but in true and pure conscience. And above all, may his honor be highly regarded by us. May all the civil constitutions[103] of the world point us there, that God's throne may be elevated

---

[96]se ranger-se soumettre.
[97]durs à l'esperon.
[98]humanité.
[99]le tout.
[100]racine.
[101]perverti-bouleversé.
[102]apprenons.
[103]les polices.

above the highest heavens.[104] And although children may obey
their fathers and mothers, and people obey their magistrates, and
in each home we find the order which God approves, along with
its various [social] grades, may this motivate us [still] higher, to the
end that we grasp that God, who possesses the world's highest
sovereignty, must preside over every creature and in brief over
our entire life. Thus in this way we see that all obedience that is
rendered to mortal creatures ought to tend toward this goal, that
God is purely worshiped.

And so much the more we see why the wretched papacy must
be detested by us. For there you confront an arrogance that has
swelled itself in the world; but to what end, unless it is that of
chasing God from both his throne and his honor, which are his?
For the Pope readily attests that it is necessary to be subject to
one's[105] superiors. But what [does he do]? Does he abide by either
God's order or nature's? No! But on the contrary, he has purposely despised everything contained in the holy Scripture, re-
versing the entire order and civil government[106] that God has
commanded us. He is called the Vicar of Jesus Christ, and yet we
see that he has deprived Christ of his seat, [and] that he is no
longer the head of his church.

Therefore let us hold in revulsion whatever the devil has instituted in the world. And although we often see that things do not
turn out as they ought, and that authorities abuse their power, let
us understand that, with respect to kingdoms, and empires, and
the covenant of righteousness, they cannot thwart what God has
ordained. Of necessity, all that will prevail. For it has its foundation in God. It isn't like this hellish papacy which has no foundation. But on the contrary we know that God wills for there to be
kings and princes and people of justice. Consequently they must
be heeded. And when they cease to be responsible for their

---

[104]tous les cieux. In a passage similar to this in the *Institutes*, the *LCC* editor calls
attention to Cicero's influence (21.1495, n. 23). Calvin writes (4.20.9; *LCC*
21.1495): "And thus all have confessed that no government can be happily established unless piety is the first concern; and that those laws are preposterous which
neglect God's right and provide only for men. Since, therefore, among all
philosophers religion takes first place, and since this fact has always been observed
by universal consent of all nations, let Christian princes and magistrates be
ashamed of their negligence if they do not apply themselves to this concern."
[105]ses.
[106]police.

power,[107] and Fathers behave with tyranny toward their children, let us bend our knees, knowing that such is the result of our sins. And when God permits the order which he has established to go unobserved and for everything to be overwhelmed, let us realize how much more urgently we need to flee back to him and pray for him to remove the current conditions that we might perceive that we should ask for nothing but to be governed by him. For it is by this means that he procures our salvation.[108]

[107]devoir.

[108]Golding's translation concludes this sermon with the following exhortation: "Nowe let us kneele downe in the presence of our good God with acknowledgement of our faults, praying him to vouchsafe to make us feele them better, that wee may with true repentance learn to mislike of our selves for them, and so returne unto him as we may profite more & more, even untill we be rid of al our sinnes & thoroughly fashioned againe like to him in righteousnes. And so let us all say, Almighty God heavenly father, etc." *Sermons Upon the Fifth Book of Moses,* trans. Golding, p. 218. Cf. Calvin, *Sermons sur les dix commandemens,* 1557 ed., p. 105.

Sermon Eight[2]

Deuteronomy 5:17[3]

We have already seen that in order to live at peace[4] with men it is important for us to be obedient to our superiors. For that is the first thing that God commands us in the second table of the law, seeing that the descending order from God is to honor those whom he has set over us.[5] It is true that when people speak of men, they are referring to some common societal [feature], for we are all descended from Adam's race. We are of the same nature, which means that men are equal.[6] But, nevertheless, since it pleased God to distinguish between certain positions, we must keep that in mind and observe the injunction that whoever enjoys any preeminence and dignity must be acknowledged for such as

---

[1]N. in *CO:* "This sermon corresponds to the eighth in the 1562 collection, p. 162–83." *CO* 26.321.

[2]The original title: "The Seventh Sermon on Chapter 5:17." *CO* 26.321.

[3]Also cf. *Institutes* 2.8.39–49; Comm. *Four Books of Moses*, vol. 3, pp. 20–22; *CO* 24.611–13; *Catechism, CO* 6.70, 72.

[4]bien vivre.

[5]Calvin stresses this same principle in the *Institutes* 2.8.35.

[6]pareils.

he is honored. And it is not enough to argue here: Why is he better than I? For the injunction doesn't stem from the fact that one [person] may be better than another, but from the fact that God willed that those to whom he has given some [measure of] preeminence should be held in honor. For it isn't enough for children to honor their fathers for [the purpose of] bearing them some respect, but it is necessary for them to help them; they need to employ themselves in their behalf insofar as that is possible. For as our Lord Jesus Christ[7] makes it clear, it is nothing but hypocrisy when children merely offer signs of honoring their fathers and mothers and yet leave them in necessity, demonstrating that they don't care about their needs or of accounting for their own obligation. Such [action] defrauds fathers of what is properly theirs and makes a mockery of God's law when people only want to keep it ceremonially. Rather it involves complete subjection, for it not only means that we should make gestures of honor, but that we render what is due to those who enjoy preeminence and that it be done willingly.

In truth (as we have already elaborated), men clearly want to be exempt from all servitude, but insofar as God has instituted a diverse order, it is imperative for us to submit to it with a good heart and not by force. For what is gained if we obey God while gritting our teeth while our heart craves the reverse? Consequently it is necessary for us to do it willingly and to find good and amiable everything that our Lord has commanded us. That's what opens the door to good relationships[8] with men, that is, that in recognizing that fathers and mothers and all superiors are higher in dignity than the rest, that we honor them; or otherwise God is violated in them. It would be like our refusing to pay homage to him and to be subject to him.

Now after Moses had given this fifth commandment, he adds: *You shall not kill.*[9] It is true that on the face of it, it would appear that God did not lead his people to great perfection, seeing he forbids murders. But we have to note that God wanted to encompass in a brief summary everything that is required to regulate our life effectively, consequently, it was essential to forget nothing, nor leave [anything] out.

[7]Matt. 15:4–6.
[8]de bien cheminer.
[9]Deut. 5:17. The French text reads "meurtriers," "murderers." Literally, Calvin says: "Let us not be murderers."

Now let us understand how men's lives are best and [most] justly ordered: when they abstain from doing evil, from [causing] any injury and violence, and when they honestly walk in chastity and do not harm others; in addition, they ought also to watch their speech lest they injure [anyone] through duplicity and lies. It is imperative for all those traits[10] to be in us if we want to conform to the will and justice of God. Thus we ought not be surprised to find God speaking here about murderers,[11] for his purpose is to keep us in check in order that we might not attempt any outrage against our neighbors or harm them.

But nevertheless we need to return to what we were saying earlier, which is, that God spoke in a gross and uncultured manner in order to accommodate himself to the great and the small and the less intelligent.[12] For we know that everyone excuses himself on the grounds of ignorance, and if something appears too obscure and difficult, it seems to us that when we fail we can wash our hands of it if [only] we can say: "O that was too lofty and profound for me; I didn't understand it well at all." Therefore in order that men might no longer have [recourse] to such subterfuges, God willed to speak in such a way that little children could understand what he says. That is why, in sum, he says: *You shall not be murderers.*

In addition, let us note that in order to lead us little by little toward upright living, God confronts us with the most detestable things in order that we might learn to guard against doing evil.[13] For example, he could have easily said: "You shall not cause any injury to or violence against your neighbors." He could have easily said that. But he wanted to emphasize murder. And why? [Because] it's a thing against nature for men to confront each other in such a way as to efface the image of God.[14] Thus we hold murders in horror, unless we are stupid.[15] But in any event it teaches us that murder is too atrocious a thing and that we have to

---

[10]choses-la.
[11]meurtres.
[12]aux plus idiots.
[13]See "Introduction," n. 68.
[14]Calvin will repeatedly emphasize this theme as a principle of interpretation in the Sixth Commandment. See "The Sixth Sermon," n. 79. However, Calvin explains it best in the *Institutes* 2.8.40: "Scripture notes that this commandment rests upon a twofold basis: man is both the image of God, and our flesh. Now if we do not wish to violate the image of God, we ought to hold our neighbors sacred. And if we do not wish to renounce all humanity, we ought to cherish him as our flesh."
[15]abbrutis-abrutis. May mean "brutalized" or "stupid."

regard it as a curse. Therefore God, in order to hold onto us better and to retrieve us from all harm[16] and injury, shows us that we must not pollute our hands with the blood of our fellowmen. And so people abstain from murder; is that all? It would be much more appropriate if we were to treat it as if he had almost said—indeed we already ought to consider it this way, for God wants to hold both our hearts and our thoughts in subjection and wants to be worshiped by us so purely—that we ought not harbor any ill will toward our neighbors. Why then does he speak of murder? It's as if he were saying: "Consider if you had no written law, if you were like the pagans. At least you would have this engraved upon your hearts, that to murder is a shameless and detestable thing. That being the case I declare to you that all who bring harm to their neighbors, all who scheme[17] against them, all who harbor hate and rancor, I consider and condemn them all as murderers." That is why God speaks in this way.

Now let us carefully note that not without cause did our Lord prohibit murders. Why? For we cannot live[18] among men unless we abstain from all injury and violence. Still God prohibited all that under one heading. Why? For if he had used a long explanation people could have said: "I can't remember it; it's just too difficult for me." Thus God wanted to put it in one word in order that his doctrine might be immediately learned and his law easily come to our memory. We do not need to keep running over it, nor do we need an abundance of thick registers and volumes. It's enough that God comprised in ten phrases[19] the guide for upright living. Who will be able to say now, "I have forgotten such an article. I didn't understand it?" What? Are we unable to retain only ten words? Thus we can now see why God wanted to hold men [guilty] for being confused by their own impudence when they have not necessarily understood what they should do. That is why God spoke with such brevity. Moreover, he was cut and dry[20] (as people say), in order that we might learn to submit[21] ourselves peaceably to him, indeed, that the most ignorant might realize that it is not necessary to be a great scholar in order to understand

---

[16]nuisance-dommage, tort.
[17]machinent-travaillent.
[18]converser-vivre.
[19]parolles.
[20]il a masché-il a mâché.
[21]ranger-soumettre.

the law of God. And seeing that he has descended so low, there is no one so ignorant that he cannot understand what the law contains. In brief, that is what we want to retain.

Now in addition, since it is God who has forbidden us to kill,[22] insofar as it is such a shameful and atrocious thing, let us understand that, in the first place, whoever raises himself up against his neighbors to kill them is not worthy to be kept[23] on this earth, for he is worse than savage beasts. We see how the bears and the lions and the other beasts get along [quite] well. And why? Although they have no rational capacity for discernment, nor any law or [sense of] justice, nevertheless, their knowledge derived from common nature sustains them. Now if beasts are able to exist quite well without fighting among themselves, then shouldn't men be restrained by some consideration seeing that God has engraved upon their hearts that murder is a shameful thing? [After all] they behold in each other a common nature; for each contemplates the image of God in his neighbor.[24] Shouldn't that serve them as a bridle for abstaining from all violence? To what is it leading? Therefore let us clearly keep in mind that God has never yet spoken to us but that we are already quite convinced that if anyone sets himself against his neighbor, he despises nature; he is not worthy of being included in the human race.

Now seeing that the authority of God is joined with what we should have already grasped earlier, and that he shows us that human blood is not to be spilled without our having to account [for it] before him, this being the case, let us learn to walk without causing injury to anyone; or otherwise God becomes our mortal enemy, [for] he declares that men are in his protection.

It is true that there is no mention of a threat here, but it should suffice that he speaks of it in other passages. [For example], it is said that since man is created in the image of God, it is unlawful to make any aggression;[25] or to put it in another way, it's as much as if our Lord were saying: "You wage war against me when you seek to hurt each other in this way, for I have implanted my image in you."[26] If someone merely breaks into a prince's chests, that constitutes such a grave offense that he will be punished like

[22]le meurtre.
[23]nourri.
[24]See n. 14 above.
[25]See Gen. 9:6.
[26]See "Introduction," n. 71.

a murderer. And why? For that also tends to confuse the public order.[27] But here is the image of God which is implanted in men and people despise it; is it not fitting that such an outrage should be doubly punished? Consequently let us note that God, in explaining that it is to him that we address ourselves when we injure other men, wishes to show us that we must indeed retain that [admonition] or we become destitute[28] of [our] senses and wholly mad. And that we might still be better advised concerning the matter, our Lord explains that murder cannot be committed without polluting the ground. For this subject is treated in that passage where it is said that the spilling of human blood in itself constitutes a blot and a stain that can only be erased with great effort.[29] Indeed, [even] when lawful killing is mentioned, such as in a war which is approved, it is still said that a man is polluted.[30] And why? In order that we might learn to hold the spilling of blood with the greatest horror—although an enemy is killed in open war and God forgives it, provided the man who kills has a just and lawful cause and does so out of necessity, nevertheless the fact remains that this is still said to be a macule, that the man is soiled. And why is that? It's in order for us to realize that God has created us to live peaceably with each other and that we cannot even quibble[31] (as the saying goes) without this becoming a spot on us and without our already being polluted before God. Thus when the holy Scripture uses all these forms of speaking, ought we not be [that] much more cautious to walk without causing injury to any of our neighbors?

Now, nevertheless, seeing that God deals rather curtly with these things according to our ignorance and weakness, let us note that it isn't enough not to spill blood; we must abstain from all outrage[ous acts] and violence. In brief, men must be dear and precious to us. For until we arrive at that, God will always consider us murderers. If anyone strikes his neighbor, although he does

---

[27]police.
[28]desprouveus-dépourvus.
[29]See Num. 35:33. See also Calvin's Comm. *Four Books of Moses*, vol. 3, pp. 58–67; *CO* 24.637–41. Calvin elaborates this text against the background of Num. 35 which specifically deals with a variety of cases involving different degrees of murder.
[30]See I Chron. 22:8; Deut. 20:10–20. Calvin likewise elaborates this theme in Comm. *Four Books of Moses*, vol. 3, p. 52; *CO* 24.632: "He now teaches that, even in lawful wars, cruelty is to be repressed, and bloodshed to be abstained from as much as possible."
[31]donner une chicguenaude.

not kill him, he is still a murderer in God's sight. And why? We
have already said that God expressly used this word in order to
explain to us that although people may consider quarreling and
street fighting to be of petty and inconsequential nature, God
hardly considers it so.[32] Why? [Because] murder is still involved.
That is why God spoke the way he did.

Moreover, if we are forbidden to kill, let us realize that we are
also forbidden to cause any harm to, or aggression against, our
neighbors.[33] If we should only raise a finger against someone
[and] offend him with indignation, that is a murder committed in
God's sight. If we only thought about that, wouldn't we possess
greater modesty? [Quite often] we see people who are so angry
that as soon as someone says a single word to them they are immediately ready to fight. For even if there hasn't been any blood
spilled, in their estimation, that's a mere trifle. Whatever the case,
we do not want to make God retract his warning[34] when he declares that all who are factious are murderers. Therefore let us
learn to tolerate[35] our imaginations no longer when we want to
judge from [the perspective of] our faults, but let us peaceably
receive the judgment that God has given. And let us realize that
all who have violently attacked their neighbors are already guilty
in God's eyes. That, in brief, is what we need to retain [from this
text].

Now do we abstain from all wrong?[36] Have we ever caused our
fellowmen any offense? We have to come to the heart [of it]. For
God did not merely provide a civil law in order to make us live
honestly, but he provided a law in conformity with his nature. We
know that he is Spirit and wills for us to worship him in spirit and
truth. That being the case, it is crucial for us to realize that he has
not only ordered our hands and our feet, but also our affections
and thoughts.[37] It is true that men, since they are carnal, upon
hearing the law of God for the first time, think they are justified,

---

[32] A possible allusion to the May 16 riot.

[33] The context in which Calvin discusses this same note in the *Institutes* illumines
his development here. "The purpose of this commandment is: the Lord has bound
mankind together by a certain unity; hence each man ought to concern himself
with the safety of all. To sum up, then, all violence, injury, and any harmful thing
at all that may injure our neighbor's body are forbidden to us." 2.8.39; *LCC*
20.404.

[34] sentence-avis.

[35] apporter.

[36] nuisance-tort.

[37] See the *Institutes* 2.8.6.

inasmuch as the world does not hold them reprehensible. In fact they tend to act with a great deal of freedom and license to do evil. And that is why even the Jews, who ought to be nurtured from their childhood in the law of God, take this—Thou shalt not kill[38]—too literally.[39] For they understand that as long as we have not committed an *open*[40] [act of] aggression that would offend our neighbor, then we have not trespassed against God. Consequently, if the fault was not apparent to the eye, they thought that it should not be charged against them by God. But our Lord Jesus rejects[41] this, showing that the law is too foolishly explained[42] [by this means]. "When it is said: 'Thou shall not kill' (he says), it seems to you that you will be exonerated if men do not hold you in judgment. But whoever calls his neighbor, 'fool,' that is, whoever only utters some indignation against him, is guilty of the Gehenna of fire."[43] Whoever harms others is [as] guilty as [if judged] by a heavenly decree, as [if] God and all his angels [should] rise up against him. Whoever even murmurs against his neighbor, whatever it is that he mumbles between his teeth, even though no offense is perpetrated, is already guilty of judgment.

We see then what our Lord Jesus is after, that is, that even though we are able to affirm solemnly[44] that we have committed no affront, that we have provided no cause for offense, that far from having unsheathed our sword our neighbor has not been wounded by us, that is still insufficient. Rather we see that God wants to prevail over our tongues and thoughts and over all our affections, which is reasonable enough. And that such is the case, whoever offends his neighbor has already demonstrated that he is a murderer, for our tongue is like a sword. Therefore, although you may not have your sword in hand poised to strike, if your tongue is armed in such a way as to speak evil against your fellowman, and if you have offended him, that is a form of murder in God's sight. And even if you have not uttered a loud and clear offense, do not imagine that such will acquit you; for even if you have only mumbled under your breath, that is enough to make you guilty before God. You will be condemned before his heav-

[38]tueras.
[39]lourdement.
[40]Italics for emphasis.
[41]redargue-blâme.
[42]exposee-expliquée.
[43]Matt. 5:21–22.
[44]protester-affirmer solennellement.

enly throne, even though you are exonerated before men and earthly justice finds no fault with you. When we hear that, let us understand that he who is speaking is the same one whom God the Father has given to be the judge of the world. Thus we must not swell with pride,[45] for we shall not gain anything by all our sophistry and subtleties. But let us learn to look to God in order to obtain a right and pure[46] explanation of the law. Who is the one who is speaking? He who rules over our hearts and our thoughts! He cannot be worshiped by our glance and is not content with our abstaining from evil in our own eyes, rather he wants to be worshiped in spirit and truth. He wills for our consciences to be pure and chaste, for us to be purged of all malice.

That being true, if we only keep the nature of God in mind, it is no longer necessary to confine the law of God to external works, but it is fitting to conclude that when God speaks of murders, he equally speaks of all enmity, of all indignation and anger, and of all rancor that we harbor against our fellowman.[47] In fact, that is the precise reason why Saint John says that whoever hates his brother in his heart is [already] a murderer.[48] It's as if he were saying: "Put on all the airs you want to. Even though your hate may be hidden and you hide your eyes[49] against it, even if you don't show the slightest sign of ill will, don't think that God consequently has his eyes closed too." Men may never detect what you keep disclosed, but when you hate your fellowman in your hearts, that is to say secretly, in such a way that no one can perceive it, indeed you are murderers in God's sight. In fact, the reason for this is abundantly clear.

It is true that when princes and magistrates create laws, their manner is different from God's. But then their purpose has to do only with the way we govern ourselves with respect to the external civil order to the end that no one might be violated and each [of us] might have his rights and keep peace and concord among men. That is their intention when they create laws. And why? [Because] they are mortal men; they cannot reform inner and hidden affections.[50] That belongs to God. Besides, they cannot

---

[45]nous eslargir.
[46]naifve-pure.
[47]See n. 26 above.
[48]See I John 3:15.
[49]dissimuliez-fermiez les yeux sur.
[50]Cf. *Institutes* 2.8.39: "For it would be ridiculous that he who looks upon the thoughts of the heart and dwells especially upon them, should instruct only the

fathom hearts; that is the peculiar task of God which the holy Scripture[51] attributes to him. But still when a civil law is made, even though not a single drop of blood may have been shed, if it is known that a man intended evil, he is considered a candidate for the gallows. Take a man who has unsheathed his sword[52] and nevertheless his thrusts are repulsed, so much so that he never even touches his fellowman's skin; nonetheless the laws, even of pagans, condemn such a man to the gallows, as he indeed deserves. Why? For the law doesn't consider what happened, but it weighs intention and attitude.[53] Thus if earthly princes and magistrates punish those who intend evil, even though we might prevent them and they are unable to fulfill their purpose, what then will God do? Does he have less authority than a mortal man? That (I say) is what we have to come to if we are going to understand that God is fully justified in condemning as murderer all who hate their brothers. Why? Simply consider (as I have said) his nature. Do we wish therefore to keep this commandment? In brief, then we must begin with murder. Why? Because God wanted us to be filled[54] with terror in order that when [the] issue of acting in a prejudicial manner toward our neighbor, or of making an extortion, or inflicting some injury on him, should arise, we would know that such a thing is detestable and horrible in his sight and that he will not tolerate it. Why? Because it's the same as murder. Therefore, that is why God wanted to subdue us from the very first and why we must begin at this point.

Besides, if we find it strange that God equates a slap in the face with murder, or for that matter a verbal insult, or sulking, and that even though our lips may not have parted, [he] still [condemns] our secret and hidden hate—although it might be well hidden within us; if we find it strange that that should be equated with murder in God's sight, let us remember his nature and that he is indeed worthy of our attributing to him more than [we do] to mortal men. Now if earthly magistrates punish an evil deed when it is finally exposed,[55] what will God do, to whom nothing is

body in true righteousness. Therefore this law also forbids murder of the heart, and enjoins the inner intent to save a brother's life. The hand, indeed, gives birth to murder, but the mind when infected with anger and hatred conceives it."

[51]See Ps. 7:10.

[52]A direct reference to the Comparet brother who drew his sword against Henry Aulbert on the night of the May 16 tumult.

[53]le conseil et l'affection.

[54]preoccuper.

[55]An echo of Calvin's own involvement in exposing the "conspiracy" of May 16.

hidden? And then we have to note what the apostle says in the Letter to the Hebrews,[56] that the Word of God resembles its author, for it is like a two-edged sword, piercing to the marrow of the bone, for there is no thought of ours which it does not inspect. And why? For nothing is hidden in the presence of God. Thus, since nothing is hidden before God, it is fitting that his Word should test and fathom the depths of hearts. Consequently, of necessity, what remained unknown to men becomes exposed before him and thereby we are admonished to walk in such a way that we bear no enmity nor ill will toward our fellowmen.

Nevertheless, it is still necessary for us to go further than that. For it is not enough for men to abstain from doing evil, for they are created for the purpose of helping each other and of supporting each other together.[57] Therefore God, in forbidding us to murder, shows us the opposite, that we must hold our neighbor's life dear, that we must go to the trouble of both maintaining and preserving it as long as we possibly can. But he wanted to begin by this end, by showing us what he commands. And why? Because we know how vicious we are, how many thoughts we have, and how filled they are with brambles and thorns. Indeed, we have many affections, yet how infected they are with brush and fallow land and similar things! Consequently, God willed with good reason to extract from our hearts and thoughts the malice and vice there lodged; he even wanted to correct those vicious and corrupt factions within us. For without that it is impossible for us to be able to lift a single finger to do good, or even have a single decent thought. That is why the prophet[58] says: "Break up the ground for tillage and do not sow among the thorns." It's as if he were saying: "I clearly see that when someone admonishes you for having offended God, you put on a few airs and become semireformed; nevertheless, you continue to live as you always have." Now it is not enough for one to sow wheat in a field; it must be properly plowed. In the same way, if you only have a fine [outward] appearance, thorns, brambles, nettles, and weeds may still infest within. Consequently the seed there will be worthless, and you will be far from being able to bear good fruit before God. That is why our Lord now says, "You shall not kill," instead of [simply] saying, "Be careful to preserve your neighbor's life."

[56] Heb. 4:12–13.
[57] See n. 33 above. In the *Institutes* (2.8.39) this is the note on which Calvin opens his discussion of the Sixth Commandment.
[58] See Jer. 4:4.

Now we know from experience how men would like to be justified in God's sight, thanks to a fine appearance, while retaining their vices and corruptions. This is in keeping with what we have already cited in Jeremiah.[59] For if we are told to act justly toward our fellowmen, we will certainly not risk a full contradiction. Therefore (in some way) we will attempt to justify ourselves; nevertheless the filth [within us] stagnated, yet all we want to do is to plaster over it like those who do not want to deplete their purse when their house needs critical repair. What do they do? They plaster over it and stop up the cracks, but the problem is still there. The same is true of us. We only want to plaster over it and thoughtlessly justify ourselves. Yet nature teaches us the complete opposite. For if we want to sow a field, do we toss the grain into the brambles and thorns? Of course not! When we see a field in thickets, we clear it, and then we cultivate it. The same ought to apply to us. Consequently, let us see[60] that not without cause God has first of all condemned our vices. For he clearly sees that they are so profoundly rooted in our nature that it is difficult [for us] to get rid of them; indeed, we can never retain them in such modesty as to walk in his righteousness unless he pulls up this wretched root of evil which he knows indwells us. That is why he says, "You shall not kill." It's as if he were saying: "Do you want to live in pure and tender love with each other? [Then] it is imperative for everyone to enter into himself, for you to examine with care whether you have any hate, any enmity, [or] any ill will toward your fellowmen. You must take care not to let any agitation[61] and vehemence tempt[62] you to threaten your neighbors, [or] attempt anything against them. You [should] understand all those things. For in order to be purged of all anger, hate, and enmity, you have to begin at this point: that it isn't enough for you to have abstained from insult and injury and violence, for you not to have attempted anything against your neighbors, or harbored in your hearts any hate or malice against them. It isn't enough for you not to have been poisoned with ill will, but it is crucial for you to live in charity. It is imperative for you to be brothers together, worshiping God as your Father." That is the direction in which we must go.

[59] du Prophete.
[60] apprenons.
[61] bouillons-agitations.
[62] fascher-importuner.

Therefore let us note that when we especially want to benefit from the law of God, we have to remember our vices and imperfections within us, and be displeased with them, and then be willing for them to be removed. Have you done that? But that is not all. For God does not want us to be lazy in this world. He did not simply create us to abstain from evil. Rocks and trees and other unconscious things achieve that quite well. Rather it is crucial for men to give and apply themselves to accomplishing good. Therefore let us understand that when our Lord wills for the life of our fellowmen to be precious and dear in our sight, he shows that, as far as he is concerned, each time we fail to help our neighbor in need, we kill him. For we are not only murderers when we harbor ill will and secretly hate our neighbors, but even when we do not help them in their need and do not attempt to engage ourselves in their behalf when they need our help, we are guilty before God.

Since such is the case, it is no longer a question of flattering ourselves. For we see what rigor the law entails, though [it is] not excessive. For can we deny before God our common bond with other men, seeing that he has created us in his image? Or can we repudiate him as our Father and disavow fraternity with each other, seeing that he has willed to unite us by such a bond? Shall we say that God crowds us too much and that he imposes too heavy a burden on us when he leads us toward that equity and justice? Whatever the case, let us be on guard against flattering ourselves, seeing that we have understood that our Lord wants us to go to the trouble of helping each other, insofar as our neighbor's life ought to be as precious to us as it is to him. That is the sum of this commandment: *Of not to kill.*

What else remains, except for us to pray to God for him to lead us that we might conform to his will? For there is no foundation to arguing that his words are obscure. Nor is there any substance to the charge that his commandments are so numerous that we cannot remember them. For God speaks so simply and uses such brevity as to deny us that excuse. He even undermines any arguments about not knowing how to begin, because he shows us. For in place of the [old] custom of being able to grant ourselves a license to do evil, making ourselves believe that what we do is neither a great nor mortal crime, he always makes us consider that opposite thought: "If I commit the slightest possible offense[63]

---

[63]nuisance-ce que fait souffrir, tort.

against my nieghbor, I am a murderer in God's sight." When we want to do evil the devil blinds us by making us think that we only do evil when we want to kill and slit someone's throat in a single blow. (As I have said) that is appalling to us, for nature restrains us from becoming so enraged as to say, "I shall kill you!" But if anyone pesters[64] us, or if we are defied,[65] then look out! Yet we regard it as nothing. And yet how much vexation[66] have we conceived? If we actually render the same, provided we do not cause too great an uproar, it still seems to us that it ought to be pardoned. Then up go the fists for fighting and hitting. And oh, well! What's a blow? It isn't mortal. That's how men waste their time. And why [do they do it]? Because they are always making light of their faults.

Now, as God has shown us, we have to maintain a completely different order than that. For whenever it becomes a matter of fighting and hitting, or a question of injuring, or of even conceiving some hatred and vexation, let the [idea of] murder come to mind and let us think: "Poor fellow, where do you think you are going? What are you about to precipitate? For you will be guilty of murder in God's eyes." Therefore let us no longer argue that we do not know how to begin, for God shows us and we cannot ignore that willingly. [For] in the end it will be known that we did not want to direct[67] our eyes [in the right direction] in order to understand all that must be visible and obvious to us. That is what we want to glean from this text.

Moreover, there is also [the fact] that not without cause did God prohibit murder before coming to [the subject of] charity. For he shows us that we are bound and obligated to help each other, insofar as necessity requires it. And why? For we are full of evil affections which need to be rooted out. Like a ground that is full of thorns and brambles, it has to be tilled before anyone can sow it. In the same way we need to be purged of our vices that are naturally in us, or otherwise we will never be disposed to walk in pure and tender love with each other.

Now it remains for each [of us] to consider what we can do. When I have the means for helping my fellowman, it is essential that I conclude that what God has given me is not mine, that is, it

[64]fasché-importuné.
[65]despittez-defiés.
[66]despit-irritation.
[67]dresser-diriger.

is hardly appropriate for me to love myself to the extent that I have no regard for others, but when I have the means of supporting those who need my aid, I must engage myself to that end. For there is a community between men. God did not intend for as many people to live apart as he individually created. Rather he united us all. Therefore since God has drawn us together, it is crucial for us to keep this community which God has set in our midst and for us always to come back to it, for it is contrary to nature for us to hate our [own] flesh.

But there is now a matter for the faithful to consider that far transcends this, for not only must they acknowledge that they are formed in the image of God, but they must remember[68] that they are members of our Lord Jesus Christ and that there exists [now] a more strict and sacred bond than the bond of nature which is common in all human beings. And so much the more must we detest those who thus forget [this] union which God has set up for his people. [For there are] those who only want to ruin what God has united and joined, who want to disperse the body of his church, as we see Satan's agents[69] [doing]. [For they] only favor complete chaos. In fact, it seems that they [deliberately] want to disdain[70] God. Especially do they want men to be obligated to them. And they want to separate themselves from those who in their estimation bear them no profit, or fail to strike their fancy. Therefore whenever such a brutal and monstrous[71] ambition enters a man's mind, is it not a sign that the devil possesses him and that the Spirit of God does not reign therein, not so much as even by a single drop?

Therefore let us now learn to submit[72] ourselves truly to what is said here, that being purged of all rancor and ill will, we might be advised to engage ourselves in the service of our fellowman and fulfill our obligation according to the means that God has given us. And in addition, [let us keep in mind that] if evil affections, even though they are hidden, are equated with murder in God's sight, then what will be the outcome of violence and excess when men overflow to that extent, when they strike and kill as much as they do? Of necessity, are they not worse off than the world's pa-

---

[68]penser.
[69]supposts-suppôts.
[70]dispitter-dédaigner.
[71]enorme-monstrueux.
[72]ranger-soumettre.

gans? But in any event, let us be warned that we shall have profited poorly in God's school if we only keep our hands from doing evil while our hearts are unreformed. Therefore now in order to demonstrate what constitutes true Christian perfection, it is inadequate for us simply to refrain from secretly harboring any ill will in our heart, rather we should be true brothers by involving ourselves in behalf of our neighbors inasmuch as we possibly can.

Now if it is unlawful to harbor any secret ill will, then it is even less permissible to act in such a way as to strike, or kill, or commit any violence. And those who do are savage beasts. And if even among pagans that sentiment was condemned, as well as by human laws, then what will be the case when the law of God condemns us? Thus let us learn to submit ourselves to him, not according to our imaginations, but according to his nature.

Now inasmuch as he is spirit, he also wishes for us to worship him in such integrity that not only should our feet and hands be restrained but our hearts should also be submissive to him. [For] lo, in such subjection and obedience that our only desire is to demonstrate in effect that we are truly his children, are we as such. [And that is essential] whenever we have fraternity with all those whom he has called with us in common union.[73]

---

[73]Golding's translation ends this sermon with the following admonition: "Nowe let us kneele down in the presence of our good God, with acknowledgment of our faults, praying him to make us feele them better, and that wee considering howe hee hath bounde us to our neighbors, and will have us to shewe the reverence that wee beare towarde him by abstaining from all evill & wrongfull dealing, may live in such brotherly love one with another, as the chiefe marke that we shoote at, may bee to honour him as our father, and to suffer our selves to bee governed by him and by his holy spirit according to his word, so as we may bee strengthened more and more in it, knowing that his reaching of his hand to us, is to the end to guide us and to hold us under his protection. That it may please him to graunt this grace, not onely to us but also to all people and Nations of the earth, Etc." *Sermons Upon the Fifth Book of Moses*, trans. Golding, pp. 223–24. Cf. Calvin, *Sermons sur les dix commandemens*, 1557 ed., pp. 119–20.

Sermon Nine[2]

Deuteronomy 5:18[3]

Speaking on the Christian life, Saint Paul, having exhorted Christians on the fear of God, adds that they should walk in justice and sobriety.[4] Now there can be no doubt about that referring to the second table of the law. Do we want, therefore, to fulfill what our Lord has commanded us in the second table? It does not suffice to refrain from wronging anyone either bodily or with respect to his property, but beyond that duty, as God attests in other passages, we are required to live in moderation[5] and honesty. In that first passage which I have referred to in Titus,[6] Paul says that

---

[1]N. in *CO:* "This sermon corresponds to the ninth in the 1562 collection p. 183–204." *CO* 26.334.

[2]The original title: "The Eighth Sermon on Chapter 5:18." *CO* 26.334.

[3]Calvin discusses the Seventh Commandment in the *Institutes* 2.8.41–44; Comm. *Four Books of Moses*, vol. 3, pp. 68–71, *CO* 24.641–44; *Catechism, CO* 6.72.

[4]Titus 2:12.

[5]attrempance-modération.

[6]Titus 2:12. Calvin cites this same text in his Comm. *Four Books of Moses*, where he summarizes what this sermon develops in greater detail: "Unquestionably what Paul teaches has been prevalently received from the beginning, that a good life

we have been redeemed by the grace of our Lord Jesus Christ in order that we might live in this world in the fear of God, and then in sobriety and justice. In another place in Timothy[7] he says, that if the civil order is just[8] and magistrates perform their duty, then we will walk justly and uprightly in piety. Now with respect to the fear of God, we mean that spiritual service of which we spoke earlier in which God should be purely worshiped by us, in which we should place our confidence in him, call upon him, [and] bestow upon him that reverence which he is due. But how to approach our neighbor is a question involving how we should live[9] with men.

There are two provisions which God puts forward. In the first place justice involves our not dealing in violence, extortion, or fraud with respect to goods, and secondly [it means] that we should not be profligate, that there should be no villainy, [and] that our life should not be wasted; that is what uprightness and sobriety entail. We have seen with respect to explaining God's prohibition against killing that that [commandment] meant for us to abstain from all outrage and injury, and not only that, but that we should endeavor to live in peace with our fellowman and not allow anyone to be molested.

Now is that all? With regard to goods, we shall be told that we should not be thieves, that we should not bear false witness against our neighbors. That is the same as justice and equity. For if we want to protect each other's rights, then we must not harm or injure anyone. Also with respect to goods, we should not attempt to rob anyone of his substance. But now God interjects [that we are] *not to commit adultery*. That is included in the word sobriety, or moderation.[10] For even though we might not rob anyone's property, or be murderers and quarrelers,[11] if we are impudent, profligate, and our life is brutal, we must not suppose that God will be satisfied with us. Justice and sobriety are not separable things, insofar as God has linked them to his law. Moreover we have seen that God confirms them through his apostle by expounding what

consists of three parts, soberness, righteousness, and godliness (Titus 2:12) and the soberness which he commands differs not from chastity," vol. 3, p. 69; *CO* 24.641–42.

[7]See I Tim. 2:2.
[8]s'il y a bonne police.
[9]converser-habiter, séjourner.
[10]attrempance-modération.
[11]batteurs-querelleurs.

is only briefly touched on [here]. Furthermore, if we want to grasp the natural sense of this passage, let us understand that God commands us here to lead an honest and chaste life, that there may be no turpitude or dissoluteness in us. That is the sum of this precept.[12]

Now in particular it is true that God forbids us in this passage *to be adulterers*, that is to say, to break[13] the marriage vow, for any man to solicit another's wife. But we need to stress[14] what we have already said, that God includes all [of this] under one heading or subject and proposes to us what quite naturally ought to be detestable to us in order that we might hold all promiscuity[15] with the greatest horror.

It was said yesterday that when men are tempted to do evil, they deceive themselves,[16] thinking that the fault will be inconsequential, but from the lesser one proceeds to the greater. On the contrary, in order to check us, God sets before us the most monstrous sins in order that we might be filled with fear and not so easily tempted to commit an error. It's as if he were saying: "Be careful not to fall, for you will break your neck. Don't think that you will only slip, for the fall will be fatal. Therefore, look out!" In brief, that is why God has originated such an order in his law, and now he speaks not about all promiscuity[17] in general, but about adultery which breaks holy marriage.

Now we know that if anything ought to be holy in all of human life, it's the faith that a husband has in his wife and her faith in

[12]In the *Institutes* Calvin summarizes the purpose of the Seventh Commandment as follows: " . . . because God loves modesty and purity, all uncleanness must be far from us. To sum up, then: we should not become defiled with any filth or lustful intemperance of the flesh." 2.8.41; *LCC* 20.405.

[13]corrompre-briser.

[14]poisons-pesons.

[15]paillardise-débauche. In English this word may be translated as "sexual promiscuity," "fornication," or even "adultery." "Débauche" means "debauchery." But it is evident from a reading of Calvin's interpretation of the seventh commandment in both the *Institutes* 2.8.41–44 and the Comm. *Four Books of Moses*, vol. 3, pp. 68–71 that "paillardise" in the sermons refers to any "sexual uncleanness." For the most part, only the context can dictate how the word should be rendered. Cf. Randle Cotgrave's citation in *A Dictionarie of the French and English Tongues,* reproduced from the first edition, London, 1611, with an introduction by William S. Woods (Columbia: University of South Carolina Press, 1950), n.p. Cotgrave provides the following entry: "*Paillardise:* f. Lecherie, whoredome, venerie, obscenitie, uncleannesse; also, roguerie, knauerie, villanie, wickednesse; any filthie, or beastlie humor."

[16]de deçoyvent-se deçoyvent.

[17]paillardise.

him. In truth, all contracts and all promises that we make ought to be faithfully upheld. But if we should make a comparison, it is not without cause that marriage is called [a] covenant with God. By this word, Solomon[18] shows that God presides over marriages, and for this reason, whenever a husband breaks his promise which he has made to his wife, he has not only perjured[19] himself with respect to her, but also with respect to God. The same is true of the wife. She not only wrongs her husband, but the living God, for it is to him that she is obligated. More especially, God himself wants to maintain marriage, since he has ordained it and is its author. Therefore when we hear the word *adultery*, it ought to be detestable to us, as if men deliberately wanted to despise God, and like raging beasts wanted to break the sacred bond that he has established in marriage.

Now we understand how he regards uprightness.[20] Why? When he wants us to be sober, chaste, [and] modest, he says to us: "If you are not virtuous[21] and sober, you are like adulterers, that is to say, whatever excuse you might be able to feign before men, regardless of how little and inconsequential your faults, I will hold you with hate; you are stinking to me; your entire life is foul as far as I am concerned."

We see therefore (as I have already touched on) that this is a strict commandment designed to hold us in honesty and modesty. And by means of it we see how frivolous is the excuse of those who say that they wrong no one when they indulge themselves and are full of shocking misdeeds.[22] For our Lord well knows why he used such language; it isn't because he was a stammerer, [or] wasn't able to direct things, but because he wanted to show that if men want to turn a small incident into a profligate matter, there is another side to it, which is that he condemns and curses all adulterers, all who indulge in shamelessness and unchastity. Thus all the more gravely must we weigh this word which is couched here when he says, *You shall not be an adulterer.*

In any event, we ought to follow the points that are contained under this precept. In the first place (as I have already mentioned), let us understand that God wants holy marriage to be

---

[18]See Prov. 2:17.
[19]periure-parjuré.
[20]honnesteté-convenance. Literally: "honorableness," or "agreeableness." See Huguet, vol. 4, p. 497.
[21]honnestes.
[22]pleins d'enormitez.

preserved. For just as our lives and our persons are precious to him, so also he wills that that faith and mutual loyalty which ought to exist between a husband and wife should be held in its proper esteem and that a thing as holy as marriage should not be exposed to villainy and shame. That is why no one is to look upon his neighbor's wife with lustful eyes. And why? Because our Lord has already united her with her husband; he wants the husband to put her in the shade. And when we think of any evil or shameful desire, he wants us to regard with horror what has been shown us, that is, that God himself will take vengeance on those who have violated the sacred intimacy which he has dedicated in his name. The same holds true for wives with regard to husbands, that is to say, a wife must not surrender herself to lascivious thoughts when she looks upon a married man. Why? Because God has assigned her her own spouse. It is imperative [then] that if we do not want to make war against our creator, that each man should live in his [own] home—provided he has a spouse—and that this order should be maintained inviolable, because God is its author. That is one point.

Furthermore, we must continually return to the nature of God,[23] realizing that he is not an earthly lawgiver who only forbids the external act while permitting us to indulge evil affections, for God has no desire to be served with the eye, nor is he like us. Men are satisfied when they cannot perceive their faults, but God who fathoms our hearts sees the truth, as Jeremiah[24] explains. He not merely wanted to restrain our bodies in his law, but above all he considered our souls. Consequently let us note that God has not simply forbidden the act that would in effect violate marriage or break it, but he has forbidden all lasciviousness and wicked intentions. And that is why our Lord Jesus Christ says that when a man looks upon another man's wife with lust, he is an adulterer in God's eyes.[25] Although he is not guilty according to human laws and cannot be chastized for having acted promiscuously, nevertheless in God's sight he is already condemned as having transgressed this commandment here.

Therefore when we hear the word *adulterer,* a condition thusly condemned, let us not only learn to restrain ourselves in effect

[23]Calvin also appeals to God's nature in the *Institutes* (2.8.44) as a principle for interpreting the basic meaning of this commandment.
[24]See Jer. 5:3.
[25]See Matt. 5:28.

from all promiscuity, but also to maintain our senses chaste that we might be chaste in both eyes and heart. For that is how Saint Paul[26] defined true chastity when he says that those who are not married must be careful how they obey God in keeping themselves pure and clean in body and mind. He does not say that those who have not defiled their bodies in adultery are those who are chaste, but those who have taken the trouble to preserve both their bodies and minds from corruption.

Now once we have considered how God curses and detests all adulterers, we need to go further and apply and extend this to all promiscuity. It is true that whosoever breaks the marriage vow commits a double òffense and is intensely guilty[27] as I have said. But nevertheless we need to come back to this [and emphasize] that God not only wills for no one to act against marriage, but he does not want men to lead an animal existence, for adultery to be in vogue, or for those who are not married to stray about yielding themselves here and there the way dumb animals do whenever they meet. For it is said that not only our souls, but also our bodies are temples of the Holy Spirit,[28] as was just a few moments ago mentioned.[29] And those are Saint Paul's words when he admonished the Corinthians that it was too shameful and infamous a thing for them to permit promiscuity, as they were doing. He says: "Do you not know that your bodies are temples of the Holy Spirit?"[30] So it is God who has bestowed this honor upon us, who has chosen these poor bodies which are not only fragile vessels, but [at best] only carrion,[31] made of dirt and corruption. Nevertheless God has honored them to the extent that he wills to make them into temples for his Holy Spirit to indwell. Yet we are going to wallow them in every [kind of] stench? We are going to turn them into sties for swine? What a sacrilege! And that is not all. Let us see where Saint Paul takes us. Our bodies are members of Jesus Christ.[32] Therefore when a man indulges in prostitution, it's the same as if he were to rape[33] the body of Jesus Christ. For we

[26]See I Cor. 7:34.
[27]est beaucoup plus enorme.
[28]I Cor. 6:19.
[29]Calvin's secretary (Raguenier) at this point includes the following explanation within parentheses: "(Note: he said this because at today's sermon a marriage was celebrated)." CO 26.338.
[30]I Cor. 6:19.
[31]charongnes-charognes.
[32]I Cor. 6:15.
[33]deschiroit. "Rape" captures Calvin's meaning more forcefully than "tear to pieces."

certainly cannot mix the Son of God with our filth and abominations, he who is the fountain of all purity. Therefore when a man
throws himself into fornication, it's as much as if he breaks the
body of our Lord Jesus Christ into as many pieces as he can. Not
that we can actually do that, for the Son of God is not subject to us
to be dishonored in that way, but in any event we are guilty of
having committed such a blasphemy and offense.

Therefore, in light of that, let us learn that God not only wills
for each of us to maintain faith and loyalty with our partner in
marriage, but in general that we should be chaste in order to walk
in purity of life so that we do not give up the reins at every moral
morass and turpitude. And why [do that]? The reasons which I
have traced ought sufficiently to motivate us to that end.
Moreover with respect to what has already been discussed about
adultery, let us also apply it in this way: that we control our senses
with such moderation[34] that whenever the devil solicits any lasciviousness within us, he shall always be repulsed and find no access to us.

A certain pagan[35] has said quite well that it isn't enough for a
man to have restrained his hands, that is to say, for him not to
have given himself to pillage, outrageous conduct, and the harming of others, but what was necessary was that he should have
chaste eyes, that is to say, that he should not have indulged in
immoral glances. Now if that was known to ignorant and blind
wretches, what will happen to us when we are admonished (as I
have already said) that God has bestowed upon us the honor of
not merely reforming our souls themselves, but our bodies as
well—although they are corrupt and only constituted of putrefaction? In light of the fact, then, that God wants to make them his
own and wants to indwell them, is it not imperative for us to learn
to walk in solicitude in order that no defilement or filth be committed that would result in expelling[36] God instead of, according
to his will, our becoming his residence and holy temple? Indeed,
we need to remember what Saint Paul[37] says, that other sins are
committed outside of man's body; fornication[38] (he says) is committed in the body. Now there can be no doubt about the fact that

[34]attrempance-modération.
[35]Golding's translation (on the margin) identifies this pagan as Pericles, *Sermons Upon the Fifth Book of Moses*, trans. Golding, p. 226.
[36]dechasser-bannir.
[37]See I Cor. 6:18.
[38]paillardise.

larceny and robbery soil our hands (as the Holy Scripture testifies), and that as the prophet Isaiah[39] says, whenever we offend
anyone our hands are bloodied. But Saint Paul, acutely aware that
fornication[40] is far more infamous and that people must be that
much more alert with respect to it, explains that fornication[41]
leaves its mark stamped upon the body, and thus the body is exposed to shame.[42]

Now [if] we truly want to preserve our honor and are irritated[43]
whenever anyone casts aspersion or gossips on us, then why do we
go about prostituting ourselves, especially when it results in our
receiving an infamous label and impression before God, before
his angels, and before men? Therefore let us carefully note that,
and we shall be restrained. Moreover, inasmuch as we see how frail
we are and how the devil is always tempting us, let that provide a
bridle for us that we might be brought back to this purity which I
have said is not only physical, but mental and spiritual.

Furthermore, we ought also carefully note that it is said, that no
one should be deceived by vain words, for by them the wrath of
God comes upon believers.[44] Today, it is not only the common
man who flatters himself into thinking that fornication[45] is not
such a great and mortal sin, but we even see *bons vivants*[46] make

---

[39]See Isa. 1:15; 59:3.
[40]paillardise.
[41]paillardise.
[42]See I Cor. 6:16.
[43]marris-irrités.
[44]See Eph. 5:6.
[45]paillardise.
[46]ces graudisseurs-ces gaudisseurs, or "scoffers," or "bons vivants." Certainly a
reference to the immorality that characterized the Favre family of Geneva. See also
Walker, pp. 301–303. Of particular interest is the following entry in *The Register of
the Company of the Pastors of Geneva.* "On Tuesday the penultimate day of October
[30] 1548 we ministers of the city were called before Messieurs to give advice concerning a divorce case involving François Favre and his wife. Favre asked to be
separated from his wife because she had numerous lawsuits and her properties
were situated in Morges where he was unable to attend to them, and he had not
taken her on this condition. Moreover, he confessed to having committed adultery,
which his wife also objected against him in agreeing to the divorce. On this Mon-
sieur Calvin began to give his opinion, affirming that adultery is sufficient cause
for divorce from the wife's side as well as from the husband's; for although the
husband has preeminence over the wife, yet in this there is equality—St. Paul, I
Cor. 7, 'the husband has not power over his body, etc.' It was necessary, moreover,
to consider when this fornication or adultery had taken place, whether or not it
was before the marriage was contracted, and if it was during the marriage,
whether since the adulterous act the wife had consented to continue living with her
husband, so that the fault was cancelled. And, again, Messieurs were urged to

light of God by calling fornication[47] a natural sin and a matter of small consequence. There are actually such shameless swine who talk in that way.

Now for this reason Saint Paul[48] says that no one must deceive you; already in his time such raillings[49] flew from the lips of those who were contemptuous of God and many [people] were blinded by them, for we know that the world is inclined toward flattery. "Let no one deceive you (says Saint Paul) by such lies."[50] Why? [Because] fornication[51] is a detestable thing in God's sight, as he shows by the punishments which he sent and which Saint Paul lists in the tenth chapter of I Corinthians.[52] He cites[53] that case, for example, in which a great army perished.[54] Can't we learn from that, then, that God cannot tolerate sexual immorality?[55] For human life is precious to him, as was explained yesterday. Men are creatures made in his image. Therefore when twenty-two or twenty-three thousand men[56] sinned and God destroyed such a number of his images, that is to say, creatures whom he had made, doesn't this tell us how intensely the fire of his vengeance burned? And why? Fornication[57] was its cause. Therefore let us conclude that it is not simply a matter of our deceiving ourselves, as if it were a light sin to be pardoned, seeing that our Lord, who is not rash, has punished it so severely. Rather let us realize that we shall have to account for it before the heavenly judge; [for] although men may easily forgive us and we consider[58] it nothing

beware lest there should be any collusion between the parties, which would open the door for the dissolving of many marriages. It was pointed out, further, that the wife, who was an interested party had not brought an action, although she accused him of disgraceful conduct. Accordingly, Messieurs were unanimously exhorted to give careful attention to the outcome of this case. Thereupon we were dismissed." Pp. 84–85; *Registres de la Compagnie* 1.41. In a footnote on Favre, the editor points out that the wife in question in the above case was Favre's third; ibid., n. 4.

[47] paillardise.
[48] I Cor. 6:9.
[49] brocards-railleries.
[50] I Cor. 6:9.
[51] paillardise.
[52] See I Cor. 10:6–11.
[53] ameine-cite.
[54] See Num. 25:1–18. Calvin cites this same incident in his Comm. *Four Books of Moses*, vol. 3, p. 70; *CO* 24.643. It epitomizes the heinousness of all sexual immorality or fornication in particular.
[55] paillardise.
[56] See Num. 25:1–18.
[57] paillardise.
[58] cuidé-cru.

more than a filthy and contagious game, yet God will have his say. Consequently let us look to him and to the examples which he has given us in order that we might live under his fear and make a much greater effort to restrain ourselves from all stains. That, in sum, is how we ought to understand this seventh commandment of the law to the end that we might not contaminate ourselves by any unchastity or immoderation.

Now if we have to maintain both our bodies and our souls unsullied, is it not crucial at the same time for us to avoid those occasions that lead us into immorality?[59] Of course! Therefore let us note that those who abandon themselves to any [form of] licentiousness are only asking to be thrown into Satan's snares, and although they may not be held accountable by the world, they are already adulterers[60] in God's sight. If that were only taken seriously, we would no longer see lewdness in dress,[61] or in gestures, or in speech, as the world currently provides far too excessive a license. For when men and women dress in such a way as to seduce each other and to entice each other into adultery, are they not all the more engaged in prostitution?[62] It is true that they argue: "Oh, I haven't committed adultery." But in so doing they [only] reveal that they are a prey to Satan and would like to entrap others as much as possible. Consequently, they are like a type of adulterer in God's sight, as all licentiousness and excessiveness in dress is only asking to be engulfed by the snares.

In addition, there are gestures and words as well. Whenever a man and a woman associate with each other in such a way as to invite room for Satan, and lose their shyness toward each other to the end that they especially become entangled in his traps, and abandon themselves in servitude to him, that is adultery in God's sight. [For] although there may be nothing in effect, nor any conclusive action taken, in any event God will not let such things rest unpunished, for they have attempted it too blatantly. And thereby we can see how frivolous and puerile those subterfuges are by which people hope to excuse themselves as having done no wrong, on the condition that they have not violated the intent. Like those who would like to have dances and [indulge in] lewd conduct—of course, provided that no fornication is involved—is that so bad?[63] That's the same as if they openly wanted to mock God and close their eyes to him in order to insult him and neverthless wonder if they have done anything wrong. Now we know quite well that dancing only serves as a preamble to fornication,[64] for in particular it opens the door to Satan and cries for him to come in and enter with enthusiasm. That is what dancing always invokes. If you say, "I have not had an evil desire," you make God a liar. After all Saint Paul[65] declares that foul language undermines[66] good morals. Indeed that is why he quotes[67] that [passage] from a pagan,[68] in order to make us that much more ashamed.[69] If we can't accept Saint Paul's teaching, [then] let us attend the school of those poor unbelievers and idolaters, for at least they were able to assert that foul speech destroys good morals.

Now when tongues are contaminated by foul language and lewd references, whether in gestures or speech, it is merely a sign and indication of complete sordidness. If people reply that no evil purpose is intended, don't they openly refute the Holy Spirit? Therefore let us note that when every [form of] sexual immorality[70] is forbidden us, the purpose is that we might conduct ourselves modestly in both speech and deeds and that there might be no immorality in us tending toward adultery.

It is true that everything is clean for those who have a pure conscience: nevertheless we have to be on guard lest Satan preoccupy us and cause some flaw within us. That is why this precept must be weighed in such a way that we not simply fasten upon the act of fornication,[71] but that we consider everything connected with it, all its accessories, everything approaching it and capable of leading us to it. In short, we need to come back to what I previ-

---

[63]A reference to the Favre family.
[64]paillardise.
[65]See I Cor. 15:33. Calvin's N.T. text apparently read, "Evil communications corrupt good manners." This is the same rendering which appears in his *Commentary on the Epistles of Paul The Apostle to the Corinthians*, trans. John Pringle (Grand Rapids: Wm. B. Eerdmans Publishing Company, 1948), vol. 2, p. 34. (Hereafter cited as Comm. *Corinthians*, vol. and p.) The Latin text cited in that passage reads: "ne erretis: Mores honestos corrumpunt mala colloquia." See *CO* 49.550.
[66]corrompent-brisent.
[67]allegue-cite.
[68]Calvin identifies this pagan as Menander in his Comm. *Corinthians*, vol. 2, p. 42; *CO* 49.554.
[69]vergongne-vergogne.
[70]paillardise.
[71]paillardise.

ously referred to in Saint Paul,[72] that as we ought not cause harm to anyone with respect to their persons or property, likewise we ought walk in complete chastity,[73] as it is fitting for all lewdness and immoderation to be cut off from us.

Now since all filthy speech, all dancing, and [all] lewd acts of immorality[74] are condemned in God's sight as forms of adultery,[75] let us note that the same applies to all other [forms of] immoderation. We see drunkards who glut [themselves] like wild beasts, and are they any better satisfied[76] and improved? It is only a matter of their rushing into every turpitude; they are redolent[77] with it, incognizant of their shame. Thus when men lead such an animal existence, they are drunkards and gluttons and their bodies are especially exposed to every [condition of] sordidness. [And] although they may not commit an act of fornication itself, do we think that they are going to escape God's hand and not be damned as adulterers? That is how the sobriety, of which Saint Paul speaks, shows us that if we want to be chaste and pure before God, then not only must we refrain from sexual immorality,[78] but we must soberly use eating and drinking to nourish us and not for the purpose of leading us into immoderation to such a degree that we no longer possess a check on ourselves or any modesty. That too is what we have to observe.

Now someone may argue at this point: "And just how are we supposed to be able to restrain ourselves from every corruption, seeing our flesh is so fragile?" For [in all honesty] we are aware of the incontinence that exists in men and by means of it are shown, better than anywhere else, how vicious their nature is. Moreover, it is true that men cannot be chaste, for our Lord, thereby, through such intemperance of the flesh, wants us to be conscious of the curse against Adam's sin—unless, as it is written, we possess a special grace[79] not given to everyone. Still it is crucial for each to consider what God has given him and to use the gift he has, knowing well that he is all the more obligated to God. But in any event, there is the remedy of marriage for those who cannot re-

---

[72] Titus 1:15.
[73] honnesteté.
[74] dissolutions impudiques.
[75] paillardise.
[76] saouls-rassasiés.
[77] empunaisis-remplis d'une mauvaise odeur.
[78] paillardise.
[79] See I Cor. 7:7. See Calvin's discussion of celibacy in the *Institutes* 2.8.42.

strain themselves. Therefore God, although he wants to leave this mark of weakness in us, nevertheless grants us an appropriate remedy for it. [And so we return to the argument.] Is a man's flesh weak? Is a woman's equally? The matter is certainly a vice, and although it may appear to be an inclination derived from nature, it is from that broken nature which we have incurred from Adam; thus in itself it is condemned, for all such intemperance is far from that excellent dignity that God set in the human race, that we should bear its signs and become like angels.[80]

Therefore all immoderation of the flesh is wrong, but insofar as our Lord supports us, he has ordained such a means whereby this weakness will not be imputed as a vice. Therefore, if the mantle of marriage is worn, then immoderation of the flesh, which is vicious and damnable in itself, will not be imputed in God's sight. And when a man, having prayed to God and cast himself upon him, sees that he cannot refrain, let him take a wife in order not to lead an immoral life, or behave like a dog, or a bull, or some wild beast. Thus when he marries, as ordained by God, that is how vice is covered, and hidden, and not brought into judgment. And herein we see the inestimable goodness of our God, that although he leaves this vice in us, which indeed ought to make us feel ashamed, he nevertheless ordains a helpful means by which it may be overcome. And although men might be immoderate, they are not indicted before him and his judicial seat, provided they contain themselves within the confines of marriage. For all immoderation is unlawful. For example, when a man wants to enjoy too much license, and a wife the same with her husband, there is no reason for them to make their home into a bordello.[81] But when a man lives honorably with his wife in the fear of God, although their lawful intimate relationship[82] might be disgraceful,[83] nevertheless neither before God nor his angels is such a relationship shameful. And why [is that]? The mantle of marriage exists to

[80]An allusion to Ps. 8.

[81]Calvin elaborates this same note in his *Institutes*, embellishing his point with a citation from Ambrose: "Ambrose censures this wantonness with a severe but not undeserved judgment; he has called the man who has no regard for shame or honorableness in his marriage practices an adulterer toward his own wife." 2.8.44; *LCC* 20.408.

[82]la compagnie du lict.

[83]honteuse-timide. In this context "disgraceful" better translates Calvin's meaning than "timorous." It may be that his own conjugal relationship had been a "timorous" one, one in which he never felt free of embarrassment. Yet he did not dwell on that aspect, as the larger context of this passage demonstrates.

sanctify what is defiled and profane; it serves to cleanse what used to be soiled[84] and dirty in itself. Therefore when we see that our Lord is that benign and has ordained such a remedy, are we not that much more malicious and ungrateful if we do not use it and if all the excuses which men put forth are not rejected? Indeed, has God not provided[85] for their needs and made available to us a good physician to heal what is wrong with us? Has he not gone on ahead, as we see [?] Therefore let us reject all [those] subterfuges [based on] our fragile nature, inasmuch as our Lord wanted to relieve us from that matter and has ordained holy marriage in order that those who do not have the gift of continence may nevertheless not succumb to every turpitude. That is what we have to observe.

Now with respect to this subject, let us carefully note what the apostle[86] says about the marriage bed, for when men and women keep themselves within the bounds of the fear of God and complete modesty, the bed is honorable. Instead of there being shame (as indeed there should be), our Lord turns[87] all of that into honor. What the apostle calls honorable in God's sight is hardly a mere trifle; for what should be shameful even in men's eyes, God has forgiven. But he pronounces a curse and vengeance on all adulterers. When we hear such advice, let us learn to cover ourselves with this honorable shadow (wherever we have such need), in order that our ignominies may not be cursed and condemned before God and his angels. And at the same time let us fear this dreadful judgment which is made against all adulterers and fornicators. Indeed, let even those who are able to abstain from marriage be careful to abstain from it for [only] a time, in such a way that they do not reject the remedy which God has assigned them, unless they know that God is holding them back. Thus let those who live outside of marriage be ready overnight to submit to God if he calls them to that estate.

Now with regard to this matter we see how Satan has reversed the whole order. For under the shadow of sanctity we see how [a host of] abominations have come about. For example, in the papacy it appears that the most angelic virtue is not to marry. For the state of perfection, claim the monks, is to remain unmarried.

---

[84]ord-souillé.
[85]proveu-pourvu.
[86]See Heb. 13:4.
[87]convertit-tourne.

The priests say that they are consecrated to God; when we are his clergy we are like the flower of the church; we must be separated from the common pollutions of the world. Consequently in the papacy they put esteem on becoming like the angels of paradise and not on being married.

Now nonetheless we see how God is mocked by such diabolical pride, for since marriage has been scorned [by them], worse than bestial abominations have emerged. You have priests, monks, and nuns who defy God and reject the good [plan] he presented to them, that if there is any weakness in them, let them marry. They scorn and disclaim all of that and regard it as dirt. Now that is to fight against nature. And, moreover, is it not appropriate for God to avenge himself against that kind of presumption when men trample underfoot a remedy which he gives them? Does an illness not worsen when in scorn for your doctor, instead of drinking what he has prescribed for your health, you cast it to the ground? That is precisely what these angels of the papacy's hell have done, [along with] all those vermin of priests and monks and nuns who have rejected holy marriage. In doing so, they have openly made war against God. And still they are not content with that, but we see how they run on. They have dared to utter blasphemies which ought to make everyone's hair stand on end. In that alone we see the devil has completely dominated. And indeed it is the Antichrist's seat, this seat of Roman apostasy, when it was proclaimed that those who are in the flesh cannot please God, and that we have to be separated from every corruption, and especially that marriage must be denied to priests. Those are the very words of a Pope[88] that were nonetheless written down as if they were an oracle from heaven.

Now if the devil were in complete vogue and were incarnate in this world, could the Pope speak in a more detestable way for defying God and holy marriage than by saying that those who are in the flesh cannot please God? It's the same as if he had condemned the entire human race. For by that pronouncement, he not only condemns those who are living today, but he condemns all the holy Fathers who lived under the law, all the holy patriarchs, apostles, [and] holy martyrs. Thus you have a devil of

---

[88]Calvin identifies this Pope as Siricius in the subsequent paragraph. Cf. *Institutes* 4.7.22–28, where Calvin discusses the Catholic Church's error in forbidding her priests to marry. See also *LCC* 21.1251, n. 45 where further references to Siricius are listed.

Rome who wants to expel the apostles and martyrs and all the holy Fathers from the kingdom of heaven. Thus, whoever wants to be in the Pope's paradise must be the companion of hell's devils. For it is certain that although it was a monstrous thing for that beggarly Siricius[89] to have proclaimed such a blasphemy, seeing that he willed to exclude from the kingdom of heaven the greater part of those holy people who have ever lived; nevertheless God has never permitted such a horrible blasphemy to be proclaimed—unless it was his will to render the seat of Rome abominable, deliberately intending for the devils to go to that extent, when, under the shadow of sanctity, they accordingly rejected marriage and by a just vengeance dropped the reins against malicious immoral conduct.[90] For they have infected the world with their detestable sodomies to the extent that even pagans hold it in horror.

Now as a result of all of this, we are admonished (as I have already said) not to despise the gifts of God, but to make use of them with all sobriety. And as for those who cannot contain themselves, let them consider bending their neck, receiving the Master's yoke, and submitting to it. And let them realize that when husbands uphold their wives and wives try to live in good peace with their husbands, that that is a sacrifice acceptable to God. And if they should be responsible for children, let them be warned to feed and provide for them, whether rich or poor, knowing that God accepts that service. Let wives engaged in their housework also realize that this too is a sacrifice acceptable to God. And if marriage is scorned by those devils who in disdaining God imagine that angelic perfection consists in abstaining from it, nevertheless, let all those who are married realize that God accepts them, that he receives them and even presides over their household. For since he says that he is the author of marriage, he blesses it when we come to it according to his will. Nevertheless let those who are not married be clearly warned to walk in the fear of God and to prize and honor marriage as if they were. And let them warn each other to preserve themselves in complete purity, of body and soul, as Saint Paul discusses it in the seventh chapter of I Corinthians.[91] In that passage he does not condemn widows,[92]

[89] Ibid.
[90] des infections meschantes.
[91] See I Cor. 7:33–34.
[92] vefves-veuves.

or others who abstain from marriage, but he exhorts them to do what they must. For widows, virgins, and those who are outside of marriage must all the more adhere to God and walk as being less prevented from dedicating themselves completely to him. Why? For they do not have as many distractions in this world. Those who are married have more impediments; nevertheless they must be careful not to drop the reins and must always walk in fear and solicitude.

That is how in every condition we have to exercise sobriety and godliness[93] with such a regard that we not only reveal signs of morality and godliness in ourselves, but also that we might offer our bodies and souls as gifts and sacrifices to God, seeing that he has so costly redeemed them by our Lord Jesus Christ and has willed for them to be dedicated to him, that he might indwell them like his temples.[94]

[93]honnesteté.

[94]Golding's translation concludes this sermon with the following exhortation: "Now let us kneele downe in the presence of our good GOD with acknowledgement of our faultes, praying to him to voutsafe to make us feele them better than we have done, yea even in such sorte, that being rightly sory for them, wee may learne to repaire unto him, with acknowledgement of the faultes whereof wee bee guiltie, seeking to give ourselves to his obedience, and to please him in all things, even untill we have finished our course and pilgrimage upon earth, and bee come to the salvation that is prepared for us, as it is already in the Kingdome of heaven. That it may please him to graunt this grace, not onely to us but also to all people and nations of the earth, Etc." *Sermons Upon the Fifth Book of Moses*, trans. Golding, p. 229. Cf. Calvin, *Sermons sur les dix commandemens*, 1557 ed., p. 133.

Sermon Ten[2]

Deuteronomy 5:19[3]

If we could understand God's will in the brief discourse in which he explains it so carefully to us, it would not be necessary to study a long time in order to understand how to govern ourselves well and how to lead a holy and righteous life. But as the proverb says, there is none so terribly stupid as he who refuses to understand, nor none so hopelessly deaf as he who will not hear.[4] And that is why we make ourselves blind, although our Lord shows us his spendor before our eyes. And we see it so [clearly] in this precept of the law, as in the others. For if each person were to enter into his conscience in order to make a thorough examination, would he not find that it is easy to determine when we have

---

[1]N. in *CO:* "This sermon corresponds to the tenth in the 1562 collection, pp. 204–25." *CO* 26.346.

[2]The original title: "The Ninth Sermon on Chapter 5:19." *CO* 26.346.

[3]Cf. also Calvin's development of the Eighth Commandment in the *Institutes* 2.8.45–46; Comm. *Four Books of Moses,* vol. 3, pp. 110–11; *CO* 24.669; *Catechism, CO* 6.72, 74.

[4]See *CO* 26.346.

cheated our neighbor, and when we have wronged him with respect to his property,[5] whatever our pretext, so that we are guilty of stealing[6] in God's sight? But what? We seem to be satisfied with the fact that we can conceal our shame from the world. In the meanwhile the judgment of God is put under our feet, and we don't [even] think about it. All the pages [of Scripture] so scarcely serve us, that in the end judgment before the heavenly judge is unavoidable. Thus we find that it is not in vain that God proclaimed through his prophet Zechariah[7] that his curse would fall upon the liar[8] and the thief, that is to say, that in whatever way we have erred or whatever article of the law we have broken, God will easily be able to take vengeance against us because of it. Therefore men may well be able to justify or flatter themselves, but the fact remains that in the end God will reveal his anger[9] against both liars and thieves.

But in order to grasp clearly the will of God, let us note that, in the same way he earlier explained murder and adultery, he now uses this word *thief* in order to make us regard with hate all fraud, graft, and any kind of wrong that we know we could do against our neighbors. If a person calls a man a thief, he will be angered by it, for it's an offensive word, so much so that he cannot bear being dishonored in that way in the world's eyes. Now God, in order to motivate us to hate all fraud, all wrong, and all extortion that can possibly be done against another's property, emphasizes this word.[10] He could have easily put it in other ways. He could have said: "Be careful lest you take any of your neighbor's goods from him. Look out that you don't gain your profit at your fellowman's expense. Beware not to engage in any violence." But in one word he said: *Don't steal.* And why? In order that we might regard fraudulent activity, robbery, graft, and all wrong with the greatest abhorrence, and be ashamed of cheating anyone, and be horrified (I say), seeing that we are guilty of stealing before God.

In addition, let us note that there are many kinds of stealing. For some engage in secret fraud when they amass the substance of others by subtle means and practices; others use force, which is properly called robbery, or pillage, or pilfering; some use an even

[5] A reference to Natural Law.
[6] larrecin-larcin.
[7] Zech. 5:3–4.
[8] pariure.
[9] ire-colère.
[10] See the *Institutes* 2.8.10.

greater coverup, for it appears that they have taken nothing; you cannot accuse them before the world; but insofar as they do not live in simplicity and righteousness, they are thieves in God's eyes. There you have the different ways in which we have to approach stealing if we hope to understand what is forbidden in this passage.

But nevertheless we need to note that God does not judge thieves in the way that men do. For those who enjoy reputation and influence will not fail to be condemned before God; indeed, although none should accuse them—unless it is the poor who out of hunger cry for vengeance (although not a word may be spoken)— the afflictions that the poor endure speak loud and clear before God and lead to a trial without a word being uttered. Consequently it is inappropriate for us to employ our imaginations here with regard to judging different aspects of stealing and for us to think[11] that we can escape the hand of God though we are not punished by men or earthly justice, for indeed God goes much further. Therefore let us remember, in sum, that (whether by God or through the Holy Scripture) all forms of wrong are called stealing whenever we desire to gain for ourselves what isn't ours. And in fact, when God, through his prophet Isaiah,[12] threatens that whoever has pillaged and ravished will experience the same, he is not talking about the little thieves who are led out to the gallows,[13] but he is speaking about the great princes and kings who were in fashion by the whole world. And then in the first chapter, where he even addresses himself to the sacred people who were the church of God, he says: "You Princes and governors are companions of thieves."[14] Now it is certain that no one had prosecuted them in trial, nor had they done the same to others, but in any event they were not failed to be condemned by God. Thus thieves who are honorable here below will not be forgotten to be cursed by the law. For God has announced his judgment concerning that in this passage. It is imperative then that we cast our eyes down, realizing that we shall benefit nothing, even though our thefts are excusable in the world's eyes, whether we cover or falsify them. For God's law will nonetheless run its

[11]cuidions-croyions.
[12]See Isa. 33:1.
[13]Possibly an allusion to the Comparet brothers who were executed on June 27, scarcely a week preceding this sermon.
[14]See Isa. 1:23.

course, and at the same time its execution will be sharp. There is nothing that God has prohibited that will not be called into account. That is what we have to emphasize in this passage.

Now it would be helpful to explain in detail what we have briefly discussed, to make it more specific by examples, in order that it might be better impressed [upon us]. As I have already said, if we were prepared to pay attention to what God illuminates for us, a long exposition would be necessary here. But what [is the actual case]? We only want to dabble,[15] and if something should be made known to us, [we only] use it as an occasion for doubt. And that is why we have to be pressed further.[16] We have already said that there is no one single form of stealing. For some steal by pilfering the goods of others, as when we say, he stole a horse; he stole so much money; he stole a bed, a pot, some dishes, and similar things. And indeed, such thefts are adequately sentenced by the world. But when a merchant overcharges for his merchandise, or when he sells it in an underhanded way, [knowing] that no one will be able to catch him, [thinking to himself] "Ah! here is a simple man who knows nothing, I will trap him!" people don't consider that stealing. In any event, the man is a thief inasmuch as he has acted out of a bad conscience, regardless whether anyone condemns him.[17] It is true that if anyone cares he can be a good and faithful judge with respect to such dealings, [for] if he knows that fraud is involved, he can say, "I've been cheated!" We don't have to go to a theologian or a great scholar to be shown that we have been wronged; we each readily know that. Still we don't think of that as a form of stealing and hardly acknowledge it. Whatever the case, God will not neglect to judge as a thief anyone who has taken advantage of a simple man, or has sold him goods in an underhanded way, seeing that he has outwitted him through a fault of judgment. Anyone who also overcharges an illiterate person is equally a thief. Moreover, if an artisan[18] makes a faulty good and the buyer cannot perceive the flaw, or especially if someone takes whatever he can and sells what unquestionably doesn't belong to him, [justifying it on the basis] that he is dealing with a rich man who has a full purse, it's all the same. Therefore if

[15]nous envelopper.
[16]d'avantage-de plus.
[17]Calvin had earlier condemned this kind of knavery in the *Institutes* 2.8.45. "For [God] sees the intricate deceptions with which a crafty man sets out to snare one of simpler mind, until he at last draws him into his nets."
[18]un homme mechanique.

a man engages in any of these practices—although he may be able to get away with it in the world's eyes—the judgment of God will nevertheless run its course. And although we should ask everyone for an opinion and they should reply, "We don't consider that stealing," God will not retreat from our fantasy. Consequently, those are the thefts that will come under judgment before God, although we currently let them pass. Nor will he side with those who relegate themselves such a license, for their evil will not be forgiven. What are we thinking? Have we not said that God's law is immutable? As we shall see, it requires its execution.

Furthermore, seeing that we should not operate in such a way by either finesse or subtlety, it is crucial for us to return to that natural law,[19] which is, that we ought to do unto others as we want them to do unto us.[20] When we follow that rule, it is unnecessary to have thick tomes in order to learn not to steal, for, in brief, everyone knows how he ought to walk with his fellowman, that is, that he should not harbor malice, or attempt to enrich himself at his neighbor's expense, or gain for himself substance which is not his own. That word alone would suffice and our very best excuses and pretexts would disappear. For even when people have deceived men, they think that at the same time they have blinded[21] God. Let us take an example in which this point may be more readily perceived. Whoever receives another's property through the courts thinks that he is the world's most just owner.[22] Why? That's justice. Now I neglect to say that this justice must still not be corrupt. For in truth there are some who through corruption make justice a pure [act of] brigandage and who through unjust practices reverse all equity and law. For often justice is only a market place where another's rights are sold and all justice is perverted. But even where that is not the case, if through astuteness and finesse a man finds a means of acquiring for himself another man's goods, and argues: "O the courts[23] judged in my favor over that; you won't find a better or more equitable title to it in the whole world than that," then there is a thief in a twofold sense. He

---

[19]equité naturelle.

[20]See Matt. 7:12; Luke 6:31. Cf. also Comm. *Four Books of Moses*, vol. 3, p. 110; *CO* 24.669; where Calvin cites this same principle.

[21]esblouy-aveuglé.

[22]See Calvin's condemnation of the same in the *Institutes* 2.8.43. God "... sees the hard and inhuman laws with which the more powerful oppresses and crushes the weaker person." *LCC* 20.409.

[23]la justice.

would just as soon have stolen or robbed his neighbor's house as to have won it unfairly in a court case. Why? [Because] that involves outright stealing and secondly stealing under the guise of justice, which is such a sacred thing that it constitutes a sacrilege which God cannot tolerate.

If a theft is domestic [in nature], it is much more seriously punished, but when we come before that seat[24] which God has dedicated to his majesty, if everything there is perverted and confused, isn't that worse than robbery? Consequently, let us carefully note that whatever trick one may be able to use on men, God's law will continue to follow its course; that is to say, if we employ fraud or malice, or make use of extortion and violence, then we will be condemned as thieves.

If a man under the guise of his authority wrongs his neighbor who is poor and thereby oppresses him, he is a thief and half-murderer. Such an action does not simply constitute a theft, but it qualifies as murder. Nevertheless such happens and is forgiven. True, from time to time someone may murmur, but only half-heartedly.[25] And in the meantime the guilty party is applauded; and still worse, he is honored so much more since he is a big thief. For according as a man's estate grows and he becomes wealthy, people woo him and he becomes even more admired. And quite often it is through thefts that people attain great honor, as far as the world is concerned. But let us not take up such bandages for the purpose of blindfolding our eyes, rather let us understand what the holy Scripture contains: that we will always be thieves if we do not do unto others what we would want them to do unto us; [apart from that] we do not render justice to everyman. For it is fitting for us to define a vice by its opposite virtue.[26] If we really want to know what stealing is, consider what doing the right [thing] for our fellowman would be. Now we do not do our neighbors justice when we rob them of their goods, or, by whatever means is available, add to ourselves what is theirs. For, in brief whenever we employ any malice or outrage[ous means], we are sufficiently refuted.[27]

Thereby we see that stealing is not simply committed with our hands, when [for example] someone is able to steal another per-

[24]Seat of the magistrate or prince.
[25]à demie bouche.
[26]See the *Institutes* 2.8.8–9.
[27]convaincus-réfutés.

son's money or coins. But stealing occurs when a man possesses what isn't his, and when we don't attempt to protect what God has put in a person's hands, for he wills everyone to retain what he has. For example. If a servant wastes his master's goods,[28] he is a thief. If a working man only asks for his daily wages and nevertheless loves to loaf[29] (as people say) and wants something to eat,[30] certainly he is a thief as anyone can tell.[31] But it would also be appropriate to consider other forms [of stealing] and make this comparison, that whenever we do not render to every man what rightfully belongs to him, God will always regard that iniquity as stealing.

Now it remains to be seen how we should walk in such a way that God would not need to curse us as thieves. That is done, in the first place, when we learn to love our neighbors—as Saint Paul shows in the thirteenth chapter of Romans.[32] It is a marvel that people make so little over cases in which other men's property has been stolen; that being the case, is it such an impossible thing for us to love our neighbors when asked to do so? One can only say, No. For nature willed to bind men together in union and God made them all in his image.[33] For that reason we must not be unyielding and offensive[34] about loving one another. Now at the same time, if we have charity,[35] as Saint Paul[36] says, we will never be thieves. And if we willingly remind ourselves what we rightfully owe men and how we are obligated to them, all those remonstrances would not be necessary: "You shall not steal; you shall not commit adultery; you shall not kill." All that would be superfluous, as Saint Paul explains in that text.[37]

But what? There are very few who think like that. But on the

---

[28]gourmande le bien d'autruy.

[29]oeuvre faicte.

[30]son escuelle dressee-avoir à manger.

[31]Calvin employs a similar illustration in the *Institutes* 2.8.45.

[32]Rom. 13:8–10.

[33]See "Introduction," n. 71.

[34]fascheux-désagréable.

[35]See Calvin's reference to "charity" as a principle of interpretation in the *Institutes* 2.8.51. Cf. Calvin's Comm. *Four Books of Moses*, vol. 3, p. 110f.; CO 24.669. "Since charity is the end of the Law, we must seek the definition of theft from thence. This, then, is the rule of charity, that everyone's rights should be safely preserved, and that none should do to another what he would not have done to himself." This statement is related to the principle of "defining a vice by its opposite virtue." See n. 26, above.

[36]Rom. 13:10.

[37]Rom. 13:9.

contrary (as I have said), we always resort to vain excuses when we have stolen another man's property, or engaged in fraud, or some malicious trick, or extortion. We always have an excuse ready. But the fact remains that through that act it becomes apparent that we lack charity and are like savage beasts. In short, it shows that we are not worthy of being considered men, seeing that we break the bond of union that God established between all the children of Adam. So much then for that point: that it is imperative for us to study charity's lesson if we do not want to be thieves.

Next is the matter of our not craving to be rich. For as soon as that lust for gain[38] takes hold of us, it is certain that we will become thieves; it cannot be otherwise. Now that may seem strange at first, but in any case whenever we are plunged in meditation, nature teaches (as the pagans[39] were quite able to say) that it is impossible for us [not] to crave to be rich, or for us not to be aflame with greed, by hook or by crook.[40] Do we want, therefore, to be free of stealing? Then avarice must be put under, that is to say, the desire to aggrandize ourselves. And lest this word should become a chicanery, [by someone asking], "And just how do we do that?" let us learn to be content with our [present] condition. For whoever does not have a specific pattern or rule will always be troubled by covetousness; his affections will drive him from place to place, so much so that he will never know any peace, or be able to say, "It is enough for me to stay within my bounds." I maintain that the condition which God has given every man must be [looked upon] as if it were the terminus for saying, "Behold your God intends for you to be satisfied with what he has given you. Be content. If you don't, you will not only upset the human order, but you will defy your God as if you were making war against him."[41]

That accordingly is what we need to note, that when we have this principle of charity as our guide, it is enough for us to learn to be content with our condition.[42] And why [is that]? Because such is God's will, and he wants to test our obedience. And that

---

[38]cupidité-de gagner.

[39]Calvin does not provide specific sources.

[40]à tors et à trovers.

[41]Cf. the following statement in the *Institutes* 2.8.45: "We must consider that what every man possesses has not come to him by mere chance but by the distribution of the supreme Lord of all. For this reason we cannot by evil devices deprive anyone of his possessions without fraudulently setting aside God's dispensation."

[42]See "Introduction," n. 70.

cannot be done unless, at the same time, we keep Saint Paul's rule,[43] which is to learn how to be rich and poor, hungry and thirsty, as well as enjoy abundance. Not only does Saint Paul say that we ought to be patient in poverty, and admits that he has experienced his share, and, even more, provides us with an example and shows [us] the way, but he says that we must learn [both how] to be rich and [how to] abound.[44] And how is that? It seems that this is a word of advice without advice.[45] For to exhort us to have patience when we are poor is something everyone knows he already needs. Why [then]? For we will be tempted. It is a hard and unpleasant reality[46] that when a man has no bread to eat, or at best only brown bread, he still wants to have his ease and comforts. Thus with regard to poverty, every man can admit that we need someone to console us, for someone to teach[47] us that we ought not to murmur against God, or be tempted to do evil. But when he says that we should learn how to become rich, people deride this notion, as if it were founded on unreasonable grounds. That is why this doctrine is more necessary than the first. And why? Let us consider for a moment who the rich are: insatiable men[48] who can never be satisfied and who are much more difficult to be content than the poor. [For example] if we were to make a comparison between the rich and the poor, we would find that just as there are some who are tormented and grieve, and who are led to steal, and engage in many adverse practices, so the majority are content to accept what God has given them and follow their course. But when we come to the rich, as for kings and princes, we find that they are so inflamed and covetous for the goods of this world that we cannot satisfy them; indeed, they are almost grieved if the sun shines on the poor. In brief, we see that the majority of the rich would not even be satisfied had God given them the whole earth to possess. For, as I have said, they are still jealous[49] that the poor have a common ray of light, and that they drink water, and work, and even succeed better than the rich; [in all of that] a rich man only feels envy toward them. And although he draws their sweat and blood, it seems to him that when they eat

[43]Phil. 4:12.
[44]Phil. 4:12.
[45]un propos sans propos.
[46]chose.
[47]remonstre-remontrer.
[48]gouffres-hommes avides.
[49]marris.

at his expense they are wringing him of his very intestines and bowels. And unfortunately, this parsimony, or rather brutal cruelty on the part of the rich, is far too common. Consequently Saint Paul is justified when he says that we would benefit tremendously if we could learn [how] to be rich, that is to say, if at the same time we would not solicit gain. [Therefore] if God has given us any abundance, let us walk in our state without covetously saying, "Oh, there is something I want! I must have that and that, etc.!"

Now there is still more to the matter than a rich man simply not wanting to increase his gain, rather it is imperative for us to be poor in our heart. For we ought not place any pride or confidence in our riches, or use them as occasions for oppressing the weak and those who have no credit or support, as far as the world is concerned. For in the final analysis, we must be ready to become poor if that should be God's will. Whoever is clearly rich today, who has full caves and granaries, a well-lined purse, fields, possessions, and a full string of merchandise, let him not be surprised if God should will to remove it all; may it not importunate or chagrin him too much, but may he arrive at Job's patience and be able to say, "May God's name be praised, since it has pleased him to take back what he has given me."[50]

That is why (I say) it is so difficult to know [how] to be rich. For unless we come [to that point where we are willing] to submit to God's will, to receive peaceably all that he gives us, that is to say, to bear our poverty with patience when he sends it to us and to be content with those goods which he has put in our hands without abandoning our hearts to them, of necessity we will always be thieves. For the poor are tempted to do evil, and it seems to them that God sends it upon them. Sometimes they even use this ruse: "O! I see that he only wants me to eat the shirt on my back; he would like to destroy me if he possibly could. And why aren't I permitted to take vengeance against him?" That is how everyone wants to be satisfied by his [own] hands. But it isn't for us to do. And even when a man is rich by virtue of graft, finesse, and fraud—all for which he will have to give an account before God—it isn't for us to deprive him of what he has stolen.

Consequently if we are poor, it is immediately understandable if

---

[50]See Job 1:21. Calvin's chapter on "Christian Freedom" (*Institutes* 3.19.9) is highly relevant.

we are pushed to steal, even to the extent that we dare to say, "Oh, well, our Lord wants to torment[51] us. That is why we are indigent with respect to this world's goods. We do not have what we would like to have. It's as much as if God intentionally wants to humble us." That is one way to put it. But may we, nevertheless, strive to overcome that temptation. For we know how even Solomon[52] asked not to be poor, for fear of being tempted to steal. When such a person [as Solomon] is afraid and, behold, makes that petition to God in the name of all the faithful, ought we not be on our guard?

Therefore those who are indigent and have need[53] of both bread and wine, and who do not know to whom to turn, and who lead a rather shabby life, who occasionally with great pain find half enough bread to their satisfaction,[54] as well as others who do not enjoy the comforts they would like, may both these [groups] be counseled to put themselves in God's hand and to pray for him to grant them the grace to walk in such a way that they may not be led to wrong or offend anyone under the pretext that necessity forces them. And let those who enjoy the vogue, who have money in their purses, be especially careful not to oppress the poor, for they always have their traps set. For that is what the rich do; if they see that a poor man is going under, they hurry there like hunters and immediately fall upon him, turning this way and that, and through their weaving have the poor man entrapped in the end.

Therefore let those who have possessions[55] be clearly warned not to increase themselves beyond measure, but rather to be tighter on themselves [by] not abusing their abundance. Let those who possess a great deal not elevate themselves for the purpose of oppressing those who hardly have anything. That is how we have to conduct ourselves in these matters.

And even when such opportunities present themselves, instead of our being subtle [enough] to investigate them from afar, let us be advised to repulse all such malice. And instead of the rich imagining[56] that they have gained everything when they have

---

[51]exercer-tourmenter, éprouver.
[52]See Prov. 30:7–9.
[53]fautes-besoin.
[54]saoul-rassasié.
[55]dequoy-la possession.
[56]cuident-croient.

been enriched at the expense of others, let us realize that they have cut the throats of the poor and have made many widows and orphans, even though they don't think so. But in any case, as long as our flesh is curious[57] and keen to look for such occasions, let us remember our God who wills to test us. Indeed, we may hold the sword in our hand, but let us guard against any wrongdoing. And let us remember that if we were in the same condition as the poor, we would certainly want to be helped.

In brief, if we hope to restrain ourselves from stealing, then let us become neither wolves nor foxes, for all those who acquire wealth through fraud and malice are like foxes. And the poor—whatever their indigence may be—whenever they are tempted to do evil and to gain by unlawful means others' property, they already demonstrate that they are no longer men. But those who commit larceny with violence are like savage beasts who only want to devour everything. Consequently, in order not to be thieves, let us not be cruel.

Nevertheless, above all, let us learn to wait upon the benediction of God for all that is necessary in this world. For if we would [only] live by this rule, [then] it is certain that all avarice and robbery and fraud, and all similar things, would be immediately corrected. That is the only medicine we need for healing these vices, for us to be able to lift our eyes to heaven and say, "God is our Father, he will provide all that we need; it is he in whom we must hope for all that sustains us in this present life; in sum it is his benediction that constitutes the fountain of all wealth." If we were adequately persuaded of that, it would no longer be necessary for there to be precepts in the law against stealing, or many admonitions, or warnings. That word alone would suffice for us.

But what? We demand our daily bread of God, while insisting that it is his proper office to sustain us; and in the meantime, we engage in robbery, fraud, and malice. Isn't that a fine way to disdain God? I say with my lips, "Give me this day my daily bread," yet I go out looking for the devil. For if we employ unlawful means and cheat and rob just anyone, from whom are we taking our welfare? Is it from God's hand? Are we not indeed companions of thieves and brigands? Consequently, we can be assured that we are only asking for the devil to enrich us when we yield in that way to fraudulent activity and graft. And what is more, that is

[57]aigue-curieuse.

a definite sign of our infidelity and [the fact] that we do not expect anything from God's benediction, nor think that he is rich
enough to sustain us. That is what we are like.

In any event, these things can benefit us. For when we hear that
our Lord curses stealing and that such is detestable in his sight, let
us regard them with horror, knowing that God does not judge
according to men's fantasies, but he wills for us to walk in such
integrity that every man may enjoy his rights and no one be
molested or hindered with respect to both his property and substance. In brief, let us be extremely cautious. And then, because
we are so inclined toward evil, he wills for us, as I have already
shown, to be cognizant of those means which hold us obedient
under our God and which prevent us from robbing [anyone].
Therefore in light of the fact that he has united us together, let us
keep that rule and principle of equity.

Moreover, let us not crave to be rich. In fact, let us practice this
doctrine of patiently bearing poverty and of not being ablaze with
greed, always [trying] to advance ourselves further. And once we
[have learned to] regard all cruelty and fraud with abomination,
above all let us learn not to be so bestial as to think that if we can
seize upon this and that we shall become rich. Let us not be deceived about that. Why? For (as I have said) God's benediction
constitutes true wealth. Therefore it is crucial to drink from that
fountain and to be satisfied by it if we want to restrain ourselves
from every form of stealing.

Now nevertheless let us consider the warnings which God puts
before us. For once he has sufficiently taught us that this precept
is more than equitable [and] that he has also given us the means
for walking in justice without offending or harming anyone, seeing that we are still obdurate and that our evil affections continually turn us completely around, he adds the warnings in order to
test us. Is it of small consequence when he says that thieves and
robbers will not enter the kingdom of God?[58] Is this present life so
dear to us that in order to get by in this world and gain a few
goods we are willingly ready to provoke the wrath[59] of God? He
explains that we will be banished from his kingdom. If we had a
single ounce of faith wouldn't that warning pierce our heart? But
our Lord goes even further. For seeing that we are so carnal and

[58]I Cor. 6:10; Eph. 5:5.
[59]l'ire.

worldly, he shows us that even in this world he will make us back down, for whoever thinks that he can advance himself by [means of] finesse, robberies, and fraudulent activities will be consumed; a secret curse will undermine him. For example, in the passage which we cited from Zechariah,[60] it is said that the curse of God will come upon the house of thieves and abide there until they are consumed. We also know how he speaks of that in all the prophets[61] to the extent that our Lord says that when men hope[62] to enrich themselves and think that they will accomplish great things, he will blow upon that with such force that it will all be swept away and, so suddenly, that people won't have expected such a destruction.

But God even goes still further. Certainly it is more than enough when we realize that our Lord derides those who are tormented by the need to amass great wealth, [especially] when all of that is going to dissolve[63] and run off like water, but [then] we see that wealth causes the ruin of those who have enjoyed some [form of] reputation. Take a father who has pillaged and robbed, who has throughout his life provoked God's vengeance on himself. Is he guilty of murder? Why, he thinks his children ought to be little kings. Now if they were left with only a little with which to set themselves up in business and had to learn to work honestly, his children would have more than enough with which to be satisfied. But insofar as they trust in the goods which have been illegally acquired, their father has set them up for the hangman's noose, or to perish in some horrible way. And why is that? Because the wrath[64] of God consumes all property acquired through graft and robbery. It is even appropriate for such a man's house to be cursed. [For] it is essential for God to reveal himself as a just judge against both thieves and all who scorn his divine majesty. For when you speak to them about this, you only hear the scoffers[65] say: "Well, well, it's time for more money," as it's all the same to them. And when a poor man has neither the strength nor influence to counter them, alas! they bathe in their iniquities. But

[60]Zech. 5:3-4.
[61]Mic. 6:12-15.
[62]cuidé.
[63]decale-descent.
[64]l'ire.
[65]les gaudisseurs-bons vivants, railleurs.
[66]éslourdis-lourds, stupides.

what? When God sees that these men are that stupid,[66] and that he cannot lead them into a heavenly life, and that it means nothing to them to be excluded from the kingdom of heaven, "Behold," he says, "I have already set the date for your trial. I intend to begin to execute my judgment. I intend to show you that my curse is upon illgotten goods and that those who possess them for a [brief] time will of necessity be dispossessed. And both they and their goods will be consumed with all their kind." Now when we see all of that, ought we not be motivated lest the devil should completely bewitch us?

What remains then? That we retain that good conscience that God requires of his own; that we each work peaceably and not endeavor to burden anyone; that we only seek to know how to get along in this life without offending God. And if we don't have a large income and much money to spend, [then] let sobriety[67] be our double portion. That is the appropriate way for us to conduct ourselves.

Now if stealing is thus condemned by God, what will happen when we rob him of his honor? For it is quite in order to compare stealing with sacrilege. After all, God has forbidden us to be thieves. And why? Because he wants us to maintain equity and justice for each other. He even wills that goods, which he has dedicated to our usage, should serve[68] us in such a way that we [cannot] possess them by underhanded means. Let whoever possesses a large quantity of them be advised to dispense them as one who only uses them and who does not possess property.[69] As we have said, let whoever has very little be content.

Now if God wills for us to exercise such justice toward our neighbors for the purpose of protecting the property which they hold in their hands,[70] if the goods which he has created are respected in that way by him, and [if] he does not will for us to soil them by fraud, violence, and similar activities, then what will his attitude be toward things of higher value? Obviously, that we should walk in complete integrity with our fellowman, that we

[67]Sobriety in the sense of austerity and simplicity.
[68]demenez-menés, conduis.
[69]See Calvin's chapter on "Christian Freedom," *Institutes* 3.19.7–9.
[70]See the *Catechism, CO* 6.74; *LCC* 22.116: "We must take care that each man have his own in safety." Cf. also *Institutes* 4.20.3; *LCC* 21.1488: " . . . it prevents the public peace from being disturbed; it provides that each man may keep his property safe and sound; . . . "

should strive to render unto each what is properly his, that we should render unto our God his due, that is to say, that we should glorify him and be admonished to abide completely in his majesty, no longer usurping that he has forbidden us. For we know how audacious men are, for in their fury they not only oppress their fellowman, but they also dare to revolt against God. Having ravished their neighbor's substance, they would also like for God to subject to them and only obey him when it serves their advantage. It is appropriate then that we should be warned with respect to these things.

And in conclusion, let us also remember not only to refrain from every form of injurious activity and wrong, but at the same time, insofar as we can, let us not permit anyone to be wronged or injured. For there are two things which God commands of us: justice and judgment. Justice, in order to render each his due. And judgment [or discrimination], in order that we might neither consent to evil, or allow anyone to fool the poor who do not have any means of maintaining themselves. For when I see with my own eyes someone who has been oppressed and make no effort to help him, indeed, I am consenting to the thief, so much so that the warning[71] contained in the fiftieth Psalm applies to me: "When you see a thief, you run after him."[72] Now isn't it the same as befriending those who steal when we do not attempt to repress them, or when we close our eyes, or when we turn the reins over to them? We are consenting to a theft that has been committed. And although men might not judge it that way, we are guilty of the same in God's sight.

Therefore, let none of us think that it is only lawful for us to guard what we have, rather, as the principle of charity[73] exhorts us, let us see that we preserve and procure our neighbor's property as much as our own. That is why we should not be thieves in God's eyes, nor man's, and why the possessions that he has put in our hands are blessed by him, and why he makes us prosper, and why we should experience such a contentment that we should al-

[71]sentence-avis.
[72]Ps. 50:18.
[73]See n. 42 above.

ways aspire toward that celestial heritage, knowing that therein we
shall possess the fullness of all goods in perfection.[74]

[74]Golding's translation concludes this sermon with the following admonition
and prayer: "Nowe let us kneele down in the presence of our good God, with
acknowledgment of our sinnes, praying him to make us feele them better than wee
have done, and that wee may profit more and more in the keeping of his holy
Lawe. And bicause wee bee so corrupt and frowarde, that all our thoughtes and
affections goe the contrarie way: it may please him to reforme us by his holy spirit,
and to draw us in such wise unto him, as we renouncing the world and despising
these mortall and transitorie things, may mount up to the heavenly Kingdome,
where we shall have all contentation and rest. And so let us all say, Almight God
heavenly father, Etc." *Sermons Upon the Fifth Book of Moses*, trans. Golding, p. 235.
Cf. Calvin, *Sermons sur les dix commandemens*, 1557 ed., p. 148.

Sermon Eleven [2]

Deuteronomy 5:20 [3]

We saw yesterday[4] that it is unlawful to harm our neighbors in
any personal way or to cause them any loss of property. Nevertheless, as we see in this passage, because the tongue can inflict
injury, God also willed to mention it specifically in his law. Thus in
the same way that he earlier forbade [us] to bring any harm to our
fellowmen (which was included under the word *murder*), or incon-
venience[5] them in any way, or deprive them of their property,
here he shows that we must not under any circumstances speak ill
of them, or say anything that would bring reproach or discredit

---

[1]N. in *CO:* "This sermon corresponds to the eleventh in the 1562 collection, pp.
226–47." *CO* 26.359.

[2]The original title: "The Tenth Sermon on Chapter 5:20." *CO* 26.359.

[3]Discussions of the Ninth Commandment appear in the *Institutes* 2.8.47–48;
Comm. *Four Books of Moses*, vol. 3, pp. 179–81ff.; *CO* 24.713–14; *Catechism, CO*
6.74, 76.
the 1562 collection, pp. 226–47." *CO* 26.359.

[4]par ci devant.

[5]fascher-importuner.

against them.[6] It is true that he specifically speaks *of false witnessing*, but that is in keeping with the rule we have observed, that is, that he sets over against us what, of necessity, we find to be the most detestable in order that we might abhor those sins which approach it.[7] Consequently, if we speak ill of our neighbors, if we slander them—although in the world's eyes that sin isn't considered grievous—God disproves of it as false witnessing.

But a question can be raised here. "Why has God mentioned false testimonies and lies,[8] seeing that he has already said: 'You shall not take the name of the Lord your God in vain'?" For it seems that this is a superfluous repetition. For in such a brief summary of the law, containing no more than ten sentences, to reiterate a thing twice doesn't make good sense. But we have to note that what we have explained about not taking the name of God in vain was in the first table, where God was concerned with the majesty of his name to the end that it be held in reverence. Thus when we speak of God, it is important to conceive of the infinite glory which is in him in order not to open our mouth except in reverence and humility. When we have to make judgments and speak of God in any way, we must always remember that his name ought to be venerable to us and not thrown about thoughtlessly. So much then for this previously developed idea.

Now God speaks of another matter, that is, not to injure our fellowman, or cause him any harm by our wicked tongue. Insofar as the purpose is twofold,[9] now we see how the two sentences differ and that nothing is superfluous. Let us carefully note then, insofar as it is treated here, how men ought to live[10] together in charity and in justice, and although the name of God might be profaned by false witnessing, nevertheless the law is not superfluous when it says: *That we should not bear false witness against our neighbors.*

Now we have explained that God willed to condemn here, in general, all calumny, all untrue reports, all defamations, and

---

[6]Cf. the purpose of the Ninth Commandment in the *Institutes* 2.8.47; cf. also the purpose in Comm. *Four Books of Moses*, vol. 3, p. 179; *CO* 24.713; and the *Catechism, CO* 6.74.

[7]See the *Institutes* 2.8.10.

[8]periures.

[9]The twofold purpose of this commandment is stated with greater clarity in the subsequent paragraph.

[10]converser-vivre.

similar things. That such is the case, it is specifically said in another passage: "You shall not direct an evil report against your neighbor, or slander him so as to put a blemish upon him."[11] If the law of God contains every perfection for upright living, it follows that the preceding judgment is included. Now where shall we put it except under this sentence? Thus we have to conclude that although God may have specifically singled out the term *of false witness*, nevertheless he intended for this doctrine to apply to all calumny, all untrue reports, and all oblique references that tend to defame our fellowmen or mar their good reputation. Therefore, in this text,[12] we see how God willed to hold [us] in responsible[13] friendship, indeed, to the extent that he does not permit anyone to be attacked, whether by reputation of the person, or in terms of their property. Whoever then discredits his neighbors, whoever slanders[14] [them] in any way whatever, [only] creates war [and] breaks the bond of charity between men.

In fact, once you have thoughtfully considered it, it is certain that false reports, calumnies, and slanders hurt far more than stealing does.[15] Thus let us understand that if we intend to obey our God, it is essential for us to maintain the honor of our neighbors as much as we can. For since he has forbidden [us] to mar the reputation of anyone, in the opposite sense he equally wills for us to endeavor to protect the honor of everyone.[16] For it is not enough to refrain ourselves from doing evil without at the same time also procuring good.

Now we need to proceed by the steps which God intended for us to understand in speaking *of false witnessing*. Consequently, the first consists in the fact that when we have to make judgments, we should be reminded not to injure by false statements, or lying, or perjury those whose honor and good we are responsible to procure. For whoever bears false witness against his neighbor kills him: in essence he robs him and is guilty of whatever evil proceeds from his lie. It is true that we do not often think about that,

---

[11]See Lev. 19:16. For an exposition of this text, see Comm. *Four Books of Moses*, vol. 3., pp. 183–84; *CO* 24.715.

[12]ici.

[13]bonne.

[14]detracte-médit.

[15]Note how closely Calvin links this commandment to the preceding.

[16]Keep in mind Calvin's principle of defining a *vice* by its opposite *virtue*. See the *Institutes* 2.8.8–9.

but such is the case. That is why God particularly commanded in the law[17] that witnesses should be the first to execute a person being punished for an offense in order that people might know that it was by their voice and their accusations[18] that he was put to death, and that the witnesses might be under more subjection and each think to be accountable to God when witnessing against someone. Consequently, when we have to serve as a witness, it is essential for each of us to regard with care that we do not give free run[19] to our conscience, but say in pure simplicity what we know to be true before God.

Now the issue is not solely false witnessing at a level that concerns a man's life, but also that which includes all his honor and all his property. Therefore whenever we have to serve as a witness, let us remember, above everything else, to procure our neighbors' honor and profit. Nevertheless, at the same time, we must not lie against God by trying to conceal an offense which someone has committed, or by defending his property. For if man's honor is dear to us, what should God's be in comparison? The reason why I am prohibited from bearing false witness against my neighbor is because God intends for friendship to be established[20] between men and for no one to be tormented[21] with regard to his honor or property.

Now if God has consideration for us who are no better than worse, do we suppose, at the same time, that he forgets himself? For if I attempt through false witnessing to support someone who has acted amiss, or to cover his crime, or attempt to conceal it, I certainly blaspheme God in no uncertain terms. Why? [Because] I solemnly swear to tell the truth and then proceed to lie. Is that not denigrating the name of God? Doesn't that degrade his glory? Therefore we must not interpret God as granting[22] his favor upon criminal activity, or as intending to conceal men's iniquities when

---

[17]See Deut. 13:9. See also Calvin's exposition of this text in his Comm. *Four Books of Moses*, vol. 2, pp. 83–84; *CO* 24.361: "He would not that everyone should privately execute vengeance without a public trial; but he referred to the ordinary custom, that the witnesses should throw the first stone at condemned criminals . . . . For it was an admirable provision, that God would have those who had denounced the crime, to be the executors of its punishment, in order that they should be more cautious and moderate in giving their testimony."

[18]langues: "tongues."

[19]eslargir sa conscience.

[20]nourrie.

[21]grevé-affligé.

[22]gratifier-accorder des faveurs.

he says: *You shall not bear*[23] *false witness against your neighbor;* rather, in brief, he wanted to show that, to the best of our ability, we ought maintain our neighbor's honor, provided it is true.

Moreover, as we shall better perceive in what we have yet to deduce, let us note that in this passage God is concerned with evil intentions[24] that proceed from vengeance and rancor, rather than the deed itself. For we have already touched on the fact that God does not merely speak here of that false witnessing which we might do in legal cases, or when we have to take a solemn oath, but [he] also [means] every form of calumny and defamation; for whatever the form in which we slander our neighbor, it will always be ruled as false witnessing in God's sight. If I were to go and speak[25] in someone's ear with the intention of slandering my neighbor, that is false witnessing. It is true that I might not have been called before the judge, or raised my hand, or gone through any of the trial ceremonies, but we know what God thinks[26] about it and are therefore guilty.

Now it is essential to ask that if, without any ill will, I warn about evil in anyone, will I be accused [of bearing] false witness before God or men? Never! For God has purposely taken into consideration malevolence and enmity. Thus if I hate anyone, and slander him, and am pressed into it by that ill will that I feel toward him, that is what constitutes condemnation in terms of bearing false witness. If I crave to slander and am so dominated by the vice that I am forced to tarnish everyone, that is bearing false witness. And that is why it is said that charity covers a multitude of sins, but hate reveals our shame.[27] That is how Solomon briefly dealt with the root of false witnessing which God has forbidden and condemned by the law, namely, when we are consumed by hate. And why? For if we love one another we will certainly attempt to support each other together. We know what an intense fire erupts whenever we slander anyone; of necessity in order to maintain his honor the other person must chafe against us, then all friendship is broken. Consequently, whenever we take the trouble to exercise charity, we cover our faults to the best of our ability. But where enmity arises, our tongues are usually to

[23]parleras.
[24]affections.
[25]flagorner-parler.
[26]parle.
[27]See Prov. 10:12; I Peter 4:8. Calvin interprets the Proverb text in an identical manner in his Comm. *Four Books of Moses,* vol. 3, p. 180; *CO* 24.713–14.

blame.[28] Where the heart is envenomed, it will vent its anger and we will hurl out the ill will which is hidden.

Therefore, whenever we hate anyone and wish to see them overwhelmed, let us carefully note that, in this passage, God has condemned all backbiting that issues from ill will and enmity. [For] if we are unable to hurt anyone bodily, if we are unable to destroy them through their property and strip them of their substance, we attempt to attack them with ridicule; we inquire whether they are involved in any slander. When that's true of us, it reflects an evil root that can only produce similar fruit. That is what we have to keep in mind in order to have a correct grasp of the commandment of God.

Now at the same time let us note that when it is said that charity covers a multitude of sins, this does not mean that we are encouraged to flatter one another or promote[29] our vices through lies, rather it means that we must not give vent[30] to them with [any kind of] desire to slander those who might lose courage, or possibly by chance seek recourse[31] in some shameful way, as the desperate do. Let us carefully note, then, that the Holy Spirit wants us to engage neither in flattery, nor lying, nor promoting our neighbors' vices, rather he wants us to strive to correct their vices as much as we possibly can and, at the same time, to support them without discouraging those who have erred.[32]* For when a man sees that people debase him and do it with vengeance, he despises himself and gives himself to evil and becomes hardened in it. Therefore, whenever we rudely find fault with those who are already in despair,[33] without demonstrating any feeling of charity for them, we are the cause for their increased self-scorn.[34] Consequently, let us be warned that when we reprove vices that it be done with gentleness. And let those who are convinced[35] of their error by this means realize that we hope[36] to retrieve them from the road of perdition.

[28]" ... viola nos langues qui se desbordent .... " *CO* 26.362.
[29]nourrir-élever.
[30]esventer.
[31]se iettroyent-se rejeteraient.
[32]*Beginning with this paragraph and continuing through the next 15 or so, Calvin in essence reviews the practice of "Discipline" as it should be exercised and as it was being abused in Geneva.
[33]en mauvais train.
[34]despiter.
[35]redarguez-convaincus de fautes.
[36]veut.

For this same reason Saint James[37] applied this passage to those who seek to win their neighbors to God by kind, gentle, and friendly admonitions. Therefore when I see someone [who has been] led astray, if I admonish him for his faults and am able to win him by that process so that he returns to the right path, that (I say) is how the statement "Love covers a multitude of sin" is accomplished.

Now it is true that Solomon has another end [in mind] when making this statement, but, in comparison, Saint James did not badly apply Solomon's doctrine, for the point is that when we want to cover our sins, it won't be accomplished if we close our eyes or fail to speak up when God is offended. When people are ruining themselves, it is indeed improper for us to conceal [it], for us to cover their vices with charity. That is to misapply the doctrine. Rather it is necessary to employ kind and brotherly reprimands and at the same time to see to it that their vices are figuratively buried in God's sight, then they will not be remembered by men. Consequently, it is imperative for us to engage in the task of transforming our neighbors and nevertheless with this measure in mind, that when their vices are corrected, we should not slander [them]; if it is possible for us, [we should try to see] that those who ought to have shame [express it] for their repentance, while with regard to men they should not be cast into despair.

But indeed this procedure is badly practiced and we see how people fail at both ends of it. Therefore this method is almost never used, that is to correct vices by gentle means, attempting to cover them in order that a person might be reformed,[38] and at the same time not slandered. Why? Because when we want to have friendship with men, we usually flatter them. We know that in one way or another they are offensive to God, yet we tolerate it; just as we want people to spare us, we also put up with the evil in our friends. Consequently, that is a reprehensible coverup,[39] seeing that Satan blinds poor sinners, and we are its cause, insofar as we conceal their faults which ought to be cited by us. But that evil isn't enough. For today the world has come to the point that it seems that we are not good friends and are not faithful and loyal to those with whom we associate unless we acquiesce in their favor when they are wrong. When they are guilty and we ought to be

[37]James 5:20.
[38]se reduise-s'amende.
[39]une couverture mauvaise.

calling this to their attention and chastizing them, we turn to eloquent perjury instead. And how [is that]? "Am I supposed to offend my neighbor? I am obligated to him. Am I supposed to go now and provide evidence against him? What is this?"

That is how we esteem God's truth. That is how we change it into a lie. [And] that is how we also abuse this principle of not slandering our neighbors. Consequently let us realize that when we want to uphold evil and exalt vice that such a goal is evil. Above all, when we have been summoned and required to testify, let us not declare as true that evil which ought to be corrected. If we do, we are as guilty and involved as much as anyone can possibly be. [For if] I conceal a murder, a theft, an evil practice, a corruption, a treacherous act, I will certainly be entangled in these crimes in both God's sight as well as man's. Therefore, what we have said, that we ought to cover our neighbors' sins by means of charity, does not prevent us from declaring the truth[40] when it is necessary, or when we are required, for it is good so to do.

Now there is another vicious extremity which consists in our willingness to broadcast evil which ought to be quietly corrected without making a lot of noise. It sometimes originates from enmity, sometimes from ambition, [and] sometimes from a foolish pride[41] to flaunt ourselves. Take enmity, for under the pretext of zealously wanting to chastise vices and not being able to tolerate offenses against God, we lie in wait for those whom we hate and against whom we carry grudges, and if we find [an occasion] to criticize and censure them, immediately we level the accusation. And we improperly abuse the name of God. Pretending to be zealous, we really only want to entrap our enemies. People also see our malice in the fact that once we have cited a vice in someone we hate, we carry it to one of our friends and dwell on it as long as we can with inordinate measure. Who fails to see our lack of affection and [the fact] that it isn't against vices and sins that we make war, but the persons [involved]? That can be so easily seen. Therefore let us learn that once we have uncovered vices and sins, it is essential for our hearts to be pure and clean of all ill will, and that we be able to confess before God that we desire both the health[42] and welfare of whomever we are accusing. That is one point.

---

[40]le mal.
[41]cupidité.
[42]le salut.

Next, we must guard against all foolish ambition, as I have mentioned, that we may not attempt to make a spectacle of ourselves before men, as there are those who seek to sanctify themselves in crying and bringing charges against others. As soon as they see something, they have to level a charge. They have an inordinate need for others to acknowledge, "O! There is a zealous man." In the meanwhile, only their foolish pride has been revealed. For this reason, God often chastises such pride, since they think that insofar as they have vigorously caught others, they are saints and demiangels. In the meantime, they permit[43] themselves a considerable leeway,[44] and when they have transgressed more than those whom they have accused, they want people to forgive them. And why? Because they have so intensely reprimanded others. Indeed, some are not even ashamed to say, "What? Wasn't I vigorous in my reprimanding? Besides, when I have lived so uprightly myself, how can I endure evil in others?" Alas, if you cannot endure evil in others, how do you hope to endure it in yourself? If you had a single drop of kindness, wouldn't you hate vice in yourself as much as in others? Consequently, when we complain against our neighbors in order to blame[45] them, let us be reminded to be free of all ambition. If we want to uncover the evil which we have perceived in someone else, let us truly be so governed as to begin with ourselves. If we want to condemn vices, let us minutely examine[46] ourselves in order to blame ourselves and then we [can] come to our neighbors. That is the order we must adopt to proceed in the way God approves.

Now let us note that in general God has condemned here all [forms of] abuse and slander to the extent that if we open our mouths to vilify in any way our neighbors, we are guilty of [bearing] false witness in God's sight. Now this doesn't mean that we ought to conceal recognized evil. For all that we have thus far shown under the guise of covering sins implies that we must not tolerate flatteries or lies. Equally, we must not call "black" "white" under the pretext that we are forbidden to offend anyone. And this is readily observed. For there are a number who would especially like to see nothing condemned and who would even approve of disguising the language. [For example], a thief should be called

[43]se dispensent-permettent.
[44]à beaucoup de maux.
[45]redarguer-blâmer.
[46]espluchions-épluchions.

by another title and crimes should not be condemned under their proper names. We know that. Moreover, when it comes to blaming the guilty parties who have not only offended God but who are responsible for corrupting everything else, who constitute an infection that contaminates everything, if we want to convict[47] them and proceed in the vigorous manner we must, immediately some of these fastidious people will become angry. Alas! Does it have to be taken as far as the highest court[48] whenever anyone wants to report crimes? We know that blasphemies are rampant. We know that impiety against God and his Word is totally manifest. We know of rebellions that could not be more shameful. We know of scandals that are so monstrous[49] that it is impossible to tolerate them, unless [of course] you want to betray God. And indeed we make an outcry. And how are we answered? "The gospel teaches that the world is to be won through gentleness. Didn't Jesus Christ call sinners to himself in complete kindness, pardoning their faults? Therefore shouldn't those who preach the gospel use his approach?" That [is how they reply]! As if Jesus Christ wanted us to abuse his grace in order for Satan to set up his reign, for vices to be in vogue, for people to hide them, and for them not to be condemned. On the contrary, he says[50] that by means of the gospel he exercises a jurisdiction which condemns the whole world. That is what he advances[51] (once we have shown our turpitude) in order to confound us thoroughly with shame, that we might not possess any refuge save his pure grace and be humbled within.

Thus we carefully note that we are forbidden to slander our neighbors either by means of hate or ill will[52]; but at the same time we are conversely commanded to reprimand[53] evil and, to the best of our ability, to convince,[54] in a vigorous manner, those who have fallen by their wrong, in order to attempt if we can to reroute them toward the good and warn others that they might not be corrupted by bad examples. This is better understood if, on the one hand, we keep in mind the passage of our Lord Jesus

[47] redarguer.
[48] la chaire.
[49] enorme-monstreux.
[50] John 3:18–19?
[51] pretend-allegue.
[52] mauvaise affection.
[53] blasmer-blâmer.
[54] redarguer.

Christ when he says, "Whoever calls his neighbor a 'fool' shall be guilty of a fire of Gehenna; whoever is only angry with him is already damnable."[55] On the other hand, it is said that we should expose the unfruitful works of darkness and should abhor evil. For Saint Paul himself says, when writing to the Corinthians, that if a gospel is preached as it ought to be, those who hear it will be constrained to give glory to God and, casting themselves to the ground, will be ashamed of their sins.[56] And why? Because they have been brought to the light where previously they had been hiding. Formerly their vices were not known, [but now] they realize that they are libelous before God, and it is no longer a question of wanting to be hid. Consequently, when I growl with ill will against my neighbor, although people cannot even accuse me of calling him wayward, or a fool, but [can only say] that I simply shook my head, or raised my eyebrows[57] upon meeting him, that is [bearing] false witness in God's sight. And why? Because I am scorning my neighbor; I am also hoping to cast aspersion on him. And what has incited me to do so? An ill will that I have conceived against him.

Now on the contrary, if I want to warn my neighbor and seek his welfare and [want to show him] that I am not motivated by any sinister intention, but [only want] to procure his salvation to the best of my ability, I can say, "Look at yourself, my unfortunate friend. It appears that you want to sell out to Satan. Is that what you wish, to be captive under this accursed bondage? You clearly demonstrate that you are insane and enraged not to want to receive any admonition of any sort. Do you really have to perish in such a miserable way? Go on, my unhappy wretch, [but] everyone ought to spit in your face." I can say all of that to a man and not hurt him. And why? For that is the only way I can redirect him. When I see that Satan has hardened him to the extent that only great hammer blows can awaken him, I can proceed with such vehemence, which is also why I strive to enumerate[58] his faults. For what is my purpose in exposing [them] except that he might be forgiven by God and no longer be slandered [for them] in the world's eyes.

It hurts me to see people point their finger at such a person, for

[55]Matt. 5:22.
[56]See Eph. 5:11; I Cor. 14:25f.
[57]"... ou fait quelque nicquet...:" *CO* 26.366.
[58]couvrir.

him to be held in shame by everyone, as on a scaffold[59] exposed to every [form of] ignominy. That pains me, but nevertheless I strive to put him back on the right path. Such action does not produce harm. Nevertheless, it is inappropriate to loosen the reins on too excessive a reprimand.[60] For although we may be nobly inspired and free of ill will, we can easily fail if we are too eager to find fault.[61] That is also why Saint Paul[62] purposely admonishes us to reprove (with forebearance) those who have fallen. And why? Remember that you can also [as] easily stumble. Therefore let us use kindness and forbearance toward our neighbors, as, under similar conditions, we would want them to do [the same] toward us. But whatever the case, may we speak about vices without disguising anything, and may we vigorously endeavor to correct those who have fallen in accordance with their capacity [to bear it], in accordance with their nature as we observe it. And may charity and brotherly love inspire us to that end. For when we pray for God to guide and govern us in that enterprise by his Holy Spirit, people cannot take offense at what has been said openly with charity. Consequently, that is how we have to keep this commandment, that is, not to open our mouth in order to say a single derogatory word out of enmity, but rather to reprove in simplicity those who have fallen in the same way that, under similar circumstances, we would want others to correct us. When we make use of this equit[able principle], we avoid bearing false witness against our neighbors.

In addition, let us note that when *duplicity*[63] is mentioned, it isn't simply that we are forbidden to invent and fabricate a lie, that what we say may be ventured without any pretext, but if we maliciously pervert something not bad in itself, that is what constitutes false witnessing. Like those who testified against our Lord Jesus Christ when he said, "Destroy this temple and in three days I will raise it again."[64] That was bearing false witness, although to be certain Jesus Christ did speak in that way, that is, he did utter those words with his mouth. Why [then] are they who recited those words called false testifiers? The reason is that they changed the Son of God's meaning into something other than what he said,

---

[59]un eschaffaut-tréteau.
[60]une aigreur.
[61]redarguer-blâmer.
[62]See Gal. 6:1.
[63]de faussetté.
[64]Matt. 26:60–61.

and sought to accuse him of madness (as people say), and to charge him with a horrible calumny, as if he had spoken of the physical temple of Jerusalem. [Actually] he was speaking about his body which is truly the temple in which the fullness of divinity dwells,[65] for he is God manifested in flesh. Consequently we see, in short, that the duplicity which God condemns here is not simply our inventing a lie, or our fabricating something which was never done or said, or our promulgating some fable and goodness knows what else, rather we are guilty of bearing false witness whenever we maliciously misconstrue a statement which was originally quite innocent and turn it into something evil. For example, there are some who are so peevish that as soon as they perceive something which displeases them, even though it may not be entirely bad or [even] against God, nevertheless they are ready to level an accusation: "O, Mr. So-and-So has done such-and-such!" I don't care what it is, however small a fault, but what was [once] a virtue becomes a vice.

When we corrupt, with [so much as] a single word, anything innocently said, that puts a man under attack; it hurts him and his good reputation. Therefore, we are guilty of bearing false witness not only when we invent what has never been said or done, but whenever we change into evil, through any subtle sophistry, or any wicked and oblique means, that which was originally innocent. For (as I have said) that is sometimes done when people are too eager to reprove and are so peevish that, of necessity, everything to them must be changed into evil.

Now it is said, according to Saint Paul,[66] that charity is not suspicious, thus it is essential for us to know evil before we condemn it. It is true that sometimes we can be mistaken in our judgments about good and evil, but when there are signs and indicators that things are quite in the open, for us to say, "There, that was done badly!" only indicates that we are still too inclined to find vice. And above all, if we possess a malignant nature that [enjoys] corroding and slandering where such is not justified, surely we stand condemned as false testifiers in God's sight.

Now if those who proceed in this manner, but do so on too strict a basis, are condemned, what about those whose hate is open, who would like to distort what[ever] has been done or said, although it may have been quite innocent and have lacked any

[65]See Col. 2:9.
[66]I Cor. 13:5.

notorious qualities? If they are going to corrupt that or demean it with their wicked statements, are they not false witnesses in God's sight? Consequently, let us learn, in brief, so to procure both the honor and welfare of our neighbors that this concern may continually guide our speaking, whether we happen to be reproving them or confronting them with their vices, in order that they might be purified of them. And let those who might become seduced and debauched by their own bad examples be rebuked. Nevertheless, may we always keep this end in mind, to secure their salvation and welfare to the best of our ability and always to observe this measure: not to libel anyone to the extent that they lose courage. Rather, insofar as we can, we ought, before God and men, to intern the vices of those who are attempting to reduce their own sins and who are ashamed of the possibility of running over with all [manner of] evil. That is what we must procure.

Now if we want to observe what this text contains, we need to consider a higher principle, that is to consider why God created our tongues and why he gave us speech, the reason being that we might be able to communicate with each other.[67] Now what is the purpose of human communication if it isn't our mutual support in charity? Consequently, then, it is essential for us to learn to bridle our tongues to the extent that the union which God commands us may constantly be nurtured as much as possible. And that is why Saint James employs such vehemence when he speaks of evil reports. He says that the tongue, which is such a little member, or such a small piece of flesh, can start such a fire as to ravage the largest forests in the world.[68] Therefore let us come back to our principle, knowing that God provided us with a unique gift when he gave us a means of being able to communicate with each other. So on the one hand men's affections may be hidden, but on the other the tongue exists to reveal our hearts. Therefore let us be encouraged[69] to use such a gift and not soil it with our vices and deplorableness. And seeing that God has given it to us for the purpose of nurturing tender love and fraternity with each other, may we not abuse it in order to gossip and hustle about here and there, so perverting our speech as to poison ourselves against each other. That is the principle to which we must return.

---

[67]This higher principle does not form part of Calvin's discussion in the *Institutes* 2.8.47–48, or the Comm. *Four Books of Moses,* vol. 3, pp. 179–81; *CO* 24.713–14.
[68]See James 3:5–6.
[69]advisons-"let us advise ourselves," or "let us be warned."

Now once we have grasped, in general, how to avoid this crime of bearing false witness—since it is such a difficult task to restrain our tongues—let us all the more diligently strive to do it. We know how easily scores of deplorable words escape us, and, because we are so accustomed to doing it, that even when we speak at random without thinking, it seems to us that such [behavior] is not a vice in God's sight. Now let us note that if by nature we are too inclined to speak indiscreetly and heap blame and scandal on our neighbors, so much the more then is it essential for us to take the trouble to subdue our tongues and restrain them. For if we are given to such a sin, it will not serve us as an excuse before God. But once we have recognized that we are guilty of a particular vice, rather than being flattered by it, it is appropriate [instead] to sigh for grief, saying, "Alas! I see that I am dominated by this evil, therefore I must battle that much more virtuously and force myself by the grace of my God to come to that point where I repress a thing once I see that God condemns it." Uppermost, let us remember the warning that is made in conjunction with it. For when Saint Paul[70] says that the ungodly, the drunkards, the thieves, and the murderers will not inherit the kingdom of God, he also readily adds "slanderers," whom he banishes from all hope of life and salvation. When we hear that, is it any longer a question of our covering ourselves with leaves in order to be convinced that it is wrong to slander our neighbors? Do we think that the warning which God uttered through the mouth of Saint Paul was to startle little children and that it will not be executed on those who want to be exempt in [their] scorn of him? Therefore let us work in this life keeping that in mind, and above all let us make a comparison (for the end) that if God wills for the good reputation of our neighbors to be respected by us and forbids us so sternly to find fault with anyone, or bring up any slander that would denigrate a person's honor, what about himself! Are we not a hundred times more obligated to maintain the honor of God, especially in light of the fact that we are unable to bring him any profit and are not particularly committed to preserving men's honor in its entirety?

Therefore let us be on guard lest we bear false witness against God. [For] as Saint Paul[71] says, those who corrupt the purity of

[70]I Cor. 6:10.
[71]See I Cor. 15:15.

the gospel are guilty of bearing false witness against God, not against men. What must we do then? Let the truth of God be maintained by us, and let us proceed to that end with such openness that when we see a good doctrine we might adopt[72] and support it, knowing that by this means God establishes us as his procurers. Thus when I see truth oppressed, to the best of my ability, I must not tolerate it. Why? [Because] God calls me in his name to see to it[73] that lies are suppressed. And above all this applies with respect to the doctrine of salvation. For when we see that the doctrine might be falsified and that people want to leven it in order to overwhelm men with falsehood and lies, then that is when we must become true zealots in order to prevent those who bear false witness against God from enjoying vogue, [especially], as I have mentioned, if we do not want to consent with them and be accomplices. Finally, let us learn that when we live with men in such simplicity that people cannot reproach us for wanting to denigrate anyone, either by calumny, or lies, or slander, we ought also maintain this same zeal with respect to God, that his truth [may] abide in its fullness and that it may be maintained in order for his reign to be active in our midst. That, in essence, is what we have to keep in mind in this commandment.[74]

[72]portions.

[73]procurer.

[74]Golding's translation concludes this sermon with the following exhortation: "Nowe let us kneele down in the presence of our good God with acknowledgement of our faultes, praying him to make us perceive them better than we have done, and to leade us more and more to such repentance, as we may learne to bethinke us of our sinnes, to be sorie for them, and to mislike of them, that having obtained forgiveness of them, we may learne to direct our life according to his holy commandementes, so as he may be honored of us with true obedience, and not onely with confession of the mouth. That it may please him to graunt this grace, not onely to us, but also to all people & nations of the earth, etc." *Sermons Upon the Fifth Book of Moses*, trans. Golding, p. 241. Cf. Calvin, *Sermons sur les dix commandemens*, 1557 ed., pp. 162–63.

Sermon Twelve[2]

Deuteronomy 5:21[3]

It would seem at first sight that this commandment here was superfluous, seeing that God, having condemned robbery and adultery, intended thereby to repress evil affections. For we have explained that it is essential to illumine these commandments according to God's nature.[4] And we know that the proper office of God is to fathom men's hearts that he might know their most profound, secret, and hidden thoughts. Thus it follows that if God forbids men to be thieves and adulterers that he also intends to bridle their affections and cupidity. And in fact, if this were not the case, God would not have any more power than men when it comes to making laws. For when a terrestrial man condemns [the

[1]N. in *CO:* "This sermon corresponds to the twelfth in the 1562 collection,pp. 247–269." *CO* 26.371.

[2]The original title: "The Eleventh Sermon on Chapter 5:21." *CO* 26.371.

[3]Cf. also Calvin's development of the Tenth Commandment in the *Institutes* 2.8.49–50; Comm. *Four Books of Moses*, vol. 3, pp. 186–89; *CO* 24.717–20; *Catechism, CO* 6.76.

[4]See the *Institutes* 2.8.6–7.

219

act of] adultery, he also condemns the principle. If a person's intention appears evil, he will be punished.[5] If the law of God amounted to little more than that, it would hardly entail any importance. For it would not constitute that civil order which is necessary in order for us to maintain honest government among ourselves. And far more, as we know, Saint Paul[6] says that the law cannot be kept without a pure conscience, without a genuine faith. If such integrity is required for faithfully keeping the law of God, it follows that under the word *adultery* all wicked affections are prohibited, the same being true of the word *robbery*. We can also cite[7] the authority of our Lord Jesus Christ who is the faithful expositor of the law. For it is by his Spirit that Moses and all the prophets spoke. Therefore why is it now added that we should not covet? If he has already spoken of all wicked lusts, why was it necessary for it to be reiterated further? But we have to note that in this passage God did not intend to repress evil affections which are conclusively recognized as such by us, but those other affections which incite us, although we may neither adhere nor consent to them. These require longer and simpler exposition. Sometimes covetousness emerges in the human will when I see my neighbor's property, and am tempted with avarice [to have it], and harbor such a temptation within myself that I drop my guard. Such sin triumphs so forcefully over me that I am totally resolved to want that for myself. That is a kind of covetousness that involves the will every time. For men consent to sin, and, if they had the means, they would put into practice the evil intentions that they have conceived. Now such wicked lusts have already been forbidden when it was said: "You shall not steal. You shall not be adulterers." For therein God not only prohibited the acts of adultery and robbery, but also the coveting of another man's wife, or property, or substance. But there are other lusts to which we neither adhere nor give consent, which nevertheless excite and lure us and make us aware of an evil inclination within [ourselves] which is contrary to God and rebellious against the righteousness which the law contains. Such lusts are forbidden in this passage. Thus we see that God, having condemned every evil will and affection, quite reasonably[8] adds that this does not yet constitute the perfec-

---

[5]The French reads: "if a will appears evil, it will be punished." *CO* 26.371.
[6]See I Tim. 1:15.
[7]amener-citer.
[8]non sans cause.

tion which he requires, rather it is necessary for us to recognize every affection that excites us toward evil, even though in ourselves we may not resolve [to do] anything. For we must not stop there. If a lust is only passed up by us for want of courage, that is still a committed sin, [and] we are guilty before God. Thus we see the [level of] integrity that is required in this passage. For after forbidding evil intentions, our Lord adds that it is necessary for minds and senses to be so enclosed by his fear and aflame with a love and desire to walk in all holiness that we may not be lured or pushed about here and there by an[y] evil passion to covet either another man's property or his wife.

Insofar, then, as we understand God's intention, let us now be advised as to what he expects of us, for the law ought to be [like] a mirror[9] for us in which we contemplate our poverty. And once we have come to perceive our duty, let us realize that we are condemned if we do not approach the perfection to which God calls us. That is what we have to insist on to derive profit from this last commandment of the law. And in order that we might be that much more attentive to it and realize that it is a doctrine that highly deserves the devotion of all our study to it, let us remember what Saint Paul says, who being reputed as a great and wise theologian,[10] having been nutured in the law of God from his childhood, was nevertheless so blind that he did not understand that our poverty was part of the law of God until he was converted and our Lord Jesus Christ illumined him by his gospel to the end that he understood where the law of God must lead us.[11] That is Saint Paul, mind you, who was instructed in such a way that he was [held] in great reputation among men, although not among pagans, to the extent that he was a philosopher, but one who had been instructed in the law of God. And if we look at his life, he maintains that he was blameless before men.[12] That is Saint Paul, a holy and wise person, according to common esteem, but nonetheless a poor beast with respect to the law of God. And why? He says that he considered himself esteemed in life and thought himself quite righteous in God's eyes and did not perceive that he stood in need of the grace which God offers to all sinners. For he abstained from adultery, he refrained from robbery and similar

---

[9]One of Calvin's favorite metaphors for the law. Cf. *Institutes* 2.7.7.
[10]docteur.
[11]See Rom. 7:7, 9; Acts 22:3; Gal. 1:13; Phil. 3:5–6.
[12]Phil. 3:6.

things. Besides, he did not display evil that people [could] perceive and that was recognized by them, so much so that he justified himself in his imagination. Now in the end when God finally had pity on him, he opened his eyes and enabled him to understand what this last commandment contains: *You shall not covet.* That is how Saint Paul began to learn the law in which formerly he had been a doctor. Having made his occupation the law in which he had been taught from his earliest years, Saint Paul says that until he had truly meditated on the meaning of these words, he had passed [over them] without realizing their impact;[13] he savored neither the force nor the virtue of the law; he did not know that they referred to sin so as to condemn him before God, in order that he might base his refuge on God's mercy in which the hope of our salvation rests and must be founded.[14]

Seeing then that Saint Paul did not understand that this was the meaning of the law and would not have correctly grasped it apart from these words, let us be warned to apply ourselves to that end all the more earnestly. And insofar as throughout his life until his conversion he was so blind that he could not understand these words, so much the more ought we be attentive to them as I have already explained. For we are not more prompt[15] than he, but it is necessary for God through his Holy Spirit to reveal to us the nature of this covetousness which he has condemned in this passage.

Now beyond this, we confront another admonition which we need to hear. For the devil attempted to obscure this principle to the extent that people did not perceive God's intention, but thoughtlessly became content with every evil concupiscence which appears as sin and which confounds one. They even confined this word *covetousness* to all evil affections which entail a completely resolute will, which is contrary to Moses' natural sense. Look at what has happened in the papacy. For although the papists cannot deny that being solicitous of and goaded by an evil desire is a damnable vice, one that proceeds from original sin and the cor-

---

[13]" ... ,qu'il a passé par dessus la braise (comme on dit) .... " *CO* 26.373.

[14]The argument of the above paragraph may be clarified by consulting Rom. 7:7–9 and its context. Calvin also refers to this text in his Comm. *Four Books of Moses,* vol. 3, p. 187; *CO* 24.719: "Hence Paul gathers from this Commandment, that the whole 'Law is spiritual,' ... because God, by His condemnation of lust, sufficiently shewed that He not only imposed obedience on our hands and feet, but also put restraint upon our minds, lest they should desire to do what is unlawful."

[15]habiles-prompts.

ruption which we have reaped from our father Adam, nevertheless they imagine that after baptism this no longer remains as
sin.[16] If a man is tempted to doubt the promises of God, or murmur against him, or scorn him, if when afflicted a man accuses
God of injustice and cruelty, that isn't sin, say the papists. And this
isn't simply the view of petty officials, but it is the general resolu-
tion [that reigns] in all their diabolical synagogues. There is no
synagogue in the papacy where it hasn't been received as an article of faith that when a man is goaded and excited by some wicked
lust he does not sin.[17] If he is tempted to murder, to poison, to
commit adultery, and to do all the crimes and monstrous offenses
of the world, provided he neither consents nor assents[18] to them
(for those are the two words they use), that is to say, provided he
does not resolve to carry out his wicked intention and does not
derive pleasure from it, none of that is sin; it is only a moral combat. Thus in that way we demonstrate that we are valiant champions and that sin does not reign in us.

Now it is true that believers clearly demonstrate that the Spirit
of God rules in them when they repulse such temptations and
hold themselves in check, when they are captive to self and resist
such things insofar as they know that they are contrary to God

---

[16]See the Fifth Session of the Council of Trent, June 17, 1546, "Decree Concerning Original Sin." Calvin appears to have in mind the statement: "If any one
denies that by the grace of our Lord Jesus Christ which is conferred in baptism,
the guilt of original sin is remitted; or says that the whole of that which belongs to
the essence of sin is not taken away, but says that it is only canceled or not imputed, let him be anathema. For in those who are born again God hates nothing, . . . " *Councils and Decrees of the Council of Trent,* trans. Rev. H. J. Schroeder, O.
P. (St. Louis: B. Herder Book Co., [1941], 1960), p. 23. (Hereafter cited as *Decrees
Council of Trent,* trans. Schroeder.) See also Calvin's rebuttal of this decree in *Acts of
the Council of Trent, With the Antidote* in *Tracts and Treatises In Defense of the Reformed
Faith,* trans. Henry Beveridge, ed. Thomas F. Torrance (3 vols.: Grand Rapids:
Wm. B. Eerdmans Publishing Company, [1851], 1958), vol. 3, pp. 85–89.
(Hereafter cited as *Antidote, Tracts and Treatises,* vol. 3).

[17]Ibid. "But this holy council perceives and confesses that in the one baptized
there remains concupiscence or an inclination to sin, which, since it is left for us to
wrestle with, cannot injure those who do not acquiesce but resist manfully by the
grace of Jesus Christ; indeed, he who shall have striven lawfully shall be crowned.
This concupiscence, which the Apostle sometimes calls sin, the holy council declares the Catholic Church has never understood to be called sin in the sense that it
is truly and properly sin in those born again, but in the sense that it is of sin and
inclines to sin." Cf. Calvin's rejoinder in *Antidote, Tracts and Treatises,* vol. 3, pp.
85–89.

[18]Cf. *Institutes* 2.8.58, where Calvin criticizes the Catholic distinction between
"mortal" and "venial" sins. "Here is their definition: venial sin is desire without
deliberate assent, which does not long remain in the heart." *LCC* 20.421.

and that he condemns them. Clearly this shows that God has given us victory over sin, and that his virtue resides in us, and that we are bold champions able to combat Satan. But this does not mean that we can uproot sin and fully redeem ourselves, as if we no longer possessed any taint or blot. Alas! The reverse is true. For on the one hand, it is true that we have to praise God, since he provides us the grace for overcoming all evil affections through his Holy Spirit, but nevertheless we must equally repine in complete humility, recognizing that we are feeble on our part and that, if he had not taken pity on us, we would only have an evil conscience within us which would provoke his vengeance against us and we should indeed merit to be wholly destroyed by him.

Moreover, it was necessary for God to uncover the shame of the papacy and to show that its greatest clerics are more stupid than its poorest unbelievers who have never heard one word of holy Scripture. Why? For it is necessary to lay hold of what the law contains. It is said that the summary of the law is: "That we should love God with all our heart, with all our mind, with all our understanding, and with all our strength."[19] Had it said: "You shall love God with all your heart," then we could conclude that sin only exists where we have specifically willed [to do something]. For the heart in holy Scripture, although it sometimes signifies intelligence, refers to the will. Therefore one could cite the sophistry, that we should love God with all our heart, provided our wills are not contrary to the good. That's enough to justify us in God's sight. For one could substitute the will for evil affections, and thus it would seem that wicked lusts which goad and excite us, but which do not control us, are not included under sin. But when we expand "with all your heart" to include "with all your thoughts" and "with all your strength,"[20] isn't then a part of my intelligence already corrupt if I conceive of some wicked lust of adultery or robbery, even though I do not engage in either at all? Now tell me if I love God with all my heart when a part of my intelligence is opposed to him? It is not a matter of the heart, as I have already explained, but a matter of the power to conceptualize,[21] a power that lies in the human soul. Now [if] I display vanity and the fact that neither fear of, nor reverence for, God

---

[19]See Deut. 6:5, Mark 12:29–30. Cf. also Calvin's use of the summary of the law as a principle of interpretation in the *Institutes* 2.8.51.
[20]vertus-forces.
[21]apprehension.

restrain me as they ought, it consequently follows that I am condemned and guilty insofar as I have not fulfilled the commandment to love God. Is there not even a certain aspect of my soul,
which gives itself to thinking first of one thing and then another,
which is opposed to God and his justice?

Consequently we see that wicked and vicious thoughts are condemned and that it is no longer fitting to excuse them that we
might escape punishment from God. Even men who have never
consented to evil with a determined will shall not be excused from
being cursed in God's eyes, if it so pleases him to judge them with
rigor.

At last now we see the true natural sense of this passage and
realize that, with respect to it, we must continually be on guard,
lest we become seduced or abused [by it]. And Saint Paul's example ought that much more spur us on, seeing that he [himself]
confesses that he was ignorant of God's law until our Lord Jesus
Christ illuminated him by his Holy Spirit, in order that he might
perceive what the word *concupiscence* entailed.[22]

Now let us apply what we have discussed to our use and benefit.
In the first place, then, let us realize that in order to serve God
well, it isn't simply a matter of our desiring to do good and to
derive profit from it, rather we have to purge ourselves of all
wicked affections and all corrupt thoughts to the extent that everything within us directs us toward the goal of fully surrendering
ourselves to God. Let us not display that we have been distracted
to turn[23] to one side or the other, but let us be wholly in control
[of ourselves] in order to run without impediments or stopping,
indeed, to run in the way that God shows us, in such a manner as
to be wholly pure. And once we have adequately grasped this, we
must be prepared[24] to be on our guard. For we know how men
lose their way and dissipate[25] their energy. And what is its cause?
The fact that they are content without their host, as people say,
for they explain the law of God according to their imagination,
which seems sufficient to them, provided they have not entertained an evil will and stopped [to carry it out]. In any event, they
say that God does not ascribe all that [as sin]; thereupon, they
walk in wicked lusts and pull a blindfold over their eyes in order

22See Rom. 7:7–9.
23fleschir-tourner.
24advertis.
25se dispensent-se dépensent.

not to be aware of their hidden illusions. Now once men have taken this stand, they will not escape the hand of the heavenly judge. Therefore let us be warned to restrain ourselves in our lusts. For God has not simply condemned evil wills, but equally all lusts that lure us to [do] evil and goad us on. [Therefore] let us proceed in greater fear; let each of us more firmly grasp hold of ourself, especially in light of the fact that there is no part of us that is not infected with sin. Were we to make an examination of all the faculties of our souls, we would find that sin has spread throughout. For just as a man's body is completely infected when poison has claimed it, [so] there is a universal leprosy[26] that permeates[27] our bones, and marrow, and thoughts, and affections, and everything else. Therefore, in view of the fact that our nature is so corrupt, ought we not be that much more vigilant to hold ourselves in check, [especially] since God has condemned through the law every wicked thought that incites us toward evil? For this applies to anything that arouses us and which we realize excites our will, even though the latter may not succumb at all.

Once we grasp this, are we not provided with the occasion for recouping ourselves, in order that we might walk under God's hand with greater care? Consequently, that is how this precept ought to awaken us, instead of our being asleep and indifferent and wanting to be easily justified before God. For it is important for us to realize that such evasions are of no avail. And why? For God continues to condemn wicked lusts, having condemned wicked wills.

Now this ought to serve us in a twofold sense: on the one hand, we ought to pray for God to govern us more ardently by his Holy Spirit and to purge us of all vices and corruptions, and then having prayed that, each of us [ought] to take hold of himself, lest we do violence to our nature, to all our senses, [and] all our desires, seeing that there is nothing but rebellion in us against God's law. For even Saint Paul[28] does not speak of wills alone when he says that men in their perverse nature are enemies of God, but he mentions affections and thoughts. He employs a word that includes the thoughts which we conceive. All that (he says) is at enmity with the law of God. Since this is true, let us realize that even though we may strive with effort to hold ourselves firmly under

[26]ladrerie-lèpre.
[27]occupe.
[28]See Rom. 8:7.

God's check—albeit many wicked lusts may yet plague us—we must [still] grieve over them before God.

That is the first [application to be drawn]: that we make the effort to call upon God in order that he might govern us by his Holy Spirit and that we go to the trouble and force ourselves so to restrain ourselves that Satan may have no entrance and be unable to make a breach and thus gain possession of our hearts. May we repulse him quite some distance. And if we are conscious of a[ny] wayward thought, may we head it off, and bar the gate, and remind ourselves: "It is imperative for your God to rule you completely; let him possess not only your heart, but also your entire senses."

Now for the second [application]. We ought to learn to hold ourselves in judgment,[29] in order to give glory to God, confessing that we are wholly culpable and that if he [should] call us to count, exercising rigor against us, then we would all perish and be destroyed. That is where we have to begin, or we shall not benefit from the law of God as we ought. But at this point one can ask, insofar as God understands human frailty, why doesn't he strengthen us better? Why does he sanction[30] such a stern and austere law? For it seems that God wants to overwhelm us when he forbids wicked lusts and is not satisfied for us to render him the obedience of our wills without adding this last commandment. And that is why scoffers[31] say that God wanted to mock men in his law and that he almost forbade them to scratch themselves after making them itch.

But we need to grapple with this wretched condition of ours in order to see whether both our thoughts and affections, as I have said, are not rebellious against the righteousness of God. We should not be surprised,[32] then, to discover such a combat between the law of God and human desires. And why? Once we have carefully examined[33] all that we are, we will uncover nothing less than complete corruption and damnable vice. For we cannot conceive a single thought that does not incline toward evil. In light of that fact, then, God provides us with a wholly perfect and just rule. Should it not sound like thunder then, just as fire and water

[29]de nous condamner.
[30]fait.
[31]gaudisseurs-bons vivants, railleurs.
[32]esbahissons-ébahissons.
[33]espluché-épulché.

necessarily appear as opposites?[34] For there is less harmony between man's nature and God's righteousness than there is between
fire and water. Therefore, let us not find it strange when we discover that God has accordingly suppressed all our desires. And
when we hear the blasphemies which these railers vomit, as I have
said, let us detest them as monsters. For instead of glorifying God
in his righteousness, they proceed to attack God like wild and enraged beasts. So much then for this matter of human frailty. For
whatever form it takes, we should not be surprised that God has
condemned it in his law. Why? For when God ordains our life and
shows us how we need to live, he does not consider what we are
capable of doing or what our level of strength may be, rather he
considers what we owe him; his concern is for righteousness
whether it is found in us or not. We are God's creatures, ought we
not, therefore, completely give ourselves to his service? Surely, we
must. The logic is preemptory. And although men may inevita-
bly[35] snarl [at it], they will always be convinced that since they
belong to God, they must dedicate to him their whole mind,[36]
their whole affections, and all that constitutes their body and soul.

In any event, let us carefully note that we are unable to justify
ourselves. The reason being our own malice. [One could say that]
we inherit[37] this from Adam. But that does not follow. For although we might be captive to sin, owing to this wretched servitude, and are impeded from doing good, being compelled in
everything to do evil, nonetheless the root is in us. And each of us
should be conscious of guilt, so that we cannot say that we were
pushed into it by force, for we are each led and goaded there by
our own concupiscence. Therefore we are without any further excuse. Thereby we see that it is no longer a question of measuring
the law according to our strength and ability. Why? [Because] God
does not weigh (as I have said) what we are capable of doing and
what our strength suggests, but he keeps in mind the extent to
which we are obligated to him: he equally considers that larger
probity that lies beyond us. That is what we have to observe.

Now this is [precisely] what the papists abuse. For they maintain

[34]"... quelle repugnance il y a?" *CO* 26.378.
[35]beau.
[36]sens.
[37]tirons.

the principle that the law of God is not impossible for men [to do].[38] It is amazing that they have been so misled,[39] that the devil has bewitched them in this way. For it is such a clear and well-known doctrine in all the holy Scripture that men are forever[40] condemned by the law and that they must take refuge in God's pure mercy. When Saint Paul wants to prove that men, as sinners, are cursed and that not a one of them is just, what argument does he use? He cites this passage from Moses: "Cursed are they who do not fulfill the contents of the Law."[41]

Now at first it would seem that Saint Paul's argument is weak and that the reference he has cited is impertinent. Indeed, it is written that all those who break the law of God are cursed,[42] but it does not follow that all mankind are thereby cursed. For if a man keeps the law and fulfills it, he is exempt from this sentence of condemnation. The result would be that some have observed the law and therefore not all are cursed. But Saint Paul presupposes that the law is impossible [to keep]. And had he not presupposed that, he would have spoken as a man destitute of sense and reason.

Thus we see that the papists maintain a maxim that is completely contrary to the Spirit of God, who in turn has totally stupefied them to the extent that they have failed to grasp the ABC's of faith and the Christian religion. Thus let us carefully mark that where the law of God is involved, we must not measure it according to our abilities, or weigh it in terms of what we can do, but we must keep in mind what we owe God. But then they say, what means[43] is left for us to do? For it seems to them that everyone will be damned. Indeed, it is true that we are damned if

[38]See the *Institutes* 2.7.5, where Calvin discusses Jerome's opinion to this effect. See also the Sixth Session of the Council of Trent, January 13, 1547, Chapter 11. "The Observance of the Commandments and the Necessity and Possibility Thereof," *Decrees Council of Trent*, trans. Schroeder, pp. 36–38. See Calvin's reply in the *Antidote, Tracts and Treatises*, vol. 3, pp. 130–35.

[39]forcenez. Huguet, vol. 4, p. 157 defines the verb "forcener" as follows: "Être fou, être furieux, être emporté par la colère, ... "

[40]tousiours.

[41]See Gal. 3:10; Deut. 27:26.

[42]Deut. 27:26. See Calvin's Comm. *Four Books of Moses*, vol. 3, pp. 208–9. Calvin elaborates Deut. 27:26, but at issue is the fact that men cannot keep the law and are therefore under its curse. *CO* 24.9.

[43]moyen-intermédiaire.

we do not seek our salvation in Jesus Christ. For how can we seek God's grace if we are ignorant of our need of it? Men do not willingly beg, for if we think[44] that we possess any righteousness, [then] we will not search for it elsewhere than in ourselves. Therefore, it is imperative that we should be totally stripped of it, that we should be conscious of God's wrath, and conscious [of the fact] that death crowds us. For without that [awareness], we are unable to submit[45] to God in order to obtain mercy. But this [subject] deserves more ample deduction.

In the first place, then, let us carefully remember that whenever we are conscious of any vicious thought within, and [are aware] that our desires are aroused toward evil, we are guilty before God. Now we certainly have the right to ask why. [For example,] if a man were to conceive just one thought—one which he not only does not support, but equally detests even before it needles him— is that sin? For there are thoughts which by no means touch our heart, which leave us unmoved and concerning which we conceive no wicked desire. An idea will come to a man while he is sleeping and haunt[46] him. Though his heart may be moved, does it follow that his desire is tempted? No. When that happens we ought certainly still grieve before God and realize that if we were not held fast by his grace then a door would certainly fall open to Satan who would immediately gain the advantage. We ought still grieve in such a situation, but at all events God does not consider that sin.

Now a second stage appears when in addition solely to imagining something wicked in our mind, something confronts us, and we are moved by it, sensing within it the presence of Satan goading us, causing sin to be conceived. That is to say, although there may not be any consent (as people call [it]), or any deliberate intent to act, nonetheless, in God's sight a damnable sin has been committed.

This calls for specific examples. It is possible for a man contemplating his neighbor's house or some [other] possession to conceive of an imaginary theft and nevertheless in no way to be moved in his heart, nor have the desire to say, "I wish that were mine." His thought moves on and he realizes its vanity. He can't

[44]cuiderons-essayerons.
[45]ranger-soumettre.
[46]voltige.

prevent having thought it, but (as I have already said) although no evil affection may have been intended, God nevertheless reprimands us for our weakness. And we need to humble ourselves to groan and realize that such is still a vice for which we ought to be condemned. For let us consider whether such is found among the angels of paradise. Certainly not. Their righteousness goes to great lengths to answer to God's law. Certainly there is a righteousness of God's (as we have seen in Job)[47] that transcends that of the law, but if the angels of paradise endeavor to keep God's law, then certainly everything that can be done ought to be in order [for us] to be conformed to this rule which is given to us here. In the light of this we see that it remains a vice for which men ought to be condemned, even when they have not entertained an evil idea. But whenever there is a desire, whenever a man says, "I wish I had . . . , " even though he immediately rejects it and does not surrender to it, he is nevertheless guilty of that kind of covetousness which is mentioned here.

Since this is the case, let us learn (as I have said) to be critical of ourselves in everything. Moreover, let us be doubly critical, not only when we have entertained some lust that excites us toward evil, but [equally] when we have indulged[48] a fully thought-out affection, when we have fed a lust in the same way that a pregnant woman carries her child until it is born. Therefore whenever we have thus relaxed our guard against our wicked desires to the point that our wills have succumbed and we have stooped to consent to the evil involved, that (I maintain) constitutes a double condemnation against us. Indeed, we would still be deploring our misery, seeing that two condemnations weigh on our heads, were it not for the fact that God in his infinite goodness upholds us. That is what we must observe.

Now, in any event, it is fitting for us to come to the remedy, for we would be in complete despair and confusion if we did not have God's grace to uphold us.[49] Thus once we have grasped that we are guilty in all kinds of ways, God calls us and points out that although our wicked lusts are sin by nature, he does not want to reckon them as sin against us. What then shall we say? Is a wicked lust reckoned as sin against believers? No. Rather we are dealing

---

[47]See Job 4:18.
[48]eu.
[49]Cf. Calvin's similar but more detailed argument in the *Institutes* 2.7.1–9.

with two different things. For if we consider the nature of vice, it will always be found to be sin, but God forgives it. That is why all these evil lusts are not counted against the faithful, seeing that believers are forgiven them owing to the free goodness of God. Moreover we know that all our stains have been effaced by the blood of our Lord Jesus Christ. And what a strong witness we have to this fact in baptism. For by means of it we possess our spiritual cleansing which purges us of any impurities and pollutions within, in order that we might appear pure and clean before God. Thus, in that manner, our wicked lusts do not count against us.

What is more, even if we have committed mortal sins, they will not be charged against us, seeing that God (as I have said) does not pay regard to them; nevertheless, he expects us to. For if we deceive ourselves and make believe that we have not conceived any wicked desire, then that is sufficient grounds for God to call us to account. And why? For insofar as men flatter themselves, it is fitting for them to be condemned. That is why the devil has plotted so hard to blind[50] men's eyes, making them believe that all these things are not sin. We even see that the papists think that the most grievous sins[51] can be effaced by the sign of the cross, or by sprinkling with holy water. They look upon it as nothing and play with God as they would a little child. On the contrary, whenever we are not only too negligent, but equally inclined to flatter ourselves in our vices, may [all] this come to mind; let us hold up this mirror[52] and take a good look at ourselves. Let us not be deceived. A man can be smudged[53] and people laugh at him while he himself will not see a thing, but let him look in a mirror and see how his face is besmeared and he will hide himself; he will wash it off. Now we need to do the same. For in truth the whole law of God is like a mirror which reflects our filth, its purpose being to confound us and make us ashamed of our shamefulness. But we have to come to this commandment in order to have the right mirror, as we have already explained. For if we only read: "You shall not be a thief, You shall not be a murderer, You shall not be an adulterer," then we would each think that we are innocent. But when we come to this commandment: "You shall not

[50]esblouir-aveugler.
[51]fautes-besoins.
[52]See n. 9 above.
[53]massuré-machuré.

covet," then that provides God with a sharper lancet for not only sounding the bottom of our heart, but all our thoughts and imaginations.[54] Everything within us becomes exposed and brought to consciousness; even what we have not considered sin,[55] God must judge and condemn, unless we have done the same before hand.

Now, notwithstanding, we have to magnify this mercy of our God, seeing that we are guilty in so many ways and that nevertheless he accepts us as righteous. Let us make a comparison here between the righteousness we obtain by means of faith and the curse that is on us. [Concerning the latter] what is our fate?[56] Are we guilty before God of only one offense, or of three, or of a number? Rather we are cast into such an abyss that once we begin to count, quite fittingly we become confused, [for] a hundred thousand sins[57] would not constitute a hundredth part of what we have committed against[58] God. Consequently, we are so guilty that there exists neither an end to nor a measure of our sins. Nevertheless God receives us with such mercy that we are reputed righteous in his sight, as if we possessed full integrity and perfection in ourselves to the extent that it can only be said that we have fulfilled the entire law.

Therefore since God, by virtue of the passion and death[59] of our Lord Jesus Christ [forgives us], let us apprehend the grace which has been bestowed upon us by faith and let us render him the honor of saying, "Lord, it is in thy pure goodness and favor[60] that our salvation rests." Therefore when God forgives us of such an infinite number of offenses and reclothes us in his righteousness, isn't that proof of how much he upholds us?

Consequently whenever the law of God confounds us, not only because our lusts are without number, but [equally because] we are buried under them as if covered by vast mountains, if God seems to deal with us harshly, let us realize that God does not intend to leave us in despair, but as quickly as we are struck down,

---

[54]This statement reveals how extensively Calvin leaned on Rom. 7:7–9 to illuminate the Tenth Commandment. He also used it polemically to reject aspects of the Council of Trent concerning the pervasiveness of sin.

[55]faute.

[56]"Où sommes-nous tous plongez?" *CO* 26.382.

[57]fautes.

[58]devant.

[59]"mort et passion."

[60]gratuite-faveur.

he helps us up. When he sees our frailty, he extends us his hand and calls us to himself and wants us to be comforted, insofar as by his loving kindness[61] our sins are not counted against us. That is why believers do not cease to glorify in [him], although they stand condemned in themselves. For it is imperative to begin by this end: to be totally overwhelmed in order that our Lord might deliver us from the abyss of death and that we might realize that our salvation consists in his pure grace.

In the meanwhile let us walk with care, let us be on the lookout, knowing that when we have truly labored and taken pains to serve God, when on the one hand we have repulsed tempting[62] occasions and have mastered our affections and desires, and on the other hand have sought to repress all of our worthless[63] thoughts, let us not cease to be self-critical[64]; let us always stand in fear. Even though we have gained the victory by God's grace and sin does not reign in us, sin is always there along with some filth and stain. Therefore let us lament and repine to such a degree that it becomes a lasting part of our duty.

We know what Saint Paul says about it, having persevered to the end and having attained an angelic holiness. For he said: "O wretch that I am, who will deliver me from the body of this death?"[65] And why does he consider himself dead, if it isn't sin that he saw?

Moreover, even if we should perceive a million sins within ourselves everyday, let us not become discouraged. [For] we must continually press beyond that. That is why Saint Paul, when exhorting believers to shun vice, does not say: "Let sin have no place in you," but says: "Let sin have no reign!"[66] Certainly he would have preferred for sin to dwell in no one, but since it does, we must not let ourselves feel overwhelmed.[67] For when it is said that sin lives in us, its first purpose serves to admonish us of our miserable condition and then, realizing that every day requires combat, we should that much more ardently flee to our God for help, praying to him that he will fortify us by his strength and by

---

[61]misericorde.
[62]meschantes.
[63]mauvaises.
[64]de nous condamner.
[65]Rom. 7:24.
[66]Rom. 6:12.
[67]desconfits-defaits.

the grace of his Holy Spirit which he has given us in the name of
our Lord Jesus.[68]

---

[68]Golding's translation concludes this sermon with the following exhortation:
"Nowe let us fall downe in the presence of our good God, with acknowledgment of
our faultes, praying him to make us feele them better, and that wee may learne to
frame our lives to the obeying of him, which beholdeth not onely our outward
woorkers, intentes and affections: but also even all our thoughtes and conceites.
And for as much as wee can not attaine to such perfection out of hand: let [us
beseeche God] that all the same may bee an occasion to humble us; and therewithall to stirre us up continually to fight lustilier, so as everie of us may inforce
himselfe to correct the vices that are in his nature, untill our Lorde having rid us
from this corrupt fleshe, doe clothe us againe with his own righteousness, and
fashion us al wholly like to his glorious image. That it may please him to graunt
this grace, not onely to us but also to all people, Etc." *Sermons Upon the Fifth Book of
Moses*, trans. Golding, p. 247. Cf. Calvin, *Sermons sur les dix commandemens*, 1557 ed.,
p. 177.

Tuesday, July 16, 1555[1]

Sermon Thirteen[2]

Deuteronomy 5:22[3]

Because we cannot find a better excuse for our cowardness[4] and
rebellion against God than to blame it on ignorance, [our temptation is] to be eternally grateful for such a pretext, pretending that
we do not hear what God is saying to us, or in any event that he
isn't addressing us, or that his voice is too removed for us to hear
him. But aware of such malice, God determined to provide[5] everything men can cite[6] in order to deprive them of any further
excuse.[7] And that is why in publishing his law he willed that the
doctrine which it contains should be announced loud and clear,
indeed, not merely spoken to three or four, *but to all the people*, the

[1]N. in *CO:* "This sermon corresponds to the thirteenth in the 1562 collection,
pp. 270-91." *CO* 26.384.
[2]The original title: "The Twelfth Sermon on Chapter 5:22." *CO* 26.384.
[3]See also Calvin's Comm. *Four Books of Moses*, vol. 1, pp. 330–36; *CO* 24.203–5;
for additional exposition on this text.
[4]lascheté-lâcheté.
[5]prevenir-pourvoir.
[6]amener-citer.
[7]deffense.

237

great and the small without exception. Moreover, he willed for the law to be written [down] and preserved[8] that it might not simply serve one age, but that it might retain its vigor and authority until the end of the world. And that is why it is said in this passage *that God spoke in a loud voice.*[9]

Now by means of this Moses shows that the law is not a hidden doctrine and that it is inappropriate for us to argue[10] that we are not scholarly enough [to grasp it], for [it is] not without cause [that] God thus exalted his voice when he wanted to regulate men's lives. And in particular he adds, *that this was* [spoken] *to all the assembly.* It's as if he were saying: "It is true that God has chosen from among you [certain] people to govern and has given them intelligence; nevertheless, he wants his law to be understood by the most uncultivated[11] and ignorant, and serve as a common wisdom for all." That is one of the points we want to emphasize here.

The second is *that God added nothing* after these ten precepts.[12] The brevity with which Moses admonishes the people ought to give us courage to receive what God says to us. For if he had set before us numerous volumes, we would be able to retort that all our life would not suffice for such a study. Therefore God used brevity when he gave us his Word; there are no more than ten statements. We can count on our fingers all the instruction that is required of our life. Furthermore, Moses means that, insofar as God gave us a specific code[13] and did not intend for anything to be added to what he said, it is important for us to cling to that; it is unlawful for creatures to add anything to it. That is the second point.

For the third he proposes again[14] what he has said, namely *that in publishing his law, God spoke out of the midst of the cloud, that the mountain was smoking, that there were flames of fire* and flashes of

---

[8]demeurast.

[9]See Calvin's discussion of this "loud" or "great" voice in his Comm. *Four Books of Moses*, vol. 1, pp. 330–33; CO 24.205. Its purpose was to validate the authority of the law and to humble its hearers that they might more readily submit to God.

[10]allegue.

[11]rudes-incultés.

[12]Cf. Comm. *Four Books of Moses*, vol. 1, p. 333; CO 24.205: "When Moses states that God 'added no more,' he signifies that a perfect rule of life is contained in the ten commandments, and that, when their instruction is fully received, the whole body of wisdom is attainted to, so that the people need seek to know no more; . . . "

[13]reigle.

[14]derechef.

lightning all about. Now what is the meaning of all that? That the doctrine might possess more majesty; that men might be led to humble themselves before God in complete reverence; [and that] they might fully yield themselves to his Word and obey it. Those are the three notable points that are affirmed here by Moses before going on to the rest.

Now with respect to the first, let us emphasize[15] what has already been touched on, namely, *that God spoke loud and clear,* and not to a handful of people, but *in general to all the people,* its purpose being that we might realize that the Word of God will [always] be clear and distinct to us, provided we do not knowingly turn a deaf ear. It is true that our senses are so feeble that we could never understand a single word that God says to us, unless we are illumined by his Holy Spirit; for carnal men cannot comprehend heavenly things. They are, accordingly, too high for us. But if our blindness isn't the source of sin[16] and vice, what is? In any event, the truth of God, with respect to itself and its nature, is clear enough and completely obvious; consequently, let us not allege that it is obscure.

Moreover, what should be done if we want God to help us profit in his Word? Let us be humble and meek,[17] for it is not in vain that he has promised to instruct the humble. Therefore let us not confide in our own strength,[18] coming [before him] with presumption and pride, believing[19] [ourselves] to be sufficiently capable of passing judgment on what is said to us, but rather let us ask God to open our eyes and to extend us his hand, and let us acknowledge that we do not possess the dexterity to benefit in his school unless he makes it possible. When that happens, we do not have to doubt that God's Word will become evident to us and that we shall know what its intent is. Hereby we see what poverty has come into the world that the common people and almost all have been held back from being instructed in the holy Scripture. For we thought that such existed only for monks and priests. And yet in the end how absurd,[20] for it seemed that theology was meant to be enclosed in studyclosets. Nevertheless, this testimony has endured and ought to until the end of the world, that God has spo-

[15]retenons.
[16]la faute.
[17]petis.
[18]sens.
[19]cuidans-croyants.
[20]bestise-bêtise.

ken in a loud voice, that he has not hidden himself, nor with-
drawn into some tiny corner.

Thus it has been an act of shameless ingratitude whenever anyone has abandoned the Word of God as if it contained no worth.[21]
Therefore all the more must we carefully mark this passage when
it is said that God did not solely address himself to a few theolo-
gians, but communicated with all the people, even the most ignorant. At the same time we have to extol the goodness of our God
when [we consider the fact that] he has restored to us the good
which we realize the greater part of the world has lost by its malice
and indifference, that today the Word of God resounds among us,
and that we can read it, and publish it, and in particular become
participants in it, that this treasure can be explained to us, and
that we can hear it. That is an inestimable boon that we ought to
magnify. Furthermore, that we might be [more] attentive to listen
to our God, let no one cite[22] here [some] subterfuge in an attempt
to exempt himself. For insofar as[23] God speaks to all the company
of the faithful, to all those who are baptized in the name of our
Lord Jesus Christ, let each of us according to our station and
capacity so study therein to profit from it. And let us all hold God
in common as our [school] master, and let us be ready to listen to
him on every occasion it pleases him to speak to us, everyday.
That is the essence of this first point where it is said that God
spoke to all the assembly.

Now let us come to the second, namely, *that he added nothing*, its
purpose being that we might have that much more courage to
hear what the law contains. Certainly everything that Moses has
written belongs to the law.[24] Likewise what the prophets have also
bequeathed us as well as what has been added in the gospel constitutes one substance. For the Bible is rather bulky. But the fact
remains that God has given it a specific end in order that we
might not be misled nor bewildered and that we might not have to
inquire extensively as to what we must hold. Why? [For] it all
hinges on ten precepts, as I have said. All we have to do is count
our fingers and we have the commandments of God, we have the
sum of what we ought to remember in order to be God's good
pupils. Since such brevity exists, are men not of necessity blatantly

[21]comme deserte.
[22]allegue-cite.
[23]puis qu'ainsi.
[24]Cf. *Institutes* 2.7.1.

perverse[25] if they reject such a doctrine and do not equally take the time to profit in the Word of God? Consequently, let us eschew all such frivolous evasions[26] as, "But how? The holy Scripture is entirely too deep a sea; it's an abyss. [Even] when you want to enter it, where will you come out?"

Let us not succumb[27] to these things. It is true that God shows us in the Scripture secrets worshiped by angels; it is true that we can only have a little taste of them; nevertheless, since we live in the world, it is enough for us to know in part (as Paul says)[28] and in darkness,[29] seeing as in a mirror what we cannot yet behold face to face. All of that is true, but it still remains that God has so truly accommodated himself and stooped to our smallness that these things should[30] be easy for us, or at least we [can] understand what is useful for our salvation. If there are matters about which we are uncertain,[31] let us have the sobriety not to plunge forward until we have first of all asked God, realizing how distant we still are from our perfection. At all events, according to the measure that has been given us, we can always glorify in the fact that our Lord does not intend to leave us in doubt and in ignorance, but provides such certainty as to enable us to walk in complete security.[32] Likewise we can know that it is not in vain that he calls us to himself, that our course will not lead us astray, but we possess an end which, if we hold to it, we need not fear will fail to lead us safely.

Therefore, let us keep in mind that our Lord has not spoken according to his nature. For if he had wished to speak his language, would mortal creatures have been able to hear it? Alas no. But how has he spoken to us in the holy Scripture? He has stammered.[33] Saint Paul says that when he preached the gospel [to the Corinthians] he was like a nurse with children,[34] and when he speaks of himself, there can be no doubt that he reveals the goodness of God, who has governed him by his Holy Spirit. And what

❧

[25]malins-mauvais.
[26]repliques.
[27]allegons.
[28]I Cor. 13:12.
[29]obscurité.
[30]sont.
[31]douteuses-incertains.
[32]asseuree-rassurée.
[33]bagayé.
[34]See I Cor. 3:1-2.

we find in Saint Paul we equally find in Moses and all the prophets. Let us carefully note, therefore, that God offers himself as a nurse, not speaking to a child in the same way he would to a man, but rather keeping in mind the child's capacity. Consequently God has humbled himself, for we could not comprehend what he is saying unless he condescended to us. That is why in the holy Scripture we encounter him rather like a wet nurse, for we do not perceive his high and infinite majesty, to which we could not attain or even approach. Therefore, insofar as God has made himself accessible[35] to us, so much the more will grievous condemnation rest on our heads if we do not take the effort to profit in this doctrine which has already been masticated for us, in a manner of speaking, so that the only thing that remains for us is to swallow and digest it.

Furthermore, let us carefully note [that] when Moses says *that God added nothing to these ten statements,* its purpose was for this brevity to incite us that we might take courage, knowing that God has no intention of leading us astray into some bottomless and boundless waste, but he simply puts before us ten verses. It is true that he explains these ten verses by Moses and subsequently by the prophets; [however] in the end, the final declaration is achieved in our Lord Jesus Christ, given to us today in the gospel. And yet we still only have one end as our goal. This being the case, are men not of necessity entirely too perverse when they scorn such a grace of God and do not come to him, [especially] in light of the fact that he treats them in such a way? Consequently, that is what we have to stress[36] vis-à-vis this accessibility[37] which Moses reveals here as part of God's Word.

And yet let us also note that he wanted to limit us in order that we might learn to be satisfied with the law's simplicity, that is to say, that we might not become God's censors[38] by adding bits and pieces to his Word. For when he has spoken, it is once for all. And his intent is for us to adhere to what he has said, as we shall soon see,[39] for he sternly forbade wavering either to the right or to the left, or adding anything whatsoever to his doctrine. And indeed, insofar as God adds nothing to it, who are we to dare to infringe

---

[35]facile.
[36]retenir.
[37]facilité.
[38]contreroller-contrôler, censurer.
[39]See "The Fifteenth Sermon," Deut. 5:32.

upon him? Do we think that God has forgotten his law since giving it and no longer knows what would benefit us? Can a man advise himself on what is unknown to God? Furthermore, since our Lord has so thoroughly[40] accommodated himself to us, do we suppose that he only intended to half-instruct us and leave us in the middle of the road? Therefore, let us remember that since God added nothing to these ten statements which he proclaimed, it is required of us to impose nothing at all upon the simple doctrine which the law contains. May we interweave nothing whatsoever of our own, rather may we realize that our highest[41] wisdom lies in obeying our God.

Had that been carefully observed, we would not today be so hindered from correcting the corruptions which reign in the world. For from whence has come the corruption of religion and the worship of God if it isn't from the papacy? The papists pride themselves on worshiping God when they celebrate their pretentious cults,[42] ceremonies, and even worthless services.[43] And why? Because they have presumed to add to God's Word. For in their estimation it isn't enough for God to be worshiped according to his will,[44] but men have to invent in their minds what seems best[45] to them. Accordingly, everything that the papacy calls "worship of God" is nothing more than a folly[46] which men have invented.[47] And not only [that], but what was said by the prophet has been fulfilled: "They have scorned the commandments of God, and abandoned themselves to their [own] inventions."[48] And we see the evil that results from this diabolical audacity whenever men have tried[49] to alter[50] God's Word with their lies and musings. So much the more [then] ought we stress this passage when it is said that once God spoke, he did not want anything added to what he had said. And in fact (as I have alluded), it is a horrible blasphemy when men willingly try[51] to find [something] better—I know not

[40]familierement.
[41]parfaite.
[42]agios-simagrées.
[43]fatras-choses sans valeur.
[44]à sa guise.
[45]bon.
[46]badinage-sottise.
[47]controuvé-inventé.
[48]See Isa. 29:13.
[49]voulu.
[50]desguiser-altérer.
[51]attentent de vouloir.

what—than what the law of God contains. For in effect they make God a liar, or suggest that he has been poorly advised, or has forgotten to command what he should have. But then what can you expect? Accordingly, let us learn so to submit[52] ourselves to God that this may forever be engraved on our minds, that after God spoke he concluded by saying: "Hold fast to them, [for] these are my boundaries and limits and whoever wants to exceed them will [only] break his neck." For there is nothing but ruin when we fail to take the path that God has accordingly provided and mapped out.[53]

Now although God does not speak today in a visible manner as he did then, nevertheless we frequently need to call to mind[54] this lesson which the law contains. It is true that God has not spoken twice, but he has spoken once for all, as we say. [Yet] on our part, it is imperative for us to hear that often, as stated in the sixty-second Psalm, "The Lord has spoken once, I have heard him; but not just for one time, I have heard him twice."[55] [Now] by this text we are admonished that it is insufficient to give one day's attention to what our Lord willed to be published in his name, rather our meditation must continue on it. Consequently, let each one [of us] so engage our life, both morning and evening, that we might not cease to call to mind[56] what our Lord reveals and explains[57] to us. For were we to employ our entire life to this end, it would be all we could do to complete half our journey.

It is true (as we have already said) that our Lord will instruct us as long as it is necessary for our salvation,[58] nevertheless, let us find ourselves committed to profiting in God's Word. Therefore let us be diligent and do not think of it as being lost effort when we take hold of it and apply our daily study to it, never ceasing to search and inquire what our Lord teaches us. That is how we must put into practice the words *that our Lord added nothing.*

Now let us come to the third point, *that he spoke out of the midst of the fire, the cloud, and the whirlwind.* It is true that this has already previously been explained, but since Moses reiterates it for us, let us note that it isn't superfluous. In fact, it cannot be emphasized

[52]ranger-soumettre.
[53]compassé-mesuré.
[54]recorder-rapeller.
[55]See Ps. 62:11.
[56]recorder-rapeller.
[57]declaire-éclaircit.
[58]salut.

often enough for us, that is, that the Word of God ought to exercise[59] a majesty over us in order to humble all our senses for the purpose of making us captive to it. And why? In the first place, we are aware of human pride, for men cannot bend their neck. True, they will not say that they want to resist or make war with him, but in any event are they as docile and unassuming as they ought to be? Far from it! Furthermore, there is [man's] stupidity, for we are bewildered and dazed by earthly things; we cannot raise our intelligence to [the point] that we can apply it to listen to God. We are so preoccupied with the affairs[60] and cares of this world that we cannot attain such spiritual wisdom; it hardly takes anything to arrest [our thoughts] here. Consequently, we are in great need for our Lord to touch us to the quick that we might reflect a proper reverence for his Word, that it might not be dead, owing in part to our rebellion [and] in part to our stupidity; that is to say, we are so dazed and boorish and earthly and, in part, so preoccupied with vain things that we are held back here below by corruptible affairs.

Therefore it was not without cause that God spoke out of the midst of the fire and out of the midst of the cloud and the whirlwind when he resolved to publish his law. For it was fitting that the people should be touched with [enough] fear to say, "It is not a question of playing with God, for he has appeared to us in such terrible majesty that what else remains for us to do but to tremble under him, and to display such a subjection that he might govern us like sheep? Indeed, let us all bend our necks and bow our heads, permitting him to subject us to his will, each of us surrendering to him. Let us be confounded[61] when he speaks and have no other desire than to honor and serve him, subjugating everything to his guidance."

Accordingly that is why God magnified his law when it was published. He could have easily spoken apart from leaping flames, [or] without causing the mountain to smoke, [or] in the absence of a thick and opaque cloud, but God willed to add these miracles that the people might tremble. Furthermore, let us note that he wanted to direct us to what the prophet Isaiah says, that his Spirit will not rest on us unless we tremble before his Word.[62]

[59]avoir.
[60]negoces-affaires.
[61]confus.
[62]See Isa. 66:2.

For therein he also wills to test our obedience toward him. For when he speaks he wants to know whether we will love him, whether we will receive what he says without contradicting it, whether we will find it good and ourselves in accord with it, saying "amen" not simply with our lips but with our heart, peaceably serving him the remainder of our life. For God requires this service by which he wills to be honored in order to show the obedience which we should reflect toward his Word, but because we are so obdurate, and sluggish, and would prefer the reverse, and cannot bend our neck to carry his yoke, it is necessary that we should be assisted by all these means which are mentioned here.

Nevertheless, let us note that the fire's flames did not appear at the time solely for those who saw them, but to the end that today the law of God might have a testimony, even though it [already] ought to be authentic to us and its memory renewed in us, so that when God reminds us of what happened then, we might be humbled under his majesty.

Moreover, when we want to elevate ourselves, and are tempted by self-conceit and pride, may that ardent fire, which in those days frightened the people, and that dense dark cloud, which came before their eyes when they beheld the smoking mountain, may all that be held by us with terror in order that all our pride might be destroyed. Indeed, may we vigorously[63] awaken and offer ourselves to God to the end that he might rule[64] us and lead us where he will, we following wherever he calls us. That is what we must stress as being hidden *in the smoke, and fire, and dense cloud.*

In fact, even though God appeared in a whirlwind and dark cloud, we should note that its purpose was to repress men's curiosity. It is true (as we have already said) that God speaks in order to be understood and does not use ambiguous words; he does not engage in equivocation but has so clearly revealed his will that we can't help but be properly[65] instructed provided we are willing to listen to him. But nevertheless it is inappropriate for us to pursue our senseless curiosities and inquire beyond what seems good to us, for we know that men are so inclined that their ears are forever twitching: "What was that? I want to know!" Whereas our Lord says the opposite: "Do you want to know? Then behold

[63]à bon escient-vigoureusement.
[64]chevisse—domine sur.
[65]deument-dûment.

this impediment of a cloud! Look how dark it is!" Thus let us learn to be God's good pupils, [recognizing] that it is not necessary to yield the reins to our imaginations in order to sound what must be hidden to us; but let us be content to know what God tells us and to wait on the day of full revelation for knowing the rest which for now is incomprehensible. In short, let us ignore what God does not will to explain.[66] For such ignorance transcends all the wisdom of the world; that is, may we not aspire to know more than our Lord has permitted us.

Now let us consider what Moses adds [next]. He says *that the law was written on two tables of stone and given to him.*[67] The two tables ought to remind us of what was treated earlier, that God could have easily written all his law on one stone. He willed to write it on two in order that the distinction might better lead us to understand what the law contains. For we know that our Lord simplifies[68] for us the subjects[69] it contains in order that we might not charge that he spoke too loftily for us. In the same way that there are two principal points in our life, our Lord has divided his law in two tables, that is, that we might know how we ought to govern ourselves toward him and how we ought to live with[70] our neighbors.[71]

Does man really want to rule his life in complete perfection? [If so] in the first place, it is necessary for him to yield to the service of God in order to know what God requires and approves, and then we should live in such justice and equity with our neighbors that we demonstrate thereby that we are true children of God. Therefore the first requires that we acknowledge that God wants to be honored by us; the second, that we render to our neighbors what belongs to them and observe the natural law[72] of not doing anything to anyone unless we would want them to do the same to us.[73] Accordingly, in one table God has explained[74] how he willed to be served, as we have shown earlier, putting himself in a category by himself, in order that we might not make new gods. Then

---

[66]declairer-expliquer.
[67]Duet. 5:22.
[68]masche-mâche. Literally, "chews."
[69]choses.
[70]converser avec-vivre avec.
[71]Cf. *Institutes* 2.8.11–12.
[72]équité de nature.
[73]See Matt. 7:12.
[74]declairé-expliqué.

he explained[75] that he did not will to be represented by images or grotesque figures, as he is spirit and wishes to be served spiritually by us, for men ought not go about setting up just anything, but God wants to have a spiritual service. He wants his name to be hallowed; he wants us to practice his work and above all so to forbear[76] that we each disavow[77] our thoughts and affections to the extent that we might experience a reprieve in which God can govern us. That is what this first table of the law contains. As for the second, we have seen that he commanded us to honor our father and mother, forbade us to murder, commit adultery, steal, lie,[78] and covet.[79] That is why God divided his law into two tables.

Accordingly, if we seriously want to regulate our life, let us continually maintain the intention[80] to honor our God and then to live with our neighbors in complete justice and equity. For there are some who refrain from doing evil but who nevertheless rarely think of God and who consider themselves free and absolved, provided no one complains[81] against them in this world. Yet I ask you, what is this? For as long as we aren't thieves, is it all right for us to be sacrilegious? Is it not a more heinous[82] crime to ravish the honor of God than to rob a man, or to cut away his purse, or to pick the lock on his chest? Consequently let us not suppose that we have done everything simply because others neither bring us to trial nor direct a complaint against us, for it is a matter of God having what he demands as well as his due. For we are obligated to pay him homage all our life. Therefore it is all the more incumbent upon us to direct our study toward observing the first table of the law that we might not lead a philosophical life as pagans do in our effort to live honestly with men, but may God's honor be our most precious concern and our starting point.

Now there are equally some who seemingly want to do good, who want to be devout toward God, who want to possess a great zeal for serving and honoring him, but when it comes to living[83] with men, they rob, steal, and fight; they are full of cruelty, envy,

---

[75] Ibid.
[76] se deporte-s'abstienne.
[77] renounce-renie.
[78] mauvaise langage.
[79] toute convoitise mauvaise.
[80] regard-intention.
[81] se pleigne.
[82] enorme.
[83] à converser avec-à vivre avec.

and malice. But let us note that God did not separate the two tables of the law. He distinguished between the two, but he did not give the first table to some and the second to others.[84] He said, "This is my law, and it is imperative that what I have joined should remain inseparable. Certainly you need to be admonished about the charity which you owe your neighbors in order to follow it. But while you are acquitted from one side, you must also conform to the other. [For] it is not appropriate for you to be heedless about walking in complete justice and equity simply because you have demonstrated a great piety for worshiping and serving me." There are many such people who would like to serve God in that way, as, for example, the papists and their brand of piety.[85] But by giving us the first table, our Lord wanted to restrain us in order that we might learn to serve him as he commands and to find nothing good save what he approves. That is the substance behind this passage: *That God wrote his law in two tables.* [86]

Now in particular he wanted to write it on two tables of stone that it might endure, for it was not given [to last] for just a brief period [of time] as something transient.[87] It is true that the ceremonies have ended, which is why the law is called temporal, but what we must keep in mind is that this order, which was established among the ancient people to serve until the coming of our Lord Jesus Christ, has now been abolished and things have become perfect, indeed to the extent that we are no longer under shadows and figures which prevailed then. In any event the truth and substance of the law were not [confined] to one age; they constitute something permanent which shall abide[88] forever.[89]

Accordingly, let us realize[90] that God definitely published his will when the people left the country of Egypt, that he truly spoke on Mt. Sinai, and that, each time,[91] he gave us order[s] and provision[s] to the end that his doctrine might continually maintain its vigor. And for this reason he put his law on two tables of stone; he did not write it on bark as people used to write on then, in the same way that today we would say on paper or parchment. Rather,

---

[84]See the *Institutes* 2.8.11.
[85]à leur devotion.
[86]Deut. 5:22.
[87]caduque.
[88]ne doit deffaillir.
[89] See the *Institutes* 4.20.15.
[90]apprenons.
[91]quant et quant-chaque fois.

he wanted it to be engraved on stone that there might exist a memorial that would last in order that we should be better confirmed in what he was saying. For he isn't satisfied with having spoken on that occasion alone, but having engraved his law on stone, he wills that throughout our life our ears may be attentive to receive what he reveals for us there.

Now it is nevertheless true that the law of God would still not render a marked service if it were only engraved on stone, but it is imperative for it to be engraved upon our hearts. What must we do, then? Let us grasp that the doctrine that God propounds for us is both useful and necessary for us. However, it would not constitute an advantage unless God had added a second grace, that is, that what he declared should be stamped upon our hearts and sinews.

In the same way then that God wrote his law on two stones with his finger, that is with his miraculous power,[92] he must today write on our hardened hearts of stone by means of his Holy Spirit. For [this is what] the prophet[93] teaches[94] when he asks God to give us hearts of flesh that are soft, pliable, and docile, that we might receive what he wants to say to us. Inasmuch then as God has visibly shown that it is up to him to write his law if it is to be readily understood, let us ask him to be pleased by the power of his Holy Spirit to write it in us today to the end that we might retain it and that the devil himself, in spite of his efforts, may never be able to efface its memory in us.

Now in the meantime Moses concludes that the law was entrusted[95] to him in order for him to preserve and guard it, as well as become its minister and steward[96] with respect to the people, that each might acknowledge him as prophet; for otherwise, he could not have fulfilled his office, nor have been able to edify the church of God, unless they had recognized that the charge had been committed to him.[97] For likewise today, if we were not persuaded that God intended for his gospel to be preached by men, or that the office of pastor existed for proclaiming his Word,[98]

[92]vertu-force, acte de puissance.
[93]See Ezek. 36:26f.
[94]remonstre-enseigne.
[95]baillee.
[96]dispensateur.
[97]Cf. Calvin's discussion of Moses' authoritative role in his Comm. *Four Books of Moses*, vol. 1, p. 333; *CO* 24.205.
[98]qui portassent sa parolle.

who would bother to assemble? Neither I, nor anyone for that matter, has the talent to persuade the world to come and accept what I might say on my own accord. [But] when I speak here in the name of God and people listen to his doctrine with the intention of submitting themselves to it and of paying homage to him, that is more important than all the laws and edicts of emperors and kings. Has any mortal man [ever] been able to do that? No! But when we know that God intended for this order to be established in his church and for us to keep it inviolable, for pastors to proclaim his Word, expounding it and serving as his messengers, announcing the forgiveness of sins in the name of our Lord Jesus Christ, reproving, admonishing, comforting, and exhorting; when we know that God has willed for such a regime to be [the order] in his church, we should be ashamed to resist him who has created and formed us. Therefore that is why Moses says in this passage that God entrusted the law to him.

It is true that God gave him the law on behalf of all the people in general, as we have said. But why is Moses now considered its possessor? [On the surface] it appears that God wants to deprive all of his people and make Moses alone privileged, the law being restricted to Moses and closed to everyone else.

Of course, such is not the case, for although the law was given for all the people, Moses was designated as its protector. And what God said of him must be extended by us further, for we know[99] that the prophets[100] were ordained with a similar charge, that is, they were also stewards of this treasure of salvation, of this covenant of God, and their office was given for the purpose of continually proclaiming[101] the will of God and bringing it to us in his name.

It is the same general rule that Saint Paul lays down, [stressing] that people should regard us as ambassadors of God and stewards, he says, of the secrets God sends into the world.[102] For when Saint Paul says that we are stewards of the secrets of God, he thereby shows that it is insufficient for us to possess the holy Scripture [and] each read it in his own home, rather it is necessary for it to be preached to us, for us to possess this order wherein we are taught by men, for there to be pastors through whom God is

[99]oyons.
[100]See Jer. 1:5, 7.
[101]declairer.
[102]See I Cor. 4:1.

served in order that when we listen to them we might increasingly benefit in the doctrine of salvation. And that is also why Saint Paul says in another passage that the church is the pillar of truth, its buttress,[103] and tower.[104] The papists foolishly cite this [text] in order to arrogate unto themselves a license to construct articles of faith and impose laws according to their own whim. But Saint Paul meant the complete opposite. For he says that the church is the pillar or buttress[105] of God's truth because when God published his truth for men through the law, the prophets, and apostles he willed[106] for this ministry to endure in perpetuity, that is, he willed for there to exist a people who would be committed and delegated to this office of expounding his Word and edifying the church.[107] Accordingly, with this in mind let us understand that it is by the means of the church that God's truth abides in its wholeness. For when God gives birth[108] to a people who are endowed with his Spirit in order to confirm us in faith, illuminate, and show us the right path, that is how the truth of God abides in the world and why it hasn't perished or been put out.

Let us note, therefore, that Moses is not intended here to be the sole possessor of God's law for the purpose of rejecting the people or closing the door on them. But in particular he explains, "My friends, it is true that the law is common to [both of] us; we are all children of God; I do not ascribe more of it to myself than I do to you. Nevertheless, I want to discharge the duty which God has laid on me, that is, that I serve you as a faithful expositor and as a guardian of the law that you might not trample on it or ever forget it without being reminded of it everyday by me."

This being the case, let all those who are established as ministers of God's Word be advised to be ready and equipped to serve the uninformed, and let everyone equally remember that it isn't enough for us [simply] to read the holy Scripture, rather it is imperative for us to be diligent in order to profit from it and to come with complete humility to hear those who are ordained[109] as

---

[103]fermeté-soutien.
[104]See 1 Tim. 3:15. See the *Institutes* 4.2.1, 10; 8.12, where Calvin discusses this text in conjunction with the Catholic Church's claim to be the "pillar of truth."
[105]firmament-soutien, appui.
[106]avoulu-a voulu.
[107]On the preaching role of the ministry and God's need to teach through human means, see the *Institutes* 4.1.5–6; 3.1–3.
[108]suscite-fait naître.
[109]constituez.

ministers whose task is to provide us with exposition and understanding.[110]

That is what must be emphasized in this passage.[111]

[110]See n. 107 above.

[111]Golding's translation preserves this closing exhortation: "Now let us kneele
downe in the presence of our good God with acknowledgement of our faultes,
praying him to make us feele them better, and to drawe us daily to such repentance, as our whole desire may be to serve him and to please him, without seeking
any whit of our own will. And that forasmuch as wee be so greatly given to worldly
thinges, it may please him to drawe us from them, and therewithall to graunt that
wee may submit our life to his will, and frame it to his righteousnesse, and that for
the bringing thereof to passe, his worde may so overrule us, as wee may bee governed by it, and all our whole life be framed thereafter, untill that being quite rid
of all our fleshly affections, wee be clothed againe with his heavenly glory, at such
time as wee shall have no more neede, neither of writing nor of preaching. That it
may please him to graunt this grace, not onely to us but also to all people and
nations of the earth, Etc." *Sermons Upon the Fifth Book of Moses*, trans. Golding, p.
253. Cf. Calvin, *Sermons sur les dix commandemens*, 1557 ed., p. 192.

Sermon Fourteen[2]

Deuteronomy 5:23–27[3]

It seems to us that if God, instead of preaching his Word to us by means of men, were to speak in his majesty, or cause an angel whom he had sent to appear, that we would be more effectively moved and that everyone would be instantly converted and would obey without any opposition[4] or rebellion. But we know neither what is proper for us nor useful to us. For if we [would only] remember our fragile nature, [we would see that] it is impossible for God to make us conscious of his power[5] without destroying and annihilating us. Therefore when men long[6] for God to manifest himself by some visible sign, or descend from heaven, they have not perceived who they are, nor how transient[7] is their con-

---

[1]N. in *CO:* "This sermon corresponds to the fourteenth in the 1562 collection, pp. 291–311." *CO* 26.396.

[2]The original title: "The Thirteenth Sermon on Chapter 5:23–27." *CO* 26.396.

[3]Cf. Calvin's elaboration of this text in his Comm. *Four Books of Moses*, vol. 1, pp. 330–36; *CO* 24.204–7. See also the *Institutes* 4.1.5–6; 3.1–3.

[4]contraité-opposition.

[5]vertu-force.

[6]appettent-désirent.

[7]caduque.

dition; for if they had pondered it well, they would be afraid of God's infinite glory, knowing only too well that they are unable to bear it.

Furthermore, let us recognize that God is procuring our welfare and salvation when he declares his will to us by human means, that he ordains and establishes ministers of his Word to bring us the message he knows is fitting for us.[8] However, at least on one occasion, he willed to convince men that it was not good for them to hear his voice thundering from heaven. And that is why he wanted to publish his law, not simply by Moses, but by descending in person as we have already discussed. Yesterday it was said that the lightning, the whirlwind, and the leaping flames, and everything that is written in the twentieth chapter of Exodus, as well as the nineteenth,[9] all of that (I say) was done in order that the people of Israel might learn to reverence the Word of God.[10]

Now this instruction is also part of our heritage. For God intended that the memory of these things should endure forever and enjoy perpetual use. Consequently God displayed his glorious majesty on that one occasion in order that we might learn to receive his Word in complete fear[11] and humility; in addition he equally wanted the people on their own part to be constrained to say: *It is not good for God to speak to us again*[12]; *all we need is a man who will proclaim such doctrine as it pleases God to send us.*[13] But the intent of his rule is to condemn us if we do not imitate[14] this people who had the audacity[15] to speak as they did. Now if we allege that what was said then is no longer binding on us, the answer is easy, [namely] that if Gods intends to do the same today, that is to speak from his mouth what we are accustomed to hearing mortal men proclaim, it would be impossible for us to bear his glory; we would be completely destroyed by it. Hence let us realize

---

[8]See the *Institutes* 4.1.5, where Calvin elaborates the theme of this sentence.

[9]See Exod. 19:18–19; 20:18.

[10]In the *Institutes* 4.3.1, Calvin discusses three principal reasons why God prefers to use human means rather than speak himself; 1) "... he first declares his regard for us when from among men he takes some to serve as his ambassadors ... "; 2) "... this is the best and most useful exercise in humility, when he accustoms us to obey his Word, ... " and 3) "... nothing fosters mutual love more fittingly than for men to be bound together with this bond. ... " *LCC* 21.1053–54.

[11]crainte.

[12]derechef-de nouveau.

[13]Calvin very broadly alludes to Deut. 5:25–27.

[14]ensuyvons-imitons.

[15]s'est avancé-a l'audace de.

that this [text] is repeated in order that in the person of the people of Israel we might learn that God accommodates himself to our lowliness[16] and weakness. For when it pleases him to send us his Word which must be preached to us and when we have men like ourselves who are his messengers, he therein expresses his concern for what is fitting and useful to us. Indeed it is an insane[17] and reckless desire[18] if we ask him to appear from heaven or perform some visible miracle; for we cannot comprehend his glory and majesty.

Furthermore, although it is the proper nature of the law to threaten,[19] the same applies to the gospel as well. For we must hold to a general rule that as soon as we feel God's presence, we should feel confused. We know how the angels themselves hide their eyes, insofar as his glory is too great for them and how it is necessary for them to confess that they, like creatures,[20] are too feeble. [If that is true of angels], then what of ourselves? For we are inferior to angels and yet do not retain the integrity of our nature; we are not what God created us, that is, terrestrial men like our father Adam. But we are completely corrupt, there being nothing but sin in us and consequently it is fitting that God should be as an enemy and that we should flee from his throne as malefactors flee from the seat of their judge as much as they can. In short, we are nothing but poor vermin and putrid flesh.[21]

Consequently, as soon as God draws near to us, we must be frightened, indeed, completely overwhelmed. And thus (as we have already mentioned) it is to our benefit that God manifests himself in such a way, that is, through human means, establishing a people who expound his will as if he himself were speaking, and that his Word should be received by us with such reverence as if we heard him thundering from heaven.

Now it is still good to understand more fully what we have touched upon quite briefly, that is, that the law threatens us at the cost of and in comparison with the Gospel, as is likewise treated elsewhere at greater length. And what is that? For in the law God requires of men what is due him. But let us ask if it is possible for us to justify ourselves? On the contrary, we are like poor debtors

[16]petitesse-humilité.
[17]fol-insensé.
[18]appetit.
[19]effrayer. See the "Introduction," n. 54.
[20]See Isa. 6:2–3.
[21]charongnes-charonges. See the *Institutes* 1.15.4; 2.1.8; 2.12.

without a single farthing. We are that overwhelmed. Yet, be that as it may, God does not absolve us, but shows us that we deserve to be cursed and damned by him. And that is why, after showing how human life ought to be ruled, he adds this curse to overwhelm [us]: that cursed are all who do not fulfill everything which the law contains. It's as if he were saying: "Men must endure condemnation here, from the greatest to the smallest, they must all realize that they are indebted to me and that I can drop[22] them into the very bottom of hell, I am already passing this sentence and none is able to stay me[23]; therefore you are all lost and damned." That is the language of the law and the style which God uses. Therefore, is it not fitting for everyone to tremble? Consequently, it is not without cause that it is said that the law frightens us, yet that it pleases God to require strictly what we owe him means we must needs be lost.

Now such is not the case in the gospel, for there God supports us and not only forgives our sins, but writes his will upon our hearts. Moreover, in spite of the fact that we only halfheartedly serve him, he nevertheless forgives our shortcomings and closes his eyes like a father who does not want to press his child too strictly. Likewise in the gospel God makes use of a paternal gentleness in order that we might not be afraid to come to him.[24] And that is why the apostle in the Letter to the Hebrews[25] says that we have not come to this smoking mountain, that we have not come to Sinai to behold its leaping flames which frighten us, or to see its lightning and all the rest which confused the people, but we hear a gracious and pleasant melody, in which we are accompanied by both angels from heaven and the souls of the holy patriarchs and the Fathers who lived in the hope of life, although they still only possessed dark shadows. But now God unites us [together] with those who waited from of old for the coming of our Lord Jesus. Since this is the case, we must not retreat, rather let each one press on, and let us come with a cheerful[26] heart to hear our God, seeing that he speaks to us so humanely and in a paternal language which is not meant to startle children but rather to entice them (as they say).

[22]abysmer-abismer-précipiter.
[23]repliquer à l'encontre.
[24]See the *Institutes* 2.8.4.
[25]Heb. 12:22.
[26]allaigre-allègre.

Therefore this difference is well worth noting in order to render the gospel conciliatory for us in comparison with the law. Nevertheless if we need to return to our general principle, it is that it is much better for the Word of God to be preached to us by the mouths of men than for him to thunder [it] from heaven. And why? Simply listen to natural thunder and we are seized with fear, yet nothing is being spoken; God only causes indistinct rumbling. Therefore what would be the case if he should speak to us and then reveal his glory? We have experienced how impossible it is to behold the sun which is a corruptible creation. How then could we behold the majesty of God if it were fully revealed in its perfection? Consequently it is said that a human being cannot see God without dying or without being consumed.[27]

[Now] it is true that God clearly appeared to Moses and not simply in the way he appeared to the prophets, [but] as it is explained in Exodus[28] he gave him this special privilege, for he revealed himself face-to-face privately, as to his friend, and this was neither by means of a dream nor by a vision, but by a privacy so great that Moses was almost exempt from the company of the human race in order that he might become more familiar with God. But, be that as it may, God only manifested himself to Moses in part and measure, for had he revealed his infinite essence, Moses (whatever grace of the Holy Spirit he received) must needs have been completely overwhelmed. Still once in his life God showed his glory more amply than ever before; nevertheless, he saw only his back.

Now this similitude conveys the idea that in beholding a man's back we do not see the most important thing; for that, we must see his face. Thus, although Moses may have had an intimate audience with God, nevertheless in that supreme vision which he was granted on the mountain, when he was removed from the condition of this mortal and transitory life, when he was like an angel of paradise, nevertheless he only saw God in part, as one seeing a man from the back.

Thus let us learn to be content when God employs that order among us by which his Word is preached to us by men. And let us receive it as if we are seeing his majesty face-to-face. And why? For it is to our advantage that there are pastors who are estab-

[27]Exod. 33:20.
[28]Exod. 33:11.

lished for us as ministers of the Word, seeing that we would be completely annihilated by God's glory if it were totally manifested to us.

And to the end that no one might have an occasion to complain, as if the doctrine of God were not sufficiently attested and one were in doubt whether to hold it as from him or not, that is why God specifically revealed himself when he published his law. For we have a testimony here that the people said: *"It is the Lord. Today he has made us aware of his glory and his grandeur; we have seen that it is he who has spoken to us,*[29] that he has not interposed anyone between [himself and] us, but we have heard his voice with our ears."* That, accordingly, actually took place once for all. Nevertheless, let us hold to what has been recounted here as a testimony that Moses did not speak on his own, nor invent the doctrine which we have received through him, but he was a faithful steward of God who acknowledged[30] him and not only ratified by miracles what Moses taught[31] but personally explained[32] that he himself was the author of this doctrine.

Now there is a similar reason why the gospel is as authentic as the law, for we have likewise received a testimony from heaven that it is not a human doctrine but proceeds from God. This is what Saint Peter discusses in his Second Letter, saying, that he and his companions heard the voice from heaven in which the Father explained[33] that his Son was the supreme master and doctor of all his church. "This is my beloved Son, listen to him."[34] When therefore this voice thundered from heaven, God explained[35] that we must not look upon the gospel as a doctrine born on earth, but we must always keep its majesty[36] before us. Therefore if we want to be God's true disciples, whenever we come to the sermon we must remember what Moses recounts, that in the proclaiming of the law it was God who has spoken. And secondly, we must add this witness which we have just cited,[37] let-

---

[29]Deut. 5:24.
[30]advoué-admis, accepté.
[31]Cf. *Institutes* 1.8.5ff.
[32]declairé-expliqué.
[33]declairé-expliqué.
[34]II Peter 1:17–18. Cf. Matt. 17:1–8; Mark 9:8; Luke 9:28–36. Cf. *Institutes* 2.15.2.
[35]declairé-expliqué.
[36]ceste maiesté: Calvin seems to have in mind the gospel's heavenly origin which the Transfiguration experience confirmed.
[37]alleguer-citer.

ting God's proclamation ring in our ears when he says that our Lord Jesus Christ is the one whom he wills for us to hear. That [is what] constitutes the lawful seal[38] which assures [us] that the Word of God shall exercise its full and perfect authority over us, as it ought, even though mortal men preach it.

Furthermore, lest anyone think that Jesus Christ must be heard solely in person, Jesus himself says, "Whoever hears you, hears me; and whoever rejects you or scorns you, rejects me and him who sent me."[39] Of course the Pope and his partisans[40] in a sacrilegious way usurp this text in order to validate their tyranny, but it belongs to them as much as to the devil of hell. And why? Because in the first place we are under obligation to represent[41] the pure doctrine of our Lord Jesus Christ. For the Son of God did not hand over his office to men to be deprived of it; it was not his intention for us to be governed by men's whim; rather he continually intends to exercise preeminence over us and that dominion which he has been given.

Consequently, when he says that in listening to those whom he has sent we are listening to him, he means that if we are obedient to the doctrine of his Gospel, not despising it when it is preached to us by men, then it's as if he himself were speaking to us and we need not stop at the outward appearance.[42] This is what Saint Paul himself affirms: Though we are fragile vessels, like broken pots without worth or value, nevertheless an inestimable treasure has been committed to us, whose value is in no way mitigated.[43]

It is true that we cannot acquire for the Word of God that reverence which we would like. Why? Because we have nothing in ourselves, of our own, I say, which enables us to exalt God; nevertheless we must put our obedience to the test by proclaiming[44] the Word of God with such confidence and force[45] as if he were speaking in us. And in that way all pride can be corrected and each of us receive in simplicity the doctrine of the gospel without debating why we are to be subject to mortal men. For unless we listen to those whom God sends as his messengers, we scorn the

---

[38]droite signature.
[39]Calvin conflates several New Testament texts on this quote. See Matt. 10:40; Luke 10:16; Gal. 4:14; John 13:20.
[40]supposts-partisans.
[41]apportassent.
[42]regard exterieur.
[43]See II Cor. 4:7.
[44]portions.
[45]vertu-force.

Son of God, whom the Father has designated the supreme doctor. We must submit[46] to this [order]. Consequently, let us learn to bend our neck in order to carry the yoke of God's Son, receiving the doctrine of the gospel in complete humility, even though it is preached to us by men.

Now as I have already said, let us remember the test[47] which accompanies it, which we must undergo if we are to realize that the law has been given by God himself; and let us equally remember that the gospel had its origin[48] and ratification from heaven when God declared with his mouth that he wanted us to listen to his Son. That, in short, is what we want to emphasize in this passage. Therefore let us pursue what is said here about our not asking[49] God to descend from heaven simply to please us, rather whenever it suits him to communicate his Word to us is what should suffice us.

Now it would seem at first sight that this text contains some contradiction.[50] For the people say: *We have seen today how God speaks to men and yet they still live.*[51] And then, *We shall die if God speaks to us.*[52] For it [would] seem that if we have experienced God as one who does not engulf[53] us when he speaks, then that should make us bold. And why? Because we are yet alive although we have heard the voice of God. If he can do it once, then why not twice or three times? And yet the people say, *We have heard the voice of God, but if he speaks to us again, we shall die;* if he does it, indeed we are lost. It seems that they do not trust in the goodness of God; in fact they are ungrateful, inasmuch as they do not recognize the good which God accomplishes for them by leaving them in their strength. But we must note that the people explain[54] that they do not wish to tempt God further and that it is enough for them to have experienced[55] on that one occasion that the law was not something invented by men but rather it was authored by God.

---

[46]se range-soumet.
[47]approbation-preuve.
[48]adveu-adve[n]u. Apparently the printers dropped the original *n*.
[49]appetions—désirerions.
[50]Cf. Calvin's treatment of Deut. 5:24–25 in his Comm. *Four Books of Moses*, vol. 1, pp. 334–35; CO 24.205–6. His approach is similar but more detailed.
[51]Deut. 5:24.
[52]Deut. 5:25.
[53]abysme-abime.
[54]declairé-expliqué.
[55]cogneu.

Accordingly this passage must be understood in this way: "We have realized that today God has spoken to men and that they yet live. That is enough for us. For it is not a matter of abusing God's patience; he spared us today, but this does not mean that he may do so always. He has tested us this once because of our malice and hardness. For were we worthy of his appearing this way in his glory? But he knew that we would not be fully mastered or brought under submission unless he appeared in his visible glory and we became so afraid as to become confused. Therefore, if he had not gained us in this way by force, then he knew only too well that we would have forever been like wild beasts. But inasmuch as it pleased him to forgive us that sin which we committed and [insofar as] he has supported us today, let us no longer rue[56] the matter, for that would be too much; that would constitute a mockery of his patience. Consequently, this testimony is sufficient, both for our life and for the life of our children, and forever until the end of the world. And may those who come after us realize that it is no longer a question of having[57] to lure God out of heaven, as if he were obligated to become our equal." This is how these two passages are best harmonized.[58]

Now we need to note in this text [that] although the Word of God reduces[59] us all to nothing, God still employs such loving kindness toward us that it results in life for us instead of our being consumed. For when I say that the Word of God can reduce[60] us to nothing, I am not simply referring to that word which Moses delineates here, but should our Lord want to make us aware of the power[61] of his Word, although it may be proclaimed to us by men, we would nevertheless be totally lost. For we know that our Lord vivifies us by speaking to us and above all today when the gospel is preached to us. For what is said in the fifth chapter of Saint John is fulfilled every day, that is, that all who hear the voice of the Son of man are restored to life.[62] For by nature we are alienated from God, banished from his kingdom; therefore it is as

---

[56]retournions.

[57]vouloir.

[58]In his Comm. *Four Books of Moses*, vol. 1, p. 335; *CO* 24.206; Calvin summarizes "... this history [is] an illustrious proof that God governs His Church by the external preaching of the word, because this is most expedient for us."

[59]reduire-abaisser.

[60]reduire-abaisser.

[61]vertu.

[62]See John 5:21ff.

if we were in a tomb. But our Lord Jesus Christ grants us the remission of our sins, [and] God his Father adopts us for his children. That, then, is the splendor of the salvation which he shows us, and we are quickened by it through the power of the gospel. And thus thereby we easily have the wherewithal[63] to glorify our God, seeing that he causes his Word to restore us to life and to deliver us from death. For although the Word of God possesses the power[64] to consume us, he has converted it and uses it for the opposite purpose.

Now meantime let us carefully note that although our Lord has provided us with that one occasion (which was already in itself more than we deserve), that does not subsequently grant us either the permission[65] or the license to tempt him or to wish him always to submit to our desires. For as we know today, the papists excuse themselves from coming to the gospel, insofar as they do not perceive any miracles accomplished by it in our time. Indeed! But for what purpose did our Lord Jesus Christ's miracles serve, as well as those which he entrusted to his disciples?[66] Must they be useless for us today? Behold God has displayed[67] an excellent array[68] at the beginning of the gospel, both heaven and earth being moved. There isn't any part wherein God has not stamped some mark of his majesty in order that the gospel might be legitimated. Behold, angels descended at the birth of our Lord Jesus Christ in order to bear witness to him.[69] Remember how the sun was darkened at his death?[70] How the veil of the temple was rent in two in order to show that the sanctuary was open and that God was more accessible than ever before.[71] The sea was calmed.[72] Even devils paid homage to God's glory which was manifested.[73] In brief, as we have already shown, from beginning to end[74] God explained[75] that the gospel proceeded from him. So many illnesses were

[63]dequoy-de quoi.
[64]vertu.
[65]congé-permission.
[66]On the function of miracles see the *Institutes* 1.8.5–6; 13.13.
[67]declairé-eclaircir, exposer.
[68]vertu.
[69]Luke 2:13f.
[70]Matt. 27:45.
[71]Matt. 27:51.
[72]Mark 4:39.
[73]Mark 1:23ff.
[74]et haut et bas.
[75]declairé.

healed. So many other signs were done. That did not take place simply for that time alone, but today its account is firmly fixed in our minds. Therefore it is imperative that we accept this witness in order to confirm[76] our faith so that we may not doubt that our Lord makes his gospel as valid today as when he originally revealed it.

Meanwhile there are unbelievers who allege that if they saw any miracles they might be converted. But certainly they would remain obstinate and upon seeing miracles would only use the occasion that much more to embitter themselves against God. What must we do? As I have said, let us learn to be content. If God has given us more than he owes us, let us accept it with thanksgiving, learning not to provoke him to anger or tempt his patience. Accordingly, that is what we want to retain from this passage concerning the people's statement that the Lord no longer speaks to us, for it is more than enough that we have heard his voice and that he nevertheless permits us to live.

And even, in order that what we have just explained[77] may be even more certain for us, let us hold fast to what is said next: *Who is there of all flesh who has heard the voice of the living God and yet lives?*[78] Now here he shows us that the people of Israel did not speak in their own name, but on behalf of all mankind. They did not simply say, "Who are we?" but, "Who is there of all flesh?" And in fact (as I touched on at the beginning), men cannot help but be intoxicated when they cannot humble themselves. For the latter is impossible unless men can look at their condition and say, "Who are we?" For there is nothing either in our bodies or souls but utter frailty, I say, although we might have been whole in our nature according to which we were created. But being as ruined[79] as we are, what more are we than water that flows away, or a whiff of smoke that passes?[80] And what is worse, we are God's enemies whom he must oppose, seeing that he finds nothing but sin and perversity in us. Thus when we want to gratify our senseless[81] desires by wishing that God would perform some miracle or by

---

[76]seeller-sceller. May also read "seal." Cf. *Institutes* 3.2.7.

[77]declairé-expliqué.

[78]Deut. 5:26. Cf. Comm. *Four Books of Moses*, vol. 1, pp. 335–36. Calvin explains that the word *flesh* always refers to man's "perishing and transitory" nature; it is a contemptuous term for the human race. *CO* 24.206–7.

[79]decheus.

[80]A common proverb. See the *Institutes* 3.9.2.

[81]fols-insensés.

wanting to hear heavenly angels, let us come back to what has been shown us in this text: *And who is there of all flesh?* I say let us earnestly consider who we are and our whole [human] frame will readily admonish[82] us to render praise to God, insofar as he has not made us conscious of his presence for the purpose of consuming or confusing us, but in order to attract us by an amiable gentleness when we hear men like ourselves and our brothers speaking as if in his own person.[83]

And when the people of Israel say: *What people have heard the voice of the living God, as we have, and yet live?*[84] it is to show that God did not intend for this to be drawn as a conclusion. Subsequently, we must not complain: "Why doesn't God speak to us today in a visible form as he did on Mt. Sinai?" It [simply] pleased him. For it is not a matter of imposing a law on him, or of wanting to obligate him to continue to do what he only did on one occasion. Thus, as I have mentioned, let us refrain from abusing God's favor. Let us not become embroiled with scorn for him by saying, "Since he used the means he did at that time, why doesn't he use the same today?" When men puff themselves up like that, it's an outrageous, diabolical conceit. Thus let us grant to God the honor of having the liberty to reveal himself to us as he pleases and as he knows is most expedient for us, and let us not confine God in any way under the pretext[85] that since it pleased him to use one form of mercy once that we do not want him to use another now. Rather let us be satisfied with his simple will, for we must be subject to it.

Finally it is said: *You approach God and listen to what he tells you, and then tell us and we shall listen to it and do it.*[86] In the first place we see here that the people asked Moses to be [their] messenger and to bring them whatever he received from God. Now this is written for us that each of us might submit to that order[87] which God has established in his church.[88] For as we have already said, he wills to speak to us through the mouth of men. That is why he wanted ministers. Men did not invent them, but our Lord Jesus Christ declared that he wanted such to be the system in his church. Thus

[82]advertira-avertira.
[83]comme en sa personne.
[84]Deut. 5:27.
[85]sous ombre-sous prétexte.
[86]Deut. 5:27.
[87]police.
[88]See n. 10 above.

it constitutes an inviolable order, proceeding from God, that there should be pastors in the church who proclaim his doctrine which we must receive for our salvation. Since such is the case, let none rebel[89] here; rather let us patiently bear it when God raises up[90] people whom he intends to serve as our ambassadors of salvation. And let us not murmur because we are not all granted such a privilege, for it is his will that his body should be governed in this way, that is to say, his church. Accordingly that is what we want to gather from this passage, that is, that since God has established ministers of his Word, we should peaceably listen to them and refrain from any envy or ill will insofar as we all cannot be doctors and inasmuch as God does not entrust this office to everyone, for we must submit to his pleasure (as previously discussed). That is one point.

But at the same time, let us also note under what condition[s] we are to have pastors, for this passage helps us discern between seducers who falsely use the name of God, applying to themselves without reason or purpose the title of prelate, and the true prophets, the true servants of God and ministers of the gospel.[91] The Pope and all his vermin insist that people must listen to them and accept their doctrine without opposition. And why? Because God willed for there to be prelates in the church and for people to listen to and obey them. All of that is true. Nevertheless, was it without discretion that the Pope was granted the title of prelate? Hardly. For God time and again explained that he intended to be the head in order that we might be subject to him and not in bondage to men.

Consequently, it is imperative to recognize what kind of prelates and doctors God sends us.[92] With that in mind the following is contained in this passage. They listen to what God says to them and then they faithfully report it to the people.[93] Thus those who

[89]se rebecque-se revolta.

[90]suscite-ressuscite.

[91]See the *Institutes* 4.4–11, where Calvin traces the rise of the Papacy, its institutions, and orders, and criticizes the same for its long history of abuses. Much of this would have been known to the readers of the *Institutes* from 1543 on.

[92]See the *Institutes* 4.3. This important chapter, the preponderance of which had been developed by 1543, is entitled: "The Doctors and Ministers Of The Church, Their Election And Office." *LCC* 21.1053–68. Cf. also 4.1.5–6.

[93]Cf. *Institutes* 4.3.1: " ... because [God] does not dwell among us in visible presence, ... he uses the ministry of men ... that through their mouths he may do his own work." Notice that the emphasis falls upon God doing "his own work" through men.

wish to be heard in God's name, who want their doctrine received with complete respect,[94] must be the first to listen to God without adding anything to his Word, being submissive to him. And after they have been taught by him, they must teach others what they have received. Truly, no one can ever be a good minister of God's Word who isn't first of all [its] student. He must not lord it over others in order to disseminate what seems best to him. Nor must he be too wise here, for God reserves to himself the office of declaring what he wants us to know. It doesn't simply say here, "Listen to what God says to you and then come and tell us." Rather it says, "*All*[95] that God says to you," not a single item or point being left out. In this way every license was denied Moses; nothing was permitted him except to proclaim what God should command him, which is what we have already seen in other passages. Now what filth will the papists[96] dare advance over and above Moses? We shall see in the end that there never was a prophet raised up with such favor. In fact, although we behold an admirable mind in Isaiah and in all the rest of the prophets, it is nevertheless Moses who is preferred to all. When it is said, "Let him remind you of the law which you were given at Horeb," Malachi[97] is only speaking as all the other prophets [spoke], yet he attributes it all to Moses as if he were the first doctor, as if the law were the fountain from which we all must draw.

Now although Moses was the one who was so preferred, the one to whom God gave[98] such an excellent dignity, he nonetheless was forbidden to attempt to proclaim anything of his own, but according to what he heard from God, that [alone] was he to disseminate faithfully to the people. Now in the light of that is it not demonically arrogant that some villains actually dare maintain that they have the right to impose laws on consciences and obligate them under the pain of mortal sin? Is that not a tyranny of excessive barbarity?

Therefore let us hold to this means [which our text presents] in order not to fall into either vicious extreme [i.e., that of the papacy or of the inordinate will]. For since God has willed to govern his church by the outward preaching of his Word, let us each

---

[94]reverence.
[95]Italics for emphasis.
[96]By context. The original simply reads, "they."
[97]Mal. 4:4.
[98]baillé-donné.

submit to it, being diligent to listen to the sermons, holding the system of being taught by the mouth of mortal men as sacred and holy. And at the same time may men [remember that they do] not have the authority to announce to us what seems good to them, but they must be faithful stewards of God's Word. And may we always be able to confess[99] that our faith is founded on his heavenly will, that we do not depend on human wisdom; but may our Lord hold us in his obedience to the extent that we may be able to say that it is he whom we hear from heaven, although he makes use of human means and labor to achieve this.[100]

[99]protester.

[100]Golding's translation ends with a variation of Calvin's now familiar closing exhortation: "Now let us kneele down in the presence of our good God, with acknowledgement of our faults, praying him to make us so to fede them, as wee maye learne to mislike more and more of our selves for them. And for as much as the verie remedie to rid us from all our diseases and corruptions, is to heare his holye woorde; it maye please him so to open our eares, as wee maye receive it with all reverence and humilitie, and so print it in our heartes, as wee may make it availe to the use for which hee ordained it, namely to quicken us and to drawe us to salvation, that wee may desire it with all our heartes, and apply our indeavour thereunto more and more. And therefore let us all saye, Almightie God heavenly, etc. *Sermons on the Fifth Book of Moses,* trans. Golding, pp. 258–59. Cf. Calvin, *Sermons sur les dix commandemens,* 1557 ed., pp. 205–6.

Sermon Fifteen[2]

Deuteronomy 5:28–33[3]

In accordance with what was said yesterday, God shows in this passage that he concurs with the people's request and grants them what will become their best alternative. And by doing so we see that he wanted to make them aware of his goodness in order to win them better.[4] Certainly, from the point of view of his authority, he ought to make us subject to himself and could, but he much more prefers to treat us with paternal gentleness. That is why he shows that he is in accord with the people. Let us likewise remember that God truly knows what is good and beneficial for us, so if we had to choose, we could not do better than to desire what he does. This will not always seem so to God's people; nevertheless it is true.

---

[1]N. in *CO:* "This sermon corresponds to the fifteenth in the 1562 collection, pp. 313–33." *CO* 26.407.

[2]The original title: "The Fourteenth Sermon on Chapter 5:28–33." *CO* 26.407.

[3]Cf. Calvin's discussion of this text in his Comm. *Four Books of Moses,* vol. 1, pp. 337–38, 345; *CO* 24.207–8, 212.

[4]See "The Second Sermon," n. 19.

Furthermore, he adds that he has not taken this step because the people wanted it, but only insofar as he approved it. For sometimes God will readily grant men what they ask, but only to importune them as it brings about their condemnation. As, for example, when the people wanted to eat meat,[5] it is true that he satisfied[6] their wish, but they dearly paid their share[7] for it, for they disrespected God in wanting to revel[8] in what had been forbidden.[9] Now it is true that God nonetheless amply fed[10] those who murmured, for they had plenty to fill their stomachs, but it would have been better had they died of hunger.

Now this is not the kind of petition[11] of which Moses speaks here. For in particular God says, *that they have rightly spoken.*[12] It's as if he had said, "Follow this system, for you will see how I will gratify you. You have asked for a man who may speak to you in my name and I concur. I will it. Therefore he must lead you [even] more to accept the doctrine which will be preached to you on my part, insofar as I have done it for your sake and election. Nevertheless, do not suppose that I deliberately pleased you without reason or purpose. For I declare that all will go well if you follow this method of profiting in his word. And whenever Moses comes to you from me, you must listen in complete reverence to what he says for your welfare."

Let us also carefully note that when God's Word is preached to us by men that it is not based on their imagination, but it is founded on that doctrine which God has given and which serves for our benefit. And that ought to prevent [even] more our being tempted by any foolish ambition to alter [it], for as always novelty pleases us more than it should. Let us realize that it is here that we are to take our stand: that throughout our life we are to listen to the Word of God which is preached to us. And why is that? Not simply because he wills it, but because he explains[13] that it is good.

Furthermore, God arouses[14] the people to think more seriously

[5]chair-vivande.
[6]saoulé-rassasié.
[7]l'escot-l'écot.
[8]iouyr-jouir.
[9]See the story as told in Num. 11:1–35. The price they "dearly paid" was a plague. Cf. Comm. *Four Books of Moses,* vol. 4, pp. 37–39; *CO* 24.177–78. For Calvin the *form* of the plague was also its cause: the people's gluttony and greed.
[10]rassasité.
[11]requeste-requête.
[12]Deut. 5:28.
[13]declaire-explique.
[14]resveille-reveille.

about keeping the commandments of the law than they have. For the people had said, "We will do them."[15] But now, for his part, God says, "Who will give them the heart[16] to do this? Who will put such an ambition in their soul?"[17] Now by these words he indicates that they had scarcely taken seriously their promise, for men make great commitments with their mouth, but when it comes to fulfilling them, they show how thoughtless[18] their promises are. Therefore God, in order to make them aware of the difficulty involved in obeying the law,[19] says here, "How I wish they could!" For the word which he uses when he says, "Who will give them the heart?" means in Hebrew what we mean when we say, "So be it," or, "How I wish it were true!" Now it is true that God speaks like a man here, for he needs only to will[20] it since everything is in his hands. But then we could say to him, "It is for you to do, O Lord; yet you ask who will give them the heart? To whom does this belong to do? For man, on his own, will never incline toward good, rather he must be pushed there by some other cause, and that is not for the creature to do, but for your Spirit. Therefore, do not ask who will give them the heart, rather only deploy the force[21] of your Spirit and they will do it." For we shall also hear God say, "I will give you the heart to fear me."[22] If that were in us to do, then why should he do it? But he declares that it is for him to do, in the same way that he adds by his prophet, "I will give them a heart to obey me."[23] Likewise we shall see him saying somewhat later, "I shall enable them to keep my commandments."[24]

God, then, attributes to himself [the capacity] to instruct men and to govern them by his Holy Spirit in order that they might be subject to him and submit[25] to his righteousness. Why then does he "wish it were so" in this passage?

Because (as in many other places) he speaks in the manner of men. And its purpose is that we might better comprehend (as I

---

[15]See Exod. 24:4, 7.
[16]courage-coeur.
[17]Deut. 5:29. Cf. Calvin's development of this text in his Comm. *Four Books of Moses*, vol. 1, p. 337; *CO* 24.207f.
[18]a la volee-sans réfléchir.
[19]See the "Introduction," n. 55.
[20]souhaiter.
[21]vertu-force.
[22]Deut. 30:6.
[23]Jer. 32:39.
[24]See Ezek. 11:19–20; 36:27.
[25]se rangent-soumettent.

have already mentioned) that when anyone speaks to us about walking in the obedience of God, that such is not without difficulty, and that all our abilities[26] should be awakened to the end that we conscientiously apply ourselves to such a study. Therefore instead of men promising to perform wonders without reflecting on it and promising to obey God and keep his law, let us realize that we need only scrutinize our capacity to discover how totally inept we are. Indeed, instead of being able to perfect to the end what we have been commanded, we don't even know where to begin. We can't even conceive of one single good idea until God has reformed us, until he has drawn us to himself and given us the heart [to do it]; and then at the same time he must add the ability to put into practice what we will. That is what this phrase means: "And who will give them the heart?" or, "I would that it were so!"

Now may all of this admonish us not to presume on our strength to be too bold. For such pride ruins us whenever we think that we can do anything. And with good reason God laughs at such arrogance. Rather let us be sensitive to the fact that we can do nothing; and although we are accountable for doing everything that God commands us, that does not mean that we have the wherewithal to do it, for we all go astray. Likewise, it is no small or petty thing to love God with all our heart, with all our mind, and with all our strength. As if we had only to say, "Yes, I will go about it." But that transcends every capacity man knows.

When we have learned that the law's righteousness is too high[27] for us and that for our part we are so debilitated that it's a pity, then we shall learn to groan before God and readily apprehend that we are under compulsion to do what he ordains. Yet we shall [need] to ask him for strength, for him to help us through his Holy Spirit, and not simply for him to make up for our frailty, but for him to begin and perfect everything in us, for him to grant us both the will and the strength and even constancy, and then add the power to achieve what we long for.

Now God also indicates in this text that when he sends us his Word, his purpose is to be united with us and for us to be united with him. He only asks for [our] obedience so that when we become his children he may reveal himself as our Father. That is the

[26]sens.
[27]See n. 19 above.

intention behind God's will for his Word to be preached to us; it exists that we might be brought under his wings; that he might watch over and save us; yes, on the condition that we come to him peaceably and permit ourselves to be governed by his Word and become submissive to it.

Now certainly (as we have already seen) that is not within our power; God has to grant us the grace. And he does not grant it to everyone. But it is not a question here of our probing into God's strict counsel as to why he reforms some by [the power of] his Holy Spirit and leaves others to go astray[28] according to their corruption, without retrieving them. We must not get into that labyrinth.[29] Rather may it suffice us [to know] that God wanted to make men inexcusable in saying, "How I wish it were the case!" It's as if he had said that once we have been taught his Word we are without excuse. God will not be responsible if we are not saved.[30] Why? Because if we walk in the way that he has commanded us, we shall know that it leads to our highest good. Therefore, whenever we are afflicted and God chastises us by adversity, let us lay our misfortunes to our own faults. Let us realize that we have no grounds for murmuring or complaining to him, for we are guilty since we have not followed his Word. That, in sum, is what we want to emphasize in this passage.

[Now] it is true that at the same time he must rush to our aid, recognizing that we are too weak in ourselves to fulfill his law, indeed, that we cannot possibly attain it or approach it in any way, rather the fact remains that if we do not walk as we ought, he will forever have to pass judgment against us, knowing that the fault is ours. And when we have been chastised[31] by God, let no one say that it was undeserved. And why? [Because] when we possess God's Word we have a testimony that he wills to be united with us, and [wills] to fulfill the office of Father and make us prosper in every way, provided we absorb his grace and do not corrupt it with anything of our own. That is why men are confounded and justly condemned for having rejected God's grace and shut the door on him, seeing they have been taught by his Word and not

[28]errer-se tromper.
[29]An allusion to the unhappy controversy which the Zébédée-Bern disputes had forced on Calvin.
[30]Both Bolsec and Zébédée had charged that Calvin's doctrine of predestination made God responsible for sin.
[31]battus des verges.

profited by it. Consequently this text offers a highly useful admonition when we realize that God wants us to do what he commands in order that it might go well with us. For herein we see that if we receive the doctrine in humility, requiring ourselves to obey it, that the outcome cannot help but be happy and we will be certain of our salvation. For we shall always have to come back to this, praying that God will give us the heart, as that is his office. But at the same time if we [should] default, let us learn to condemn ourselves in order to be justified before him.

Moreover, let us rejoice seeing that he procures our salvation and wills to advance it whenever his Word is preached to us.[32] And let us remember what is said in the Proverbs of Solomon, that wisdom's pleasure and delight is to dwell with men.[33] There you have God himself asserting that when he sends us his Word his purpose is to instruct us in the complete perfection of wisdom, as if he were sending his wisdom from heaven. Indeed! And for what end? Well, wisdom is introduced there as saying, "Behold, my highest pleasure is to live with men." It's as if God himself had bared his heart and said, "My desire to be bound to men by a sacred bond is expressed in my instructing them by my Word. And if they are not ill-disposed[34] on their part, they shall realize that I forever want to be in their midst, without ever being separated from them." Certainly that ought to inspire in us a reverence for the Word of God to the extent that we might find it of [great] advantage and never allow ourselves to be diverted from it, especially in light of the fact that it brings us an inestimable gain, that is, that our Lord is united with us.

Now it follows in Moses' text that God commands the people *for each of them to retire to their tent and for Moses to remain there*[35]; then he adds: *I shall give you all the commandments, statutes, and ordinances*[36] *that you should teach all the people.*[37] Once again[38] God shows here that he does not cease to continue to teach the people, although he employs that means which has been explained, namely, that Moses was the expositor of God's will and the carrier of his message. It is certainly worth noting, inasmuch as its pur-

[32]See Rom. 10:14–15.
[33]Prov. 8:31.
[34]revesches-revêchés.
[35]See Deut. 5:30–31.
[36]droictures.
[37]Deut. 5:31.
[38]derechef-de nouveau.

pose is to help us grasp that God always wants to reserve us for himself and that he doesn't want our faith to be founded on men['s ideas], or dependent upon them. It's a point well taken.

It is true that those who follow their good intentions, or say that they adhere to what the church determines by its ancient fathers, should be deceived[39] from time to time. And if we confront them with the fact that they are in a flutter and highly uncertain of themselves when they so yield to [other] men, they become obstinate[40]; for they are like the papists, whom the devil has so bewitched that they are satisfied with having their resolutions based on human fancy, ardently scorning the Word of God. And even though one were to witness to them on the basis of God's Word in the hope of expelling their superstitions, it is all the same to them; they are so dense[41] that it hardly matters to them if God is opposed. Therefore men are quite capable for a limited time of exercising the audacity of energetically going wherever their foolish imaginations carry them and of holding out against God, but when this is brought under examination, they hardly know which way to turn. Consequently, let us note that we are without any permanent and stable[42] moorings if our faith is not founded on the Word of God, if we cannot say that what we possess we have from him, and that that is the truth, that we do not stray about [as victims of] our own opinion,[43] or stop with the doctrine of men.

When we hear God saying in this passage, *I shall deliver*[44] *to you what you must teach them*, let us note that it is simply imperative for us to rely upon him and his infallible truth for all our support in order that our faith might not fall into danger[45] or doubt. And it is that which we must look[46] for when we attend the sermon, that we might be able to have this point ratified and even signed in our consciences: that we possess God's Word on which our life is dependent.

And at the same time let us equally note that God willed to hold on to those who are charged with proclaiming his Word to the

[39]eslourdis-rendus stupides.
[40]opiniastre-opiniâtres.
[41]eslourdis.
[42]certain.
[43]cuyder-croyance, opinion.
[44]exposeray-donnerai, expliquerai.
[45]en bransle-en danger de.
[46]cercher-chercher.

degree that they dare not advance anything of their own, but should be content to be faithful stewards concerning what he commands them and always be able to testify that they have served God, seeing that they have fulfilled what he commanded them and have reported it directly.[47] That is what we have to observe, I say, that God has established his ministers for proclaiming his Word to us and has given[48] them the office of teaching, and we are to add nothing of our own invention,[49] but should simply report[50] what we know proceeds from God. And in order that the people might realize that God did not intend to half-teach them, he reiterates what we have just previously seen, the statutes, ordinances, commandments, and ceremonies. It's as if he were saying that nothing would fail in his doctrine and that the people ought not hunger[51] for anything more.[52]

This [doctrine] has [already] been explained[53] more fully, but when God made use of [these] different words, instead of simply repeating [the word] law, we should note that his reason was to arrest men's attention more effectively, in order that they might not be tempted by frivolous curiosity to add anything to his law. For we know by nature how easily we succumb to this temptation and how our flesh perpetually elicits us to invent all manner of new things.

It is for that reason that in the papacy, as each has undertaken to add his bit and portion, that laws have been piled on top of laws.[54] And why? For it seemed [to them] that plainly walking in the Word of God was inadequate and that it would be better still to introduce a mixture.[55] Now to the contrary, God says that if we possess his law we [already] have statutes, commandments, ordinances, and rules.[56] It's as if he were saying that it is unnecessary for mortal men to be so presumptuous[57] as to wish to be wiser than God. For once they have presented their discourse, they still can-

[47]de main en main.
[48]baillé-donné.
[49]imaginé.
[50]apportions-repportions.
[51]appetter-désirer, rechercher.
[52]d'avantage-de plus.
[53]exposé-expliqué.
[54]See the *Institutes* 4.10.1–32. Calvin charges that the papacy's laws deny God's law and are meaningless and worthless. They constitute a burden on consciences.
[55]meslinge-mélange.
[56]droictures.
[57]outrecuidez-présomptueux.

not correct or add anything; for whatever they advance of their own is not only superfluous and useless, but only spoils[58] it all, like pouring sour wine into good.

Thus God having spoken in this way now adds *that they should carefully observe whatever he commands them without leaning to the right hand or to the left.*[59] Once again our Lord reveals here that he does not intend for his law simply to be honored by men's mouths (a means by which we love to acquit ourselves), rather he shows that he has published his law in order to hold us under his subjection and in his service and wants his law preached even today. For that is the means by which he wills to prove[60] whether he will rule[61] over us, as over a peaceful people who are subject[62] to him.

Therefore let us carefully note [that] when we come to the sermon our purpose is not to say whether the doctrine is good and holy. [If that were the case] God would be obligated[63] to us for pronouncing his Word worthy of reception. [But] he does not intend for us to be his judges. Of course we owe him that kind of declaration; once we have heard his Word, we ought each to acknowledge that it is the pure truth, that there is no other righteousness,[64] or justice, or wisdom than what his law contains. However it is necessary for us to press beyond that and to yield[65] ourselves to his service. Certainly that is a point we want to highlight[66] in this text.

Then there is also [the phrase]: *to observe to do,*[67] in which God shows that we must seriously apply all our strength. For men cannot follow God while asleep. No matter how hard they try, it is only with great effort that they shall be able to drag[68] their legs; such is the weakness of their nature. Therefore let us not suppose that we can justify ourselves before God without confronting pain. It is simply too difficult in light of who we are, that is, seeing that we are lazy and slow to [do] any good. Yet I say that God has already loved us and is active in governing us by his Holy Spirit.

[58]gaster-gâter.
[59]Deut. 5:32.
[60]exprouver-prouver.
[61]chevira-dominera sur.
[62]reduit-abaissé.
[63]sera bien tenu à-sera bien obligé à.
[64]droicture.
[65]ranger-soumettre.
[66]recueillir.
[67]Deut. 5:32.
[68]treiner-traîner.

For if he were to leave us as we are, not only would we be slow, but we would do precisely the opposite of what he wants. If he were to call us to himself, we would retreat and ever be forced to pursue evil. That is how little power we have to will good.

But let us note what we have already mentioned. [For] although our Lord has given us some sound inclination[69] and has set us on the right track,[70] we are so lazy that instead of only taking a minute to move our foot, we need an hour before we can stir; or for every step we take forward, we stumble[71] and fall back two, or suffer some pitiful setback.

For that reason, God is justified in saying here: *Observe to do.* For it's as if he were saying: "True, my law has been given to you to be put into practice and to be obeyed. But don't think that that is easily done. What's at issue then? Let each [person] prepare himself to walk in my commandments, to think on them with all his effort.[72] May you be diligent to that [end], filled with zeal and vigor, on the lookout lest you be turned aside. May you be that attentive."

In summary, then, we see that in regard to walking in his obedience, our Lord exhorts us to work diligently. And why? Because what he asks of us is not easy. Moreover, we are so poorly disposed that it's a pity, for unless someone goads[73] us, or almost pushes us with force, we will[74] not go forward. The issue, then, is to wake up, to be alert, and always on guard in order to fulfill what our Lord has commanded us.

Next he adds, *that this should be done without turning either toward the right hand or the left, rather each should walk in all the way that God has shown.*[75] It is true that this passage is treated more fully in chapter twelve, but it would be inappropriate to by-pass it if we hope to understand what God wanted to say here. By forbidding us to be turned aside, either to the right hand or to the left, he shows us that he wants to be heard in all and by all without exception. Now this suggests two things: that we should neither add anything to nor subtract anything from the law. For when we add

[69]bonne affection.
[70]en bon train.
[71]choppons-rébuchons.
[72]qu'on y mette peine.
[73]picque-pique.
[74]pouvons, "cannot."
[75]Deut. 5:32–33.

anything, it's as if we want to turn to the right. For those who add to the law of God do so thinking that it is unnecessary to observe all its contents and that they are justified in extending it. That is how men would like to give status to their whims.[76] For when they think[77] of anything expedient, they suppose that God forgot to include it and that it is all right for them to do. And that is precisely why so many ordinances and laws and ceremonies have been instated in the papacy. The Jews were guilty of a similar error as they are reproached for despising God's commandments and statutes for the sake of their traditions.[78] Therefore let us be on guard lest we take the right hand road and be turned from the path which God shows us. And why? [Because] the right hand road symbolizes our ambition to be wise, and above all righteous,[79] and our supposing that it is good to do more than the commandments limit us to do. For when we do so, we become the devil's servants, for God disclaims[80] anything we might add to his Word; he repudiates such lies.[81]

Now we lean to the left whenever we limit[82] the Word of God, that is, whenever we are content to serve only part of it, still expecting it to defend[83] our liberty to indulge our appetites. [Take] a man who is not inclined toward some vices, and who truly wants to be justified in God's sight, and serve him as well, but because he cannot master himself with regard to a particular vice, he [still] wants God to be satisfied and makes a pact with himself, saying, "Ah well, if I sin in this matter, I will compensate for it in another." Now let us guard against taking the path on the left, that is, doing anything that diminishes the Word of God. For when it is forbidden to kill,[84] or rob, and commit adultery as well, it is imperative for us to be subject[85] in all and by all without any rejoinder concerning what we have been commanded. For just as

---

[76]phantasie-fantaisie. This statement is reminiscent of a similar one in the *Institutes* 4.8.10: "Meanwhile, contemptuous of God's Word, [the popes] coin dogmas after their own whim, which ... they afterwards require to be subscribed to as articles of faith."

[77]s'advisent-s'avisent.

[78]Matt. 15:3.

[79]justes.

[80]desadvoue-désavoue.

[81]meslinge-mélange.

[82]diminuons.

[83]donne.

[84]meurtrir.

[85]assuiettir-assujettir.

we must not add anything at all to the law, so also it is illicit to take anything from it, rather in everything we are called to walk in the path which God shows us.

Now when he says *the way*, his purpose is to exhort us to hold to it, as we shall see at the end of the book where Moses says: "This is the way; walk in it."[86] [For] it's as if he were saying: "Whoever turns aside from the doctrine which I set before you goes astray[87]; he only runs across country and, rather than advancing toward his goal, is that much farther from it." The same is true in this passage: *Walk in the way*, that is, "You poor people, do not willingly go astray, do not err. [For] if you follow where your God leads you, you cannot err. But if you follow your own mind, then in the end God will necessarily have to show you that you are no better off than a stray animal and that you have not held to the right road. Therefore understand that the doctrine of God is what constitutes your *way*."

If this word were sufficiently implanted in our mind we would be held on a very short leash and our fidgety desires would not triumph over us as they do; our life would be more stable. For God daily shows us the way, and yet men dispute [it] and pose long questions, [asking], "What are we to do?" Indeed, as if it had never been declared, as if God never opens his mouth to show us the right way. And when he does, do we not offend and insult him by not following it? Do we not accuse him of wasting his time and effort with us? Now [perhaps] we see the meaning of this word *way*, that is, that apart from the doctrine of God, there is nothing but error and deception, and that men deceive themselves whenever they think they are doing what is right, unless they are governed by the Word of God which shows us the good and true road.

Now in particular he says: [in] *all the way*. For he has no intention of making a division here as men might wish, for they would always like to reserve something—no matter what—to themselves. But on the contrary God says, "It is crucial that I be completely obeyed in everything by everyone, or I shall renounce you." Therefore if we want our life sanctioned before God, it isn't enough to be subject to him in part, rather let us see to it that our whole life is brought into conformity with what he commands to the extent that we can say that we have held to *all his way*.[88]

[86]Deut. 28:9.
[87]s'esgare-s'égaré.
[88]Italics for emphasis.

Now one should be able to ask a question here. Is it possible for us to walk entirely in the way of God? For on the contrary, since men do not do the good they want, it is demanding quite a lot for us to attempt[89] to come to the right[90] road and follow it to the end when we can't even attain it. Saint Paul himself laments the fact that he could not do what he willed to do in order to be justified before God.[91] Now the issue here is not the perfection which the law requires, rather let us simply understand that God wants men to apply themselves and yield themselves to him and to endeavor to run [on that road] even though they may not attain the end. Therefore, although throughout our life we march forward, expending tremendous effort and never fully reach God, in the same way we must hold to all that the law contains.

Of course we cannot justify ourselves vis-à-vis the law to such an extent that there would be a complete harmony[92] between our life and the Word of God, but whenever we desire to submit[93] ourselves to God and to conform ourselves to him (not on the basis of an [isolated] article, but in everything without exception, doing so with thorough dedication[94]), then we can speak of walking steadfastly in *all the way*[95] of God. For he truly supports us and acknowledges such a desire when he sees that we briskly go about to that end with undivided attention, not wishing to reserve any ambitions for ourselves, nor taking the license to do them, but working to the best of our ability according to that grace which has been given to us.

Now at the same time he adds: *In order that they might prosper and that it might go well with them and their children.*[96] Herein he shows (as we have already discussed) that all our miseries and afflictions, which we endure in this world, are only so many punishments[97] for our faults.[98] The only thing that can be said is that we are responsible for our own unhappiness. Certainly we each long to be well off and prosperous. It is hardly necessary for us to be taught that wish, for our nature inclines toward that end. Never-

[89]tasché-tâché.
[90]bon.
[91]See Rom. 7:19.
[92]correspondace-correspondance.
[93]ranger-soumettre.
[94]mis toute peine.
[95]Italics for emphasis.
[96]Deut. 5:33.
[97]chastimens-châtiments.
[98]See Calvin's doctrine of providence, the *Institutes* 1.17 and 18. In particular, 1.17, 3–5 is apropos to the remainder of the above paragraph.

theless it appears that we have conspired our [own] misfortune. For the means for prospering may be summed up in our being obedient to our God and then he will bless us in such a way as to make us aware of the fruits of his grace in all and by all. But what? We do not want to render him the obedience which he is due. Thus it is appropriate that we should be deprived of his benediction and that he should reject us as if we were not worthy of being numbered among his creatures. Thus let us note that our Lord intended here to convince[99] men of their faults and to show them that they are guilty for all the misfortune and poverty which they suffer in this world, which they must attribute to their [own] sins.[100] But at the same time he wanted to attract his own by proposing a reward. [For] it's as if he had said: "Now, then, I certainly deserve to be worshiped[101] by you, even though you should not expect anything from me, for since you are my creatures, does that not constitute an [adequate] reason for you to be subject to me? Is it not appropriate that your entire life should be surrendered to me? Nevertheless, I do not want you to serve me gratuitously; I renounce[102] my right, that is that you are obligated to do all that I command you without expecting some reward; rather I declare to you that I am ready to bless you and make you prosper when you serve me."

Accordingly our Lord, speaking in this way, shows that he wants to attract his own by an amicable means, that he wants to break their hearts[s] that they might be that much more inclined[103] to serve him, seeing he is not as stern as he could be. Rather he surrenders[104] what is his and instead takes on the office of father, saying, that if we are children to him, then he will be benign and liberal toward us. And although he owes us nothing, he will not fail to reward us for that service which we shall offer him.[105]

Now therein we are readily informed[106] that God wills to draw us to himself, but we must not infer that men can merit anything by serving God. For the papists, when they hear passages like

[99] redarguer-convaincre de faute.
[100] pechez.
[101] servi.
[102] deporte-renonce.
[103] affectionnez.
[104] se demet de-renonce à.
[105] See the *Institutes* 2.8.4.
[106] admonnestez-informes.

these, stress[107] their merits and suppose that God is obligated[108] to them in the same proportion.[109] On the contrary, God clearly wishes to show us that he is ready to accommodate himself to us along human lines, that he only wants to induce us to obey him. And this is not for his own benefit. For, in fact, what profit would he receive if we were to fulfill all his law? Would it provide him with any advantage? No! Accordingly, that is what God affirms and what we have to note in this sentence. Therefore let us learn [that] when we are obedient to God and he causes us to prosper, that the latter isn't because he owes us anything, or because we have earned it, and are therefore able to boast that he remunerates us on the basis of what we merit, rather he is pleased to pour out his gratuitous goodness upon us to the extent of calling reward what he gives us of his pure and free liberality, which he does without being bound[110] by anything.

Moreover, when he chastens[111] us and we are subject[112] to so many miseries, let us remember that we are receiving the fruits of our sowing. Inasmuch as we have behaved badly, it is quite appropriate that our Lord should give us some sign of his anger in order for us to realize that he is the judge of the world. But he equally keeps in mind our welfare, that we might groan over our faults and be displeased by them and hastily return to him in true repentance. That is why God, in displaying his anger against us, does not fail to declare his love for us; for he strives[113] to redirect us toward himself, he sees that we are asleep in our sins and he awakens us, for he knows that it is expedient for him to do so. That is what we want to underline in this passage.

Moses finally speaks of the land, saying: *In order that you might prosper in the land which I shall give you.*[114] He even puts it into a second sentence: *In order that you might be well in the land which you shall possess.*[115] Now it would appear here at first that the only reward which God permits is this terrestrial and transitory life. But

[107]ils viennent.
[108]tenu.
[109]See Calvin's refutation of the scholastic doctrine of good works in the *Institutes* 3.11.13–20.
[110]tenu.
[111]chastie-châtie.
[112]suiets-sujets.
[113]tasche-tâche.
[114]Deut. 5:33.
[115]Ibid.

if such were the case, the people of Israel's hope would have been dashed.[116] Rather let us observe that our Lord has used a different means with Israel's people than he has with us, although they tend toward the same end. For the sacrifices which were enjoined in the law were not for the purpose of retracting the people from the salvation which we enjoy in Jesus Christ, but rather were given for the purpose of leading them to him, for God's will was to signal that men are under condemnation and that they have no means for their reconciliation apart from the blood of our Lord Jesus Christ.[117]

Yet at the same time they did not cease to kill dumb beasts, God saying, "Whenever you kill a calf, or a lamb, or a sheep in my behalf your sins will be forgiven." [Now] it would seem thereby that God intended to establish the remission of sins on the basis of these sacrifices of dumb beasts. But this was not the case. Its purpose was to lead the people, however crudely, toward the redemption which we have finally acquired in the person of our Lord Jesus Christ. That likewise applies to the land of Canaan. For God willed from the very beginning to offer[118] the eternal heritage of salvation to Abraham's children when he said to Abraham: "I am your true shield[119] and reward."[120] He does not promise the earth to Abraham as the latter's highest goal,[121] but he wills for Abraham to place all his confidence in him, for the patriarch to praise him above everything else and to look forward to heavenly life for both himself and all his race; but insofar as our Lord Jesus Christ had not appeared, nor the veil of the temple had been rent, it was necessary for this land of Canaan to serve as an award,[122] seeing that it was fully promised to him in inheritance.

Therefore let us carefully note that when he says: *In order that you might prosper in the land,* God's intention is not to satisfy his people with this present life, but by this means he wants to lead them higher, that is, to the hope of this immortality which he has promised. In any event, our Lord promises his benediction on his

[116]One of Calvin's central tenets in the *Institutes* (2.10.7–14) is that the Patriarchs interpreted the promises under the Old Covenant to incorporate eternal life.
[117]See n. 19 above. Cf. also the *Institutes* 2.7.16; 8.28–29.
[118]proposer-offrir.
[119]loyer.
[120]See Gen. 15:1.
[121]pour s'y arrester.
[122]arre-arrêt.

people in such a way that they even become aware of it in this world and experience something of a foretaste, expecting the full joy[123] to be revealed to them when they are taken away from this world. Even today we ought to keep in mind Saint Paul's testimony: That when we fear God, we enjoy the promises of both this life and the life to come.[124] For in this world God wants to make us conscious of his goodness in order that we might be lured [still] higher. Likewise, we should learn to receive the benefits of God in this world in such a way as to be able to lay them aside when we have finally come into his Kingdom, where we shall enjoy the fullness of everything.[125]

[123]iouyssance-jouissance.

[124]See I Tim. 6:17–19.

[125]Golding's translation concludes this sermon with the following exhortation: "Nowe let us fall downe in the presence of our good God with acknowledgement of our faultes, praying him to make us feele them better than we have done, even till they have drawen us to true repentance, and that wee acknowledging our wretchednesse more and more, may learne to strive against all the affections of our flesh, and against all our wicked and frowarde lustes, and moreover to with-stande the cursed presumptuousness that is in us which also woulde have us to doe that which we our selves best like of, so as nothing may stay us from following the pure and simple worde of our God, assuring our selves that it is the true and perfite rule whereunto we must submit our selves, and that we must not attempt to ad any thing to it, but simplie rest upon that which is conteined there, and go forwarde more and more therein, untill that having finished this earthly race, wee be come to the heavenly rest whereunto hee calleth us. And let us pray him to reach us his hande in the meane while, whensoever we seeke him and call uppon him in our neede. That it may please him to graunt this grace, not onely to us but also to all people and nations of the earth, etc." *Sermons Upon the Fifth Book of Moses*, trans. Golding, pp. 264–65. Cf. Calvin, *Sermons sur les dix commandemens*, 1557 ed., p. 221.

Sermon Sixteen[2]

Deuteronomy 6:1–4[3]

We have often seen in these sermons how Moses would speak to the people touching on the content of the law. Just yesterday we saw him do this and now again we witness the same in today's text. We must not regard this as useless repetition insofar as men immediately forget[4] what they have learned from God unless their memory is refreshed. And we know that it takes practically nothing to divert us. For we are so inclined toward vanity that nothing is more difficult for us than to remain obedient to God; as soon as we have conceived some vain idea,[5] we are carried away and no longer remember[6] what God said to us. Moreover, insofar as his

---

[1]N. in *CO:* "This sermon corresponds to the sixteenth in the 1562 collection, pp. 333–56." *CO* 26.419.

[2]The original title: "The First Sermon on Chapter 6:1–4." *CO* 26.419.

[3]Cf. Calvin's brief treatment of Deut. 6:4 in his Comm. *Four Books of Moses,* vol. 1, p. 420; *CO* 24.263.

[4]"forgot" in Fr.

[5]conceu une phantasie.

[6]savons.

ambition[7] is to win us to himself, he is forced to uproot those spurious opinions which preoccupy us. For when a piece of ground has laid fallow, it requires a considerable amount of work to make it usable again. The same is true of us. And that is why Moses says anew *that here are the commandments, statutes,* [and] *ordinances which the Lord committed to him in order that he might give them to the people that they might be kept.*[8]

Now by these words Moses means that God wills to hold the people in his obedience. [It's as if God were saying:] "Poor people, what do you hope to gain by wandering[9] so? Behold, I give you my law. When you possess that doctrine, you cannot err. It is the way of salvation. Therefore take it." Nevertheless, men are fickle,[10] rushing this way and that, and God [has to] tighten the reins with force. Just as when a horse is difficult to manage, the rider can hardly control it with a single tug. It will only prance[11] about and resist handling. The rider must steady it with persistent control. So likewise must God act toward his people.[12] And thereby he shows that the human mind is full of rebellion, or, better yet, instability, as man cannot hold[13] to the Word of God which simultaneously provides his salvation and well-being. This being true, let us note that in the person of the people of Israel we are admonished that when God set his Word before us, it was not simply recorded for that day [alone], but must be put into practice by us every day of our life. And what we must ever keep before us is that *these are*[14] the statutes, the ordinances, and the commandments [by which we were meant to live]. It is not our prerogative to set up the rules and laws which govern our life, but that authority belongs to God.

Furthermore, he has also admonished us by showing us the right road; therefore let us follow it and stop inquiring as to what we ought to do. For once our Lord has spoken there is no longer any doubt. We must not allege, "Well, I don't know if that is good

[7]qu'il ne demande sinon.
[8]Deut. 6:1.
[9]esgarer-égarer.
[10]vollages-volages.
[11]s'esgaye-s'égaye.
[12]Calvin frequently enjoys using illustrations of this type to portray the human condition.
[13]arrester-arrêter.
[14]Italics for emphasis.

or if that is to my advantage." Let us be content with what God has shown. For he will always be a good [school] master to us, provided we do not become bad pupils on him. And for this reason the commandments, statutes, and ordinances are mentioned here anew, lest we think that God only partly intended to teach us.

Therefore a perfection of wisdom is to be found in his law. It only remains for us to obey it, for us not to be so curious as to desire what God has not shown, for us not to harbor foolish ambitions[15] that lure us this way and that, rather let us remember that God did not envy those whom he took under his charge, but above all he only taught them what was useful. [Therefore] let us govern ourselves according to his will and apply all our energy[16] to that end. And let his law be sufficient for us. And though the whole world should reject us, what do we care, we have our judge. And even if the world should go astray[17] in [its pursuit of] vain causes,[18] and everyone decides what seems best to him, let us constantly remember that it is requisite for us to stand before our God's judicial seat, that it is to him that we shall have to render an account. For he has given us his law and will judge us according to it. For that reason[19] let us forget what the world devises, knowing that it amounts to nothing but vanity and lies.

At the same time, Moses adds, with respect to his office, that he has contributed nothing of his own, but according to the charge which God laid on him, he has faithfully set forth his law. And his assertion is well worth noting. For we have to keep in mind what has thus far been discussed, that Moses was the most excellent prophet whom God ever brought[20] into being. Yet in this text he does not take the liberty to teach what his own judgment dictates, for he knows that he is a mortal man, subject to the law like other men. That is why he maintains that what he reports[21] he received from God; he only passes it on from [God's] hand to [our] hand. Since Moses [only] does that, who will dare to say that it is lawful for him to convey more? And yet we have seen that very thing come to pass. For in all the papacy, is it a matter of listening to

[15]folles devotions.
[16]sens.
[17]desvoye-égare.
[18]phantasies.
[19]pourtant-pour cette raison.
[20]suscitast-fit naître, paraître.
[21]apporte.

what God might say in order to distinguish that from men's teachings? Rather they have their holy mother church,[22] as they call it, their own decisions and statutes, and this pretext of the church seems quite sufficient to them. In the meanwhile they strip[23] God of his authority in order to reinvest it in men who are nothing but putrefaction. What an insufferable sacrilege! For God ceases to be the lawgiver who guides his people and holds them under his yoke. Instead men usurp that authority.

So much the more must we keep what is contained here, namely, that Moses, although he was a heavenly angel and God had exalted him above all men, and although he was on the mountain for forty days without eating or drinking, clearly showing that he was no longer of the same status as others; nevertheless, when he returned from that celestial glory as in the company of angels, he still humbles himself and declares that he interjects nothing of his own, that he has no desire to fantasize, but is content to have heard what God proclaimed and to report it as a good servant who adds nothing, refusing to falsify the commission which God has been given. Again that is what we want to stress in this passage.

There is next an exhortation which adds in effect *that the people ought to become engaged in doing the Law,*[24] as if he were saying that it isn't given in order for people to affirm that all its contents are good, righteous, and equitable, but in order for men to demonstrate whether they will be obedient to God or not.

It is for this reason that he says: *That you may fear the Lord your God and keep his commandments and statutes.*[25] By this word *fear*[26] he means that God in declaring his law wanted to show that it was up to us as to whether we choose to serve him or not. For should we be able to do all the commandments in such a way as to leave nothing else to be said to men, nevertheless if the fear of God is not rooted in our heart and we do not bear him the reverence of wanting to be his own, then our entire life is nothing but a wasted pomp. For we must not suppose that God is pleased with appear-

---

[22]Calvin does not object to the church being called our "Mother" (*Institutes* 4.1.1–4), rather he rejects the pretentious claims which the medieval papacy invested in the church (4.2.1–12).

[23]despouillent-dépouillent.

[24]Deut. 6:1.

[25]Deut. 6:2.

[26]On the "fear" of God and "honor" of God, see the *Institutes* 3.2.6.

ances. They might be praised by men, but they are only so much smoke in God's eyes.

Accordingly, if we want to keep the law correctly and want our life acceptable[27] to God, then we must begin in this way: by showing him reverence and by wanting nothing but to be under his hand and guidance, rendering him homage as to our sovereign King and honoring him as our Father. When that can become our desire, then that is the beginning of all the law and of all righteousness.[28] That is why it is said that the fear of God is true wisdom.[29] Thus when we want to know if we have gained anything from God's law, we must always test and sound whether we entertain the desire and zeal for God to be honored and glorified by us. For if we do possess such a fear in our heart, the results will be seen in [the works of] our hands and feet, that is in all our members, as God also decreed this rule when he proclaimed his law. And if those who boast of their fear of God lead debauched[30] lives, they contradict[31] themselves with their own mouth and reveal how shameless they are for boasting of fearing God. Thus this passage is well worth keeping in which Moses explains[32] that, first of all, in order to serve God properly,[33] our hearts must be surrendered to him, as it is insufficient to suppose that an external appearance can contain all the virtues[34] which can be conceived; rather affection must precede [everything else].

Furthermore, the fear of God is not something hidden or idle.[35] For although it might be enclosed in our hearts, it is imperative for it to be apparent in our life; for it is our heart which governs both our hands and our feet and everything. Consequently let us learn to manifest, in word and in deed,[36] that we fear God by submitting our life to his will.

This being the case we can even assert[37] that God rejects[38] ev-

---

[27]agreeable.
[28]iustice.
[29]See Prov. 1:7.
[30]desbauchez-débauchés.
[31]desmentent-démentent.
[32]declaire.
[33]bien.
[34]vertus-forces.
[35]oysive-oisive.
[36]par effect, et par experience.
[37]recueillir.
[38]desadvoue-désavoue.

erything men attempt once they have turned aside from the Word of God. Take for example the papists who are always engaged in "the service of God"[39] as they call it. Yet what do they do? They keep busy, but to no avail, inasmuch as their effort centers on human inventions. To serve God [for them means] to babble,[40] or bow down, before images and idols, to run from altar to altar, to sing masses, to tramp about on pilgrimages, to celebrate[41] different saints on different days, [or] not to eat meat on Fridays and Saturdays. In brief, it's an abyss of nonsense[42] which they cherish[43] under the guise and title of "the service of God." But will you ever find that God has uttered a single word or syllable like that? No! For everything they say has been invented[44] by men.

Now on the basis of our text let us ask whether God will accept such "service" as lawful and good. On the contrary he says, "may you fear the Lord your God and keep all his commandments and statutes." Therefore we can conclude that when men turn aside from such a path and pursue their own imaginations and whatsoever they have forged, they clearly reveal their absence of any fear of God. For otherwise they would offer to him that sacrifice which he above all prefers, which is that obedience mentioned in the fifteenth chapter of I Samuel.[45] For if we do not listen to the voice of God in order to submit[46] ourselves to it, but instead follow what someone has invented on his own or what [other] men have established, then that is an [act of] idolatry as heinous as sorcery which God detests. That is how the Holy Spirit judges it, even though mortal men may conclude the reverse. Consequently we see that Moses has explained[47] here that when we willingly fear God we should also grant him the privilege of governing us according to his will, that we should not grant that freedom to men to guide us as they best see fit. Rather when God speaks, let every

---

[39]au service de Dieu, "the worship of God." See Calvin's criticism of the papacy's form of worship in the *Institutes* 4.10. 9, 12, 14–15, 23–32. Cf. also his rejection of images in Catholic worship (1.11–12) and the doctrine of the intercession of saints (3.20.21–27).

[40]barbotter-barboter.

[41]iusner.

[42]badinages-sottises.

[43]ont.

[44]controuvé-inventé.

[45]I Sam. 15:22.

[46]assuiettir-assujettir.

[47]declairé-expliqué.

mouth keep closed, and let us keep our ears open to hear and receive everything that God says to us.

Yet it is still insufficient for each [of us] to serve God [in self content], rather we must set about to the best of our ability to see that he is worshiped by everyone. Indeed, we must even strive to see that his service endures after our death,[48] after we have been taken from this world, and that the name of God is not destroyed with our passing,[49] but abides forever. That is why Moses says [that], "Your children and your posterity after you should continue to serve God and observe his Law."[50] We should carefully note here then that Moses does not simply exhort everyone to serve God, conforming his life to the law which he has given us, but he wills for fathers to take the effort to teach their children, and for us to leave as much seed behind us as we possibly can, to such an extent that God can be worshiped by our race and his name continually be invoked properly. Thus by this means those who are our descendants will be blessed and God's covenant, which constitutes our salvation, will endure forever and never perish in spite of our mortality.[51]

Now instead of fulfilling this doctrine, we see that fathers provide such examples for their children as to suggest that they have conspired to annihilate altogether any fear of God and any observation of his law. Therefore we should not be surprised[52] if God withdraws from us and if it seems that he wants to curtail those benefits he has bestowed on us, for we are unworthy of his continual kindness insofar as we are indifferent about his service surviving in its entirety. In any event, we must not treat what is said here lightly. Therefore let us endeavor[53] so to teach those who come after us that God shall surely be worshiped forever and people know him as everyone's father and savior, everyone fully surrendering to him.

[48]trespas-tréspas.

[49]vie caduque.

[50]See Deut. 6:2–3.

[51]Cf. Calvin's more detailed development of this theme in his exposition of Deut. 6:20–25, Comm. *Four Books of Moses,* vol. 1, pp. 362–63; *CO* 24.224–25: "The sole point which Moses urges in these verses is, that the people should testify their gratitude, which he commands the fathers to teach, should descend to their posterity. The sum is, that there was good reason why all the precepts of the Law should be observed, since by them it was that God desired His people, after their deliverance, to shew forth their sense of His loving-kindness."

[52]eshabir-ébahir.

[53]efforçons.

Now at the same time Moses adds what he has previously said, *that this is in order that their days may be prolonged and God may cause them to prosper in accordance with his promise to their fathers to give them a land flowing with milk and honey.*[54] Now we have already explained what Moses meant by this text, namely, that although God could compel us in a [single] word to serve him, he nevertheless uses a more amicable approach with us, that is, he promises us a reward when we serve him, not because our works merit anything, or because he is obligated to us, but [because] when he bestows[55] his favor on us in this way it serves to move us more effectively and results in our serving him with a far more ardent heart.[56]

Now is it not an [act of] shameless ingratitude when we hear that God willingly obligates himself to us and wills to provide a reward, are we not being shameless and ungrateful (I say), if we do not totally commit ourselves to his service? We are his and everything we are able to do we owe him, as our Lord Jesus Christ says. "Who are you (he says)? I ask you, if a man has a servant, indeed a slave, whom he works like an ox or a horse, who performs a service for him, will the master rise from his table and serve him in turn? Hardly.[57] For anything a man does while a servant he owes his superior. Likewise you owe everything to God (says Jesus Christ), and he owes you nothing."[58] But if on the basis of a free act[59] God promises us that if we serve him we shall be generously[60] compensated, then our effort is not in vain.

What [then] is his reason for doing this? In order to break our heart[s]. For as I have already said, we are entirely too shameless if we are not wholly inspired to serve God, seeing that out of the bounty of his pure goodness it pleases him to grant us a reward which we do not merit.

Furthermore, let us also note that although God should make a thousand contracts with us to remunerate our works, we still could not claim that he owes us anything, rather he would be justified in cursing and detesting us. For who among us keeps the law as it ought to be kept? Even if we successfully keep one article, we de-

---

[54]Deut. 6:2–3.
[55]gratifie-accorde ses faveurs.
[56]courage-coeur.
[57]Nenni.
[58]See Luke 17:7–10.
[59]une obligation gratuite.
[60]bien.

fault[61] in a hundred [others]. And when we resolve[62] to do what God has commanded us in his law, we [still] drag[63] our feet. There remains so much imperfection that we shall never be able to run as we ought. Thus we are cursed and damned if God should want to judge us strictly. Therefore it is entirely inappropriate for men to boast here of obtaining any renewal which they have earned, or of glorifying in their works. Rather let them realize that all of God's promises in his law are conditional. Consequently,[64] since no one can fulfill his obligation, they are useless unless God should receive and support us out of his pure goodness.

Think for a moment of the mania that exists among the papists to glorify in their works.[65] They give the impression that they have made a contract with God and heartily enter into it with a diabolical impudence, convinced that God is obligated to them. And on what basis?[66] On the basis of their satisfactions, their works, and their merits. And where will you find these? "O we have done this and that [they reply]. It's simply a matter of working[67] it out with God." But on the contrary, God requires us to serve him in everything[68] that we undertake. It involves what we cannot do, as we have previously seen, and as so many other passages bring out.[69]

Let everyone examine himself to see if there is any who has fulfilled the law. We are so far from it that you will not find[70] one who can affirm that he has fulfilled a hundredth part of it. Rather it is appropriate for all to confess that they are cursed. Besides, whatever small portion men can fulfill, the fact remains that there will always linger some amount of vice and stain.[71] Thus God would still be justified[72] in rejecting all [of us] and holding us in disgust.

[61]deffailons-faisons défault.
[62]pensons.
[63]treinons-traînons.
[64]Et pourtant que-par consequent.
[65]See Calvin's rejection of the scholastic doctrine of good works in the *Institutes* 3.11.13–20.
[66]enseignes.
[67]conter-compter.
[68]en tout et par tout.
[69]See the "Introduction" n. 56.
[70]treuve-trouve.
[71]macules.
[72]pourra.

Therefore let men remain confused[73] in their shame and let them confess that they are all guilty in God's sight. And for that reason[74] let us note that this promise could not be fulfilled apart from God's support of us and the fact that he overlooks so many of our weaknesses and vices, covering them over with his steadfast love.[75] Therefore God received our works, not really considering their substance, but accepting them as good and holy because of the passion and death of our Lord Jesus Christ. And although they may always contain some stain and spots, and would even be found to be stinking were it not for the fact that the blood of Jesus Christ has effaced that, it still remains only by this means and none other that he accepts us.

Therefore let us learn to glorify in God's pure mercy[76] [alone] and not boast of any merits. And at the same time let us not fail to be intensely more encouraged to serve him, seeing that he wants to attract us to himself in this way, mastering[77] us by such gentle kindness.

Even Moses shows that everything that God promises his people, provided they keep his law, comes from such a source rather than from any [kind of] obligation. The fact is he says as much: *As God promised to your fathers.*[78] [For] it's as if he were saying: "My friends, serve God and he will be a good master to you. And don't consider the time you spend in keeping his law wasted, for an ample reward[79] has been prepared[80] for you. Only remember its source. For that fountain's reality (he says) lies in the fact that before you were born into this world God promised to lead your fathers into a land flowing with milk and honey." Thus in this manner Moses reminded the people of the promise which had been made to the patriarchs, readily showing that God was promising nothing new but only ratifying his earlier pledge.[81]

And why? Was it because he was obligated to those who had not yet been born in the world? Hardly. Rather it was because he had loved their fathers, as he has already said. Of course it is true now

---

[73]confus-confondus.
[74]pourtant-pour cette raison.
[75]misericorde.
[76]misericorde.
[77]gagner.
[78]Deut. 6:3.
[79]loier-loyer.
[80]appresté-apprêté.
[81]ce qu'il avoit dit.

that Moses shows that the people were participants in such a promise, provided they kept God's law. But what? We must always keep in mind that men are above all lost.[82] [For] if they resolve to oppose God, citing[83] some [basis of] dignity [of their own], they will forever abide in their condemnation and all be found to be cursed. It is imperative then for them to stake their entire refuge on God's loving-kindness,[84] understanding that when they are compelled to walk according to the law, that God owes them nothing, but at all events he will not fail to accomplish what he promised them, acting purely out of his sheer gratuitous kindness. That is how this passage should be understood.

Now since the land promised to the Jews is mentioned here, let us note that today we ought to be far more inspired to serve God inasmuch as he has dedicated the whole earth to himself and wills for his name to be entreated everywhere, for the blood which our Lord Jesus shed has sanctified the whole earth which was formerly corrupt. For we know [that at that time] this was the only land which God had reserved for himself and over which he willed to rule until the coming of his Son. But when our Lord Jesus Christ appeared, then he acquired possession of the whole world and his kingdom was extended from one end of it to the other, especially with the proclamation of the gospel. Therefore, in light of that, we should carefully observe that today we are far more tightly[85] bound to serve God [than previously], especially since he has consecrated[86] the entire earth through the precious blood of his Son to the end that we may inhabit it and live under his reign. And inasmuch as we [equally] desire his protection and safekeeping, let us also be admonished[87] to surrender[88] ourselves to him.

But (as we have already said) since men are so constantly fidgety as to make it impossible to restrain them adequately, Moses affirms[89] all the doctrine which he has just enunciated in saying: *Hear, O Israel, the Lord your God is one God.*[90] He has already for-

---

[82]abysmez-abismés.
[83]allegans-citans.
[84]misericorde.
[85]estroitement-étroitement.´
[86]dedié-consacré.
[87]advisions-avisions.
[88]adonner-abandonner.
[89]conferme-affermit.
[90]Deut. 6:4.

merly said, "Listen: be on your guard." He has [even] reiterated[91] the necessity of keeping the law. But here he far more clearly affirms his entire thought[92] when in particular he explains that Israel's God is one God. Now herein he wishes to exclude all those gods conjured up by the world and wants to show that it is unlawful to conceive of anything unless we hold to the Word of God. Therefore when Israel's God is called one God, it's as much as if Moses wanted to make a comparison between the God who published his law, and who had earlier revealed himself to his servant Abraham and to the other patriarchs, and all those gods in whom the world believed.[93] For since the beginning of time God has been invoked. His name was known to the pagans.[94] But [to] what [end]? The pagans went amiss,[95] each one claiming to worship God. And how? Through dreams and imaginations. For when men attempt to worship God without knowing him, they undoubtedly worship idols. [For example] the Turks[96] today maintain that they worship God, the creator of heaven and earth; but it is only an idol that they worship. And how [is that]? They call him creator of heaven and earth; they [likewise] repudiate[97] images. That is true. Nevertheless, insofar as they refuse to accept our Lord Jesus Christ, who is the living image[98] of God, his Father, they are [still] only worshiping an idol instead of God. We [also] know what Saint John says, that whoever denies the Son denies the Father.[99] Therefore they are not worshiping God but an idol.

The same is true of the Jews. The Jews happily boast of possessing the law and of worshiping the God of Abraham, Isaac, and Jacob. But what? They are apostate. They renounced God's law when they rejected Jesus Christ who is the law's soul.[100] It is he in whom God the Father wills to make himself known to us; it is in

[91]dit.
[92]propos-pensée.
[93]cuidé-cru.
[94]See the *Institutes* 1.3–4, where Calvin specifically refers to Cicero, Gryllus, Plutarch, and Statius.
[95]extravagué-sorti des bornes.
[96]Cf. a similar statement in the *Institutes* 2.6.4; *LCC* 20.348: "So today the Turks, although they proclaim at the top of their lungs that the Creator of heaven and earth is God, still, while repudiating Christ, substitute an idol in place of the true God."
[97]n'ont point.
[98]See Col. 1:15.
[99]See I John 2:23.
[100]See the *Institutes* 2.7.2.

him that he wishes to be worshiped. He also says: "Kiss the Son whom I send you."[101] And next, "Whoever does not honor the Son, does not honor the Father who sent him."[102]

Let us note carefully then that Moses wanted to make a comparison between the God who is revealed through his Word and all those gods who are eulogized[103] by the whole world; for they amount to nothing but monkey business[104] and lies. And why? For we cannot correctly worship God unless we first of all know him. We must always come back to what Jesus Christ said to the Samaritan woman: "You do not know what you worship."[105] When Jesus Christ uses this word, it's the same as if he were spitting on all those services which the world has since instituted. There hasn't been a nation which has not boasted of serving God. [But] Jesus Christ comes to reject everything which was thought to be good and holy. "You do not know (he says) what you worship." In that statement he shows that enlightenment[106] is needed, as it is unfitting for us to go about [worshiping God] in a haphazard manner, rather we need to be reassured[107] of the God we are serving.

Now since it is necessary for us to know God before we can truly worship and serve him, from whence does that knowledge come? Does it come from our garden, as people say? Is it the result of our own effort? Are we free to think of whatever seems best to us and say, "I know God"? No, no! Rather God must himself draw near to us and reveal[108] himself. Thus the only means for adequately knowing God is for us to be taught by his Word.

That is why he says: *The Lord your God.* For the people had received the law and God had [already] made his covenant with their fathers, separating this flock from the entire rest of the world. Thus it is not without cause that Moses reminds[109] the people here of the knowledge of God in order that they may lay aside[110] all the pagans' superstitions, having nothing in common

---

[101]See Ps. 2:12.
[102]John 5:23.
[103]renommez-nommés avec éloge.
[104]singerie.
[105]John 4:22.
[106]declaration-explication, eclaircissemet.
[107]asseurez-rassurés.
[108]se declaire.
[109]rameine-ramène.
[110]s'aliene-s'éloigne.

with unbelievers, and instead realize that since God has revealed himself to them in such an intimate way, they possess one sure and infallible truth.

Now if that was true during the time of the law, we possess[111] even more. For although God may have given a sufficient admonition to the Jews to prevent them from becoming involved in the pagans' pollutions and idolatries, today we possess a far brighter light since our Lord Jesus Christ has appeared, who is the living image of God his Father (as we have said). And we can readily concur with what is written in the first chapter of Saint John: "None has ever seen God, but the Son who has always been in the Father's bosom has revealed him to us."[112] The ancient Fathers might have had [some] knowledge, as we have said, but that knowledge is considered invalid in comparison with what we possess today in the gospel. For since the sun of righteousness illumines us, God has been intimately revealed[113] to us.

That is why the prophet Isaiah [says] in particular, when referring to the redemption which was to be made in the person of God's Son: "Behold, behold our God (he says)."[114] The prophet exclaims: "It is he, it is he, our God."[115] He is not content to say in a single phrase: "Here is our God." Rather he speaks as if God were present and revealing himself to him. And what is that? Wasn't God [already] present in the midst of his people? For he often said: "I shall dwell in the midst of you."[116] And again, "Behold my rest, Zion is the place of my habitat."[117] He even affirms anew that he will never depart from them, [and] that the people are his temple and a royal priesthood.[118] What then is the purpose of the prophet Isaiah's cry: "Behold, behold our God! It is he, it is he!" when our Lord Jesus Christ had yet to come into the world? Its purpose is that God has revealed himself to us even more perfectly.

Therefore we have even less excuse today if we wander about, failing to hold to the pure truth, each person turning aside after his own reveries, saying, "It seems this way to me" or "That is

[111]compete-appartient.
[112]John 1:18.
[113]se rend familier.
[114]Isa. 25:9; 42:9.
[115]Isa. 25:9; 42:9.
[116]See Exod. 25:8.
[117]Ps. 132:13–14.
[118]See Exod. 23:22.

what I find good." We must understand that that is nothing and our obligation is to come to this certainty which our Lord Jesus Christ has brought.

Now the world was so far from knowing this, that it appears that everyone willfully despised God and tried[119] to turn their back against him, rejecting all submission, in order to have the freedom of living in their own shocking way without having their shamefulness detected. The Jews are inexcusable, for we know that the prophets reproach them for having knowingly abandoned God and that they cannot absolve themselves as poor pagans [do], saying that they have not heard anything, for God solemnly affirms[120] that he did not speak in vain.

Now today when God fully[121] speaks to us and we possess so perfect a revelation in the gospel, is it not an insufferable shame for men to err as they do? In fact have there ever been as many blatant and stupid[122] superstitions as exist in the papacy today? True, the Jews engaged in pagan superstitions [and] frequently were attracted by their filth and corruption, but when all of that is carefully examined you will discover that the papists have far outdistanced them. For today the Word of God is buried in the papacy. When they deal with faith, their articles are drawn from human forges; the holy Scripture is held in about as much respect by them as if it were dead and in total ruin.[123] That is how they proceed. And when you speak to them about worshiping God, they go after their inventions. "Indeed, our intentions are good," they say. And they suppose that God is willing to be treated like a small child [and] that he will not undertake an examination of all the papacy's doctrine. Next, if you mention faith, and ask if it is important to consider God's free promises [their answer is], No! For they attribute everything to themselves.[124] If you want to deal

---

[119]machiné-travaillé.
[120]proteste-affirme solennellement.
[121]a pleine bouche.
[122]lourdes.
[123]Possibly a reference to the Fourth Session of the Council of Trent, April 18, 1546, "Decree Concerning The Canonical Scriptures" and the "Decree Concerning The Edition And The Use Of The Sacred Books." See *Decrees Council of Trent,* trans. Schroeder, pp. 17–20. See Calvin's elaboration of the Fourth Session in *Antidote, Tracts and Treatises,* vol. 3, pp. 67–77.
[124]See the Sixth Session of the Council of Trent, January 13, 1547, the "Decree Concerning Justification," chapters 1–16. Note Canon 32 in particular: "If anyone says that the good works of one justified are in such manner the gifts of God that they are not also the good merits of him justified; that the one justified by the

with Jesus Christ's office, they vitiate[125] the force of his passion and death as much as they possibly can. When it comes to discussing their salvation, they begin with free will and mention their merits and satisfactions first.

On the contrary, we have to begin[126] with the Holy Spirit's sheer grace, acknowledging that we are in bondage to sin unless liberated by God's loving kindness.[127] And that is the source for what the Scripture calls the remission of sins [and] our righteousness. It has even been appropriate to begin here knowing that if we have erred we cannot offer any other payment than what we receive[128] through the passion and death of our Lord Jesus Christ. But nothing of that exists in the papacy. Whenever it's a matter of calling upon God, they make their circuits of the saints, both male and female. In the meanwhile Jesus Christ is neither known as he truly is nor reinvested in his office which God the[129] Father gave him; instead the papists degrade him, as their sacrileges and forgeries attempt both to bury and rob him of all his glory which God the Father has given him. This is true of everything they do. For we know that their sacraments are contaminated from end to end.[130] Instead of the Holy Communion of our Lord Jesus Christ, we find this infernal abomination of the Mass in which they claim Jesus Christ is sacrificed, as if he had done nothing or as if he had not been designated the unique and perpetual priest[131] by God the Father. Thus we see how the papists laugh at the Word of God in which he has revealed himself; it seems that they have deliberately intended to efface the knowledge which the gospel contains. All the more then must we pay heed to this phrase: *that the Lord is God, indeed one sole God.*[132]

Now whenever this word [*God*] is called[133] to our attention, let

good works that he performs by the grace of God and the merit of Jesus Christ, whose living member he is, does not truly merit an increase of grace, eternal life, and . . . the attainment of eternal life . . . let him be anathema." *Decrees Council of Trent,* trans. Schroeder, p. 46. See Calvin's reply In *Antidote, Tracts and Treatises,* vol. 3, p. 162.

[125]renversent.

[126]venir.

[127]misericorde.

[128]empruntons.

[129]son.

[130]See Calvin's attack on the Mass and the medieval church's sacraments in his *Institutes* 4.18–19.

[131]Sacrificateur. See Heb. 7:17.

[132]Deut. 6:4.

[133]vient en avant.

us realize that its purpose is to illuminate whatever our own mind might think, or men invent, which we have not been taught by the holy Scripture. For God wants to be esteemed by us to the extent that we might not be engulfed in idolater's fantasies and mistakes. In fact, we cannot have the true God unless we have him alone, that is, unless we do not [attempt] to add a companion to him, for as soon as we begin introducing little gods, we renounce the living God. And why [is that]? Because he wills to be the only God.[134] As the prophet Isaiah declares in another passage: "I am [the] living [God] (says the Lord); I will not give my glory to another."[135] For we have seen earlier how he called himself a jealous God.[136] Why? In order to save[137] us from every corruption as Saint Paul speaks of it in II Corinthians.[138] For as soon as we have turned aside from the simplicity of God's Word, it's the same as when a woman listens to a pimp who has come to whisper in her ear. We are that corrupt. And thus we shamelessly play the whore[139] against God whenever we forswear[140] the faith which we promised him at baptism; we reject his law, [and] all religion is profaned by us whenever we refuse, however slightly, to accept his Word as pure doctrine. Therefore let us especially retain this word *God* whenever it is called to our attention, for God alone[141] can be God. Consequently,[142] whenever we incorporate[143] any created things along with him, he abandons us as if we were apostates and were people who are unworthy of having anything in common with him, seeing that we have not willed to ascribe him the honor which he deserves, that is, that he is the Lord. For we profane that name whenever we associate him with created things or our dreams.

Now at the same time let us note that it is not enough to reserve a single-word title ["the only God"] to the living God, but it is important for everything that belongs to him to abide in him fully.[144] How is that? He means not only to be called God, but to

---

[134]seul.
[135]Isa. 42:8.
[136]See "The Third Sermon."
[137]retirer.
[138]See II Cor. 5:17-18.
[139]paillardons.
[140]luy faussons.
[141]tout seul.
[142]pourtant-pour cette raison.
[143]aurons accompagné-aurons associé.
[144]en son entier.

be acknowledged [as the] Almighty, as our Father and Savior, as the one who has the authority to govern us, the one in whom we ought to place our trust and call upon. Those are the principal points on which we ought to meditate when we are told to honor one sole God.

It is true that the papists will frequently insist[145] that Saint Michael and Saint William are not their gods, nevertheless they worship them; even their grotesque figures.[146] They think they are going to escape [any condemnation] through the subterfuge that these images are not the saints to whom they pray, but only their reminders[147] which represent them; in any event, this is contrary to God's express prohibition. We even see that they do not know how to determine, in any way whatever, how God wants to be worshiped, since they mingle as they do among their idols of stone and wood which they believe[148] represent their saints. True enough they attempt to justify their actions through the use of Dulia and Latria, terms which they do not understand, when they say that they are "serving" their images and rendering "honor" to God, for that is the meaning they attribute to these words.[149] But they have truly compromised God when they explain[150] that they render "honor" to God alone, whereas they [merely] "serve" their idols. Isn't it a [more] sacred thing to call upon God [than it is to call upon saints]? For that is the true "service" which God wants as brought out in the fiftieth Psalm.[151] Thus we see that the world mocks God with insufferable impudence when it so shamelessly corrupts all his service and that it is more than a detestable act for men to be misled this way, seeing that the gospel contains such a clear and gaping[152] revelation. Thus so much the more ought we cling to this doctrine, knowing that our Lord wills for us to be wholly attached to him and that an inviolable union might exist between him and us. This will be accomplished when we are simply confined between the boundaries of his Word, when we permit no access to human inventions, [and] when we forbid our

---

[145]diront.
[146]See the *Institutes* 3.20.21–27 for Calvin's rejection of the veneration of the saints.
[147]remembrances-souvenirs.
[148]cuident-croient.
[149]For Calvin's interpretation of *dulia* and *latria*, see the *Institutes* 1.12.2–3.
[150]declarent.
[151]See Ps. 50:14–15.
[152]patente-béante.

minds to stray. It will come to pass only after we have listened to
what the holy Scripture contains, promptly saying amen, not simply with our mouth, but when our faith has fully relied upon what
has proceeded from the mouth[153] of our God.[154]

---

[153]See Deut. 6:13, 8:3.

[154]Golding's translation concludes with the following exhortation: "Now let us
kneele downe in the presence of our good God, with acknowledgement of our
faults, praying him to make us feele them better than wee have done, so as wee
may knowe more and more wherein wee bee bounde unto him, and not thinke to
discharge ourselves thereof lightly, but bend our selves wholly to him and to his
service, not having any other intent or desire than to keepe his holy Lawe. And
seeing wee bee yet verie farre off from it, so that strains wee our selves never so
much, wee stop in the middes of our waye: let us flee for succour to the forgiveness of our sinnes, praying him to vouchsafe to receive us to mercie, and to beare
with us in such sort, as he never ceasse to guide us with his holy Spirit, though we
deserve to bee utterly shaken off at his hand. And therewithall it may please him
to open our eyes, that wee beholding the brightness of our Lorde Jesus Christ,
may bee wholly ravished thereat, to renounce these worldly things and our fleshly
affections, which carrie us awaye: so as wee may have none other desire than to
humble our selves under him, to the ende that being stricken downe in our selves,
wee may bee lifted up at his hand by his woorde, wayting till it please him to
transfigure us after his owne image at the latter days. That it may please him to
graunt this grace not onely to us but also, Etc." *Sermons Upon the Fifth Book of Moses*,
trans. Golding, p. 271. Cf. Calvin, *Sermons sur les dix commandemens*, 1557 ed., pp.
236–37.

Bibliography

Bainton, Roland H. *Hunted Heretic, The Life and Death of Michael Servetus, 1511–1553.* Boston: The Beacon Press, 1953.

———. "Michael Servetus and the Trinitarian Speculation of the Middle Ages." *Autour de Michel Servet et de Sebastien Castellion.* Edited by B. Becker. Haarlem: H. D. Tjeenk Willink & Zoan N.V., 1953.

Barrois, George A. "Calvin and the Genevans." *Theology Today,* January, 1965, pp. 458–65.

Barth, Karl. *Community, State and Church.* With an Introduction by Will Herberg. Garden City: Anchor Books, Doubleday, 1960.

Barth, Peter, and Wilhelm Niesel, eds. *Institutiones Christianae religionis 1559.* In vols. 3–5 of *Joannis Calvini Opera Selecta.* Munich: Kaiser, 1928–36; 2d ed., vol. 3 (1957); vol. 4 (1959).

Battles, Ford Lewis, and Hugo, André Malan, eds. *Calvin's Commentary on Seneca's De Clementia.* The Renaissance Society of America, Renaissance Test Series, 3. Leiden: E. J. Brill, 1969.

———. ed. and trans. *The Piety of John Calvin: An Anthology Illustrative of the Spirituality of the Reformer.* Music edited by Stanley Tagg. Grand Rapids: Baker Book House, 1978.

Benoit, Jean-Daniel. *Calvin: Directeur d'Ames.* Strasbourg: Oberlin, 1944.

Beza, Theodore. *The Life of John Calvin.* Translated by Francis Sibson. Philadelphia: J. Whetham, 1836.

Biéler, André. *La Pensée Économique et Sociale de Calvin.* Publications de la Faculté des Sciences Économiques et Sociales de l'Université de Genève, vol. 13. Geneva: Georg & Cie. S.A., 1959.

———. *The Social Humanism of Calvin.* Translated by Paul T. Fuhrmann. Richmond: John Knox Press, 1964.

Bohatec, Josef. *Budé und Calvin: Studien zur Gedankenwelt des Franzosischen Fruhhumanismus.* Graz: Verlag Hermann Bohlaus, 1950.

———. *Calvin und das Recht.* Feudingen: Buchdruck and Verlags-Anstalt, 1934.

309

Bonnet, Jules, ed. *Letters of John Calvin.* Vols. 1–2; translated by Mr. Constable. Vols. 3–4 translated by Marcus Robert Gilchrist. Philadelphia: Presbyterian Board of Publication, 1858.

Bowman, C. "Calvin as a Preacher." *The Reformed Church Review,* Fourth Series, 13, no. 2 (April, 1909), pp. 245–61.

Bratt, John H., ed. *The Heritage of John Calvin, Heritage Hall Lectures 1960–1970.* Grand Rapids: William B. Eerdmans, 1973.

Breen, Quirinus. *John Calvin: A Study in French Humanism.* Grand Rapids: Wm. B. Eerdmans, 1931.

———. "John Calvin and the Rhetorical Tradition." *Church History,* 26, no. 1 (March, 1957), pp. 3–21.

Buscarlet, Daniel. *Genéve Citadelle de la Réforme.* Geneva: Comité du Jubilé Calvinien, 1959.

Cadier, Jean. *Calvin: L'homme que Dieu a dompté.* Geneva: Labor et Fides, 1958.

———. *The Man God Mastered.* Translated by O. R. Johnston. London: Inter-Varsity Fellowship, 1959.

Calvin: Commentaries. Newly translated and edited by Joseph Haroutunian. In collaboration with Louise Pettibone Smith. The Library of Christian Classics, vol. 23. Philadelphia: The Westminster Press, 1958.

Calvin, Jean. *Commentaries on the Epistles of Paul to the Galations and Ephesians.* Translated by Rev. Wm. Pringle. Grand Rapids: Wm. B. Eerdmans, 1948.

———. *Commentaries on the Four Last Books of Moses Arranged in the Form of a Harmony.* Translated by Charles William Bingham. 4 vols. Grand Rapids: Wm. B. Eerdmans, 1950.

———. *Commentary on the Epistles of Paul the Apostle to the Corinthians.* Translated by John Pringle. 2 vols. Grand Rapids: Wm. B. Eerdmans, 1948.

———. *Commentary on the Gospel According to John.* Translated by William Pringle. 2 vols. Edinburgh: Calvin Translation Society, 1847–60.

———. *Commentary upon the Epistle of Saint Paul to the Romans.* Edited by Henry Beveridge, Esq. Translated by Christopher Rosdell. Edinburgh: Calvin Translation Society, 1844.

———. *The Epistles of Paul the Apostle to the Romans and to the Thessalonians.* Translated by Ross Mackenzie. Edited by D. W. Torrance & T. F. Torrance. Calvin's Commentaries. Grand Rapids: Wm. B. Eerdmans, 1961.

———. *Institutes of the Christian Religion.* Edited by John T. McNeill. Translated and indexed by Ford Lewis Battles. The Library of Christian Classics. Vols. 20–21. Philadelphia: The Westminster Press, 1960.

———. *Institution de La Religion Chrestienne.* Ed. par Jean-Daniel Benoit. Bibliothèque des Textes Philosophiques. 5 vols. Paris: Librairie Philosophique J. Vrin, 1957–1963.

———. *Institution de La Religion Chrestienne.* Ed. par Jacques Pannier. Les Textes Francais. 4 vols. Paris: Société Les Belles Lettres, 1936–1939.

———. *Instruction in Faith (1537).* Translated with a historical foreword and critical and explanatory notes by Paul T. Fuhrmann. Philadelphia: The Westminster Press, 1949.

———. *Ioannis Calvini Opera quae supersunt omnia.* Vols. 1–59. Editerunt Guilielmus Baum, Eduardus Cunitz, Eduardus Reuss. Corpus Reformatorum, vols. 29–87. Brunsvigae: C. A. Schwetschke et filium, 1863–1900.

———. *Sermons de M. Iehan Calvin sur les dix commandemens de la Loy, donnee de Dieu par Moyse, autrement applez le Decalogue: Recueillis sur le champ et mot a mot de ses predications, lors qu'il preschoit le Deuteronome, sans que depuis y ait este rie/n/adiouste ne diminue.* Geneva: Conrad Badius, 1557.

———. *Sermons from Job.* Translated by Leroy Nixon. With an Introductory Essay by Harold Dekker. Grand Rapids: Wm. B. Eerdmans, 1952.

———. *The Sermons of M. Iohn Calvin Upon the Fifth Booke of Moses called Deuteronomie:* Faithfully gathered word for word as he preached them in open Pulpet; Together with a preface of the Ministers of the Church of Geneva, and an admonishment made by the Deacons there. Also there are annexed two profitable Tables, the one containing the chiefe matters; the other the places of Scripture herein alledged. Translated out of French by Arthur Golding. At London: Printed by Henry Middleton for George Bishop, 1583.

———. *Sermons on Isaiah's Prophecy of the Death and Passion of Christ.* Translated and edited by T. H. L. Parker. London: James Clarke & Co. Ltd., 1956.

———. *Tracts and Treatises in Defense of the Reformed Faith.* Translated by Henry Beveridge. Edited by Thomas F. Torrance. 3 vols. Grand Rapids: Wm. B. Eerdmans, 1958.

Canons and Decrees of the Council of Trent. Translated by Rev. J. H. Schroeder, O. P. St. Louis: B. Herder Book Co., 1960.

Chenevière, Marc-Edouard. *La Pensée Politique de Calvin.* Geneva: Editions Labor, 1937.

Chevallet, A. De. *Origine et Formation de la Langue Francaise.* 2d ed. 3 vols. Paris: J. -B. Dumoulin, Libraire, 1858.

Choisy, Eugène. *La Théocratie à Geneve au temps de Calvin.* Geneva: Imprimerie J.-G. Fick, 1897.

Doumergue, Émile. *Jean Calvin, Les Hommes et les choses de son temps.* 7 vols. Vols. 1–5, Lausanne: Georges Bridel & Cie., 1899–1917; vols. 6–7, Neuilly-sur-Seine: Editions de "La Cause," 1926–27.

Duffield, Gervase E., ed. *John Calvin.* Courtenay Studies in Reformation Theology, 1. Appleford: The Sutton Courtenay Press, 1966.

Dufour, Alain. *Histoire politique et psychologie historique.* Geneva: Droz, 1966.

Farley, Benjamin W. "John Calvin's Sermons on the Ten Commandments: Translated, Edited and Critically Introduced." Th.D. Dissertation: Union Theological Seminary in Va., 1976.

Fleming & Tibbins' French and English Dictionary. Phildelphia: n.p., 1843.

Forstman, J. Jackson. *Word and Spirit: Calvin's Doctrine of Biblical Authority.* Stanford: Stanford University Press, 1962.

Fuhrman, Paul Traugott. "Calvin, the Expositor of Scripture." *Interpretation* 6 (April, 1952), pp. 188–209.

Gagnebin, Bernard. "L'Histoire des Manuscrits des Sermons de Calvin." *Jean Calvin: Sermons sur le Livre d'Esaie.* Publies par Georges A. Barrois. Supplementa Calviniana. Vol. 2. Neukirchen Kreis Moers: Neukirchener Verlag, 1961., pp. 14–28.

Geisendorf, Paul -F., ed. *Livre des Habitants de Genève.* 2 vols. Book 1, 1549–1560. Book 2, 1572–1574 et 1585–1587. Travaux D'Humanisme Et Renaissance, pp. 26, 56. Geneva: E. Droz, 1957, 1963.

Godefroy, Frédéric Eugene. *Dictionnaire de l'Ancienne Langue Francaise et de Tous Ses Dialectes du IXe au Ve Siècle.* 10 vols. Paris: F. Vieweg; E. Bouillon, 1880–1902.

Graham, W. Fred. *The Constructive Revolutionary: John Calvin & His Socio-Economic Impact.* Atlanta: John Knox Press, 1978.

Halaski, Karl. *Der Prediger Johannes Calvin, Beiträge und Nackrichten zur Ausgabe der*

Supplementa Calviniana. Neukirchen-Vluyn: Neukirchener Verlag des Er-
ziehungsvereins, 1966.

Harkness, Georgia. *John Calvin: The Man and His Ethics.* Nashville: Abingdon Press,
1931.

Henry, Paul. *The Life and Times of John Calvin, the Great Reformer.* Translated by
Henry Stebbing. 2 vols. New York: Robert Carter & Brothers, 1854.

Higman, Francis M., ed. *Jean Calvin, Three French Treatises.* Athlone Renaissance
Library. London: The Athlone Press, 1970.

————. *The Style of John Calvin in His French Polemical Treatises.* Cambridge: Oxford
University Press, 1967.

Hoch De Long, Irwin, "Calvin as an Interpreter of the Bible." *The Reformed Church
Review,* Fourth Series, 13, no. 2 (April, 1909), 165–82.

Hudson, Winthrop S. "Puritanism and the Spirit of Capitalism." *Church History,*
vol. 18 (March, 1949), pp. 3–16.

Hughes, Philip Edgcombe. "John Calvin: Director of Missions." *The Heritage of
John Calvin.* Edited by John H. Bratt. Grand Rapids: Wm. B. Eerdmans, 1973.
pp. 40–54.

————. ed. and tr. *The Register of the Company of Pastors of Geneva in the Time of
Calvin.* Grand Rapids: Wm. B. Eerdmans, 1966.

Huguet, Edmond Eugene Auguste. *Dictionnaire de la langue francaise du seizième
siècle.* 7 vols. Paris: Champion; Didier, 1925–67.

Imbart de la Tour, Pièrre. *Calvin Et L'Institution Chrétienne.* Vol. 4 of *Les Origines de
la Réforme.* 4 vols. Paris: Firmin-Didot et Cie., (1935).

Kingdom, Robert M. "The Control of Morals in Calvin's Geneva." *The Social History
of the Reformation.* Edited by Lawrence P. Buck and Jonathon W. Zophy. Colum-
bus: Ohio State University Press, 1972. pp. 3–16.

————. "The Economic Behavior of Ministers in Geneva in the Middle of the Sixteenth Century." *Archiv für Reformationsgeschichte,* vol. 50 (1959), pp. 33–39.

————. *Geneva and the Coming of the Wars of Religion in France, 1555–1563.* Travaux
d'Humanisme et Renaissance, 22. Geneva: Librairie E. Droz, 1956.

Kraus, Hans-Joachim. "Calvin's exegitische Prinzipien." *Zeitschrift für Kirchengeschichte,* 79 (1968), pp. 329–41.

Kromminga, Carl G. *Man Before God's Face in Calvin's Preaching.* Calvin Theological
Seminary Monograph Series: 2. Grand Rapids: Calvin Theological Seminary,
1961.

Kuizenga, Henry. "The Relation of God's Grace to His Glory in John Calvin."
Reformation Studies: Essays in Honor of Roland H. Bainton. Edited by Franklin H.
Littel. Richmond: John Knox Press, 1962. pp. 95–105.

Lafaye, M., comp. *Dictionnaire Des Synonymes De La Langue Francaise.* Paris: Librairie
de L. Hachette et Cie., 1858.

Lefranc, Abel. "Calvin et l'Eloquence Francaise." *Société de l'Histoire du Protes-
tantisme Francais* 83 (April–June, 1934), pp. 173–93.

Leith, John H. "Calvin's Theological Method and the Ambiguity in His Theology."
Reformation Studies: Essays in Honor of Roland H. Bainton. Edited by Franklin H.
Littel. Richmond: John Knox Press, 1962. pp. 106–114.

————. "Creation and Redemption; Law and Gospel in the Theology of John Calvin." *A reexamination of Lutheran and Reformed Traditions.* New York: Published
jointly by representatives of the North American Area of the World Alliance of
Reformed Churches holding the Presbyterian Order and the U.S.A. National
Committee of the Lutheran World Federation, 1965. 3, pp. 43–53.

————. *Introduction to the Reformed Tradition: A Way of Being the Christian Community*. Atlanta: John Knox Press, 1977.

————. "John Calvin—Theologian of the Bible." *Interpretation* 25 (July, 1971), pp. 329–44.

Little, David. "Calvin and the Prospects for a Christian Theory of Natural Law." *Norm and Context in Christian Ethics*. Edited by Gene H. Outka and Paul Ramsey. New York: Charles Scribner's Sons, 1968. pp. 175–97.

Luther, Martin. *The Freedom of a Christian (1520)*. Translated by W. A. Lambert. Revised by Harold J. Grimm. In *Career of the Reformer: I*. Edited by Harold J. Grimm and Helmut T. Lehmann. Luther's Works, vol. 21. Philadelphia: Muhlenberg Press, 1957. pp. 327–77.

————. *Lectures on Galatians, 1535, Chapters 1–4*. Edited by Jaroslav Pelikan. Luther's Works, vol. 26. Saint Louis: Concordia, 1963.

Mackinnon, James. *Calvin and the Reformation*. London: Longmans, Green, and Co., 1963.

McNeill, John T. *The History and Character of Calvinism*. London: Oxford University Press, 1954.

————. "The Significance of the Word of God for Calvin." *Church History*, 28, no. 2 (June, 1959), 131–46.

————. *Unitive Protestantism: The Ecumenical Spirit and Its Persistent Expression*. Richmond: John Knox Press, 1964.

Martin, Paul E. "Calvin et le prêt à intérêt à Genève." In *Mélanges d'histoire économique et sociale en hommage au Professor Antony Babel*, vol. 2, pp. 251–63. Geneva. 1963.

Melanchthon on Christian Doctrine, Loci Communes 1555. Translated and edited by Clyde L. Manschreck. Introduction by Hans Engelland. A Library of Protestant Thought. New York: Oxford University Press, 1965.

Menżies, Allan. *A Study of Calvin and Other Papers*. London: MacMillan and Co., Limited, 1918.

Monter, E. William. *Calvin's Geneva*. New Dimensions in History, Historical Cities. Series Editor: Norman F. Cantor. New York: John Wiley & Sons, Inc., 1967.

Mülhaupt, Erwin. *Die Predigt Calvins, Ihre Geschichte, Ihre Form und Ihre Religiösen Grundgedanken*. Arbeiten Zur Kirchengeschichte, 18. Berlin: Verlag Von Walter de Gruyter & Co., 1931.

Nelson, Benjamin N. *The Idea of Usury*. Princeton: Princeton University Press, 1958.

The New Cassell's French Dictionary. Completely revised by Denis Girad, Gaston DuLong et al. New York: Funk and Wagnalls, 1968.

Niesel, Wilhelm. *Die Theologie Calvins*. Muchen: Chr. Kaiser Verlag, (1938) 1957.

————. *The Theology of Calvin*. Translated by Harold Knight. Philadelphia: The Westminster Press, 1956.

————. "Der theologische Gehalt der jungst veroffentlichten Predigten Calvins." *Revue d'Histoire et de Philosophie Religieuses*. 44 (1964), 270–78.

Nixon, Leroy. *John Calvin. Expository Preacher*. Grand Rapids: Wm. B. Eerdmans, 1950.

————. *John Calvin's Teachings on Human Reason*. New York: Exposition Press, 1963.

Orr, James. "Calvin's Attitude Towards and Exegesis of the Scriptures." *Calvin Memorial Addresses, Delivered Before the General Assembly of the Presbyterian Church in the United States at Savannah, Ga., May, 1909.* Richmond: The Presbyterian Committee of Publication, n.d. pp. 89–105.

Pannier, Jacques. *Calvin Écrivain. Sa place et son role dans l'Histoire de la Langue et de la Littérature francaise.* Paris: Libraire Fischbacher, 1930.

Parker, T. H. L. *Calvin's New Testament Commentaries.* London: SCM Press, Ltd., 1971.

———. *John Calvin: A Biography.* London: J. M. Dent & Sons Ltd., 1975.

———. *The Oracles of God: An Introduction to the Preaching of John Calvin.* London: Lutterworth Press, 1947.

———. *Supplementa Calviniana: An Account of the Manuscripts of Calvin's Sermons Now in Course of Preparation.* London: The Tyndale Press, 1962.

Pauck, Wilhelm, ed. *Melanchthon and Bucer.* The Library of Christian Classics, vol. 19. Philadelphia: The Westminster Press, 1959.

Protestantism and Capitalism: The Weber Thesis and Its Critics. Edited by Robert W. Green. Heath Series: Problems in European Civilization. Boston: D. C. Heath & Co., 1959.

Prust, Richard C. "Was Calvin a Biblical Literalist?" *Scottish Journal of Theology,* (September, 1967), 312–28.

Registres de la Compagnie des Pasteurs de Genève au temps de Calvin. Edited by Robert M. Kingdom et Jean-F. Bergier. Book 1: 1546–1553. Ed. Par Jean-F. Bergier. Book 2: 1553–1564. Ed. Robert M. Kingdom. Jean-F. Bergier Alain Dufour. Book 3: 1565–1574. Ed. Olivier Fatio et O. Labarthe. Travaux d'Humanisme et Renaissance, 55, 107. Genève: Droz, 1962, 1964, 1969.

Rilliet, Jean, *Calvin, 1509–1564.* n.p.: Fayard, 1963.

Robertson, A. T. "Calvin as an Interpreter of Scripture." *The Review and Expositor,* no. 4 (October, 1909), 577–78.

Rodolphe, Peter. "Jean Calvin Prédicateur: notice bibliographique à propos d'un ouvrage récent." *Revue d'Histoire et de Philosophic Religieuses,* (1972), 111–17.

Roget, Amédée. *Histoire du Peuple de Genève depuis la Réforme jusqu'à l'Escalade.* 7 vols.: John Jullien, 1870–1883.

Rothlisberger, Hugo. *Kirche am Sinai: Die Zehn Gebote in der Christlichen Unterweisung.* Zurich-Stuttgart: Zwingli Verlag, 1965.

Rucket, Hanns, ed. *Johannes Calvin: Predigten uber das Z. Buch Samuelis.* Supplementa Calviniana, vol. 1. Neukirchen Kreis Moers: Neukirchener Verlag, 1961.

Sayous, A. *Études Literaires Sur Les Écrivains Francais De La Réformation.* 2d ed. Tome Premier. Paris: G. Fischbucher, 1881.

Smits, Luchesius. *Saint Augustin Dans L'Oeuvre De Jean Calvin.* 2 vols.: Louvain: Editions Nauwelaerts, 1957–58.

Stauffer, Richard. "Les discourse à la première personne dans les sermons de Calvin." *Revue d'Histoire et de Philosophie Religieuses,* (1965), 46–78.

———. *L'humanite de Calvin.* Neuchatel: Delachaux et Niestle, 1964.

———. *The Humanness of John Calvin.* Translated by George Shriver. Nashville: Abingdon Press, 1971.

Tawney, R. H. *Religion and the Rise of Capitalism.* New York: Menton Books, 1961. (First published in 1926.)

Thompson, James W. *Economic and Social History of the Later Middle Ages, 1300–1530.* New York: Frederick Ungar Publishing Co., 1960. (First published in 1931.)

Vischer, Wilhelm. "Calvin, exégète de l'Ancien Testament." *Études Theologiques et Religieuses,* (1965), pp. 213–31.

Walker, Williston. John Calvin *The Organiser of Reformed Protestantism 1509–1564.* With a Bibliographical Essay by John T. McNeill. New York: Schocken Books, 1969.

Wallace, Ronald S. *Calvin's Doctrine of the Christian Life.* Edinburgh: Oliver and Boyd, 1959.

—————. *Calvin's Doctrine of the Word and Sacrament.* Edinburgh: Oliver and Boyd, 1953.

Weber, Max. *The Protestant Ethic and the Spirit of Capitalism.* Translated, with an introduction, by Talcott Parsons. New York: Charles Scribner's Sons, 1930.

Wencelius, Léon. *L'Esthetique de Calvin.* Paris: Société d'Edition "Les Belles Lettres," n.d.

Wendel, Francois. *Calvin: The Origins and Development of His Religious Thought.* Translated by Philip Mairet. New York: Harper & Row, Publishers, 1963.

Willis, E. David. "Rhetoric and Responsibility in Calvin's Theology." *The Context of Contemporary Theology: Essays in Honor of Paul Lehmann.* Edited by Alexander J. McKelway and E. David Willis, Atlanta: John Knox Press, 1974. pp. 43–63.

Zweig, Stefan. *The Right to Heresy: Castellio against Calvin.* Translated by Eden and Cedar Paul. New York: The Viking Press, 1936.

Subject Index

Scripture Index

Solid Ground Christian Books is a publishing company committed to the preservation and presentation of the cardinal doctrines of Holy Scripture. Our goal is to spread the fame of the Name of the Lord by finding, uncovering and restoring the best Christian literature from the past and bringing it into the modern world.

We believe that there are many treasured works from the past that the Lord has used in mighty ways, and yet are unavailable to the modern reader. We are always searching for works that have been used by the Holy Spirit in converting sinners, sanctifying saints and preserving them unto the end.

Our desire is to serve pastors, churches, missionaries, chaplains, the military, professors and students of the 21st century. We will seek to keep our prices fair, and our service prompt, personal and courteous.

Our prayer is that the God of sovereign grace will be pleased to smile upon our efforts to further His kingdom and that multitudes throughout the world will be forever changed by reading the books we produce.

Soli Deo Gloria — To God Alone Be The Glory!

Call Us at **205-443-0311**
Visit us on-line at **www.solid-ground-books.com**

Other Related Titles from Solid Ground

In addition to the book in your hands Solid Ground has published more than 300 titles since 2001. Some as follows:

Covenant Theology: A Reformed and Baptistic Perspective by Greg Nichols

The Complete Works of Thomas Manton

Deluxe Leather Edition of the *1689 Baptist Confession of Faith*

Deluxe Leather Edition of the *Three Forms of Unity*

Robert Hawker's *Poor Man's Commentaries*

Scriptural Exposition of the Baptist Catechism by Benjamin Beddome

The Marrow of True Justification by Benjamin Keach

The Travels of True Godliness by Benjamin Keach

Gospel Sonnets by Ralph Erskine

A Body of Divinity by Archbishop James Ussher

Heaven Upon Earth by James Janeway

A Short Explanation of Hebrews by David Dickson

Commentary on Hebrews by William Gouge

Commentary on Jude by Thomas Jenkyn

Commentary on Second Peter by Thomas Adams

Commentary on the New Testament by John Trapp

The Christian Warfare by John Downame

An Exposition of the Ten Commandments by Ezekiel Hopkins

The Harmony of the Divine Attributes by William Bates

The Communicant's Companion by Matthew Henry

The Secret of Communion with God by Matthew Henry

The Redeemer's Tears Wept Over Lost Souls by John Howe

Call 205-443-0311 for a Free Catalogue

CPSIA information can be obtained at www.ICGtesting.com
Printed in the USA
LVOW130911150413

329087LV00001B/1/P